Planet Water

Planet Water

*Investing in the
World's Most Valuable
Resource*

Stephen J. Hoffmann

WILEY

John Wiley & Sons, Inc.

Published by John Wiley & Sons, Inc., Hoboken, New Jersey.
Published simultaneously in Canada.

For general information on our other products and services or for technical support, please
contact our Customer Care Department within the United States at (800) 762-2974,
outside the United States at (317) 572-3993 or fax (317) 572-4002.

Wiley also publishes its books in a variety of electronic formats. Some content that appears
in print may not be available in electronic books. For more information about Wiley
products, visit our web site at www.wiley.com.

Library of Congress Cataloging-in-Publication Data:
Hoffmann, Stephen J., 1955-
    Planet water : investing in the world's most valuable resource / Stephen J. Hoffmann.
       p.   cm.
    Includes bibliographical references and index.
    ISBN 978-0-470-27740-9 (cloth)
       1. Water resources development—Economic aspects.   2. Water-supply—
Economic aspects.   3. Water quality management.   I. Title.
    HD1691.H64   2009
    363.6'1—dc22
                                                                            2008047039

Printed in the United States of America

10 9 8 7 6 5 4 3 2 1

To Paul, Alex, Lauren, Kate, and Tess; for whom ecological sustainability will be more than words.

Contents

Introduction

When I wrote the treatise "Water: The Untapped Market" back in 1987, I advocated market-based solutions to the governance of expanding global water resource challenges. Actually, as a resource economist, it is more accurate to say that I was enchanted by the potential application of the principles of resource economics to the free market system. As I prophesied over 20 years ago in the introduction to that document, "the dynamics of the water industry are changing rapidly in coincidence with the growing problems inherent in a severe imbalance of supply and demand. Given the natural constraints of the hydrologic cycle and the artificial limitations imposed by the degradation of supplies, it is becoming increasingly apparent that the effective utilization of water resources requires a more productive set of governing institutions." That set of productive institutions was collectively embraced through the marketplace.

At the time, "governing institutions" were effectively limited to federal, state, and local regulatory frameworks and oversight. It was my belief that water pricing mechanisms and the unfettered transferability of water rights, among other market-based solutions, would inevitably lead to equilibrium in the supply and demand for water. Granted, there were hurdles to overcome such as pollution externalities and public (common) good issues where market failure is predictable, but nothing that a close relationship between governments and markets could not work through.

Over 20 years later, I have seasoned to the fundamental realities of a critical industry in transition, subject to pricing challenges and politically restrained to trend toward the equilibrium that is so natural in most other markets and so needed in this one. The allocation of water to this day does not even remotely adhere to the forces of a market seeking equilibrium, and it is clear that a price-driven optimal allocation will not always equate to an optimal distribution. Not coincidentally, the global condition of our water resources has never been more in peril nor the investment opportunities greater.

The inflection point is upon us. Water will be the resource that defines the twenty-first century driven by a substantial increase in its value. This value will inevitably be unlocked as the global population adjusts to the linkages between human health, economic development, and resource sustainability. But what is meant by value? As investors know, value can be an instructive yet elusive concept. Indeed, one of the dilemmas that Adam Smith faced in writing *An Inquiry into the Nature and Causes of the Wealth of Nations* (which set the foundation for the field of modern economics) involved tracing the roots of value. By discovering the source of value, Smith hoped to find a benchmark for measuring economic growth. He identified two different meanings of value (value in use and value in exchange) and observed that things that have a high value in use frequently have very little or no value in exchange. And, conversely, goods that have the greatest value in exchange often have inconsequential value in use.

Smith summed this up in the form of a puzzling contradiction: the diamond-water paradox. Why is it that diamonds, which have limited practical use (and no survival value), command a higher price than water, which is a prerequisite for life? Smith could not solve the paradox and instead identified labor as the source of value. What is instructive, and telling, was how he phrased the explanation: "The real price of every thing, what every thing really costs to the man who wants to acquire it, is the toil and trouble of acquiring it." Price was related to a factor of production (i.e., labor), thereby circumventing the original quest for the source of value to the consumer.

While we must not forget that in Smith's day natural resources were effectively viewed as unlimited, he certainly understood the value of water to someone thirsting in the desert. But again, at the time, such a scenario was a simple issue of supply and demand (neither curve was at issue), not an explanation of why the price of diamonds was greater than the price of water. It was not until the neoclassical economists of the late nineteenth century that the "answer" was told. The resolution of the paradox involved one of the most enduring metaphors in the history of economics and indirectly set in motion a divergence between economics and ecology, with implications far greater than anyone could have imagined.

Enter the theory of marginal utility. This subjective theory of value states that the price of a good is determined by its marginal utility, not by the amount of labor inputs and not by its total usefulness. *Utility* refers to the ability of a good or service to satisfy a want, and the immeasurable units of satisfaction are metaphorically called *utils.*

Water may have a very high total utility, but its general availability creates a low marginal utility and, since price is determined at the margin, a price that is artificially low. As economists suggest, do not confuse *utility* with *usefulness;* in other words, don't confuse the metaphor as a metaphor. The intuitively obvious inelasticity of demand for water is rendered nonsensical by a price that is not rendered at the margin; again, the marginal utility of water is ordinarily low because a single incremental unit seldom commands extraordinary satisfaction. The diamond-water paradox was solved. That was the story then.

The reality today is that virtually every country in the world is presented with some combination of water quality and quantity issues. Total utility, in the form of ecology, is not afforded the proper treatment. This is the cause of the divergence between economics and ecology; the total usefulness of nature, and water, must be part of the equation. Now today, once again, it is a simple issue of supply and demand because both curves are the issue. If the model of global warming and the metaphor of climate change are necessary to understand the true meaning of ecology, then so be it. Not that six million years of geologic history in our lineage is enough to convince us, but can it be any clearer from the "greenhouse gases" metaphor of climate change that nature "manages" us, not the other way around? To explain why we must fuse the human economy with nature's economy we must also retell the story of water.

I have intentionally stopped short of a more detailed exposition of the implications for water because it is critical that the investor constantly refer back to this paradox throughout the reading. The response to the diamond–water paradox will be a prominent part of the fundamentals associated with investment in water; for now, the answer will remain a question so that the reader refers back to the paradox as often as the content inspires reflection. This foreshadows the transition under way in the water industry; that is, the substantial increase in its value.

Why is all of this so important to investors in water? While the implications will be addressed in more detail in the concluding comments, investors must keep several things in mind as the journey progresses. First, there are no substitutes for water. Second, prices set at the margin should include the marginal cost of water. Third, value in exchange requires a measure of value and the ability to exchange. And fourth, total utility is relevant to ecology.

Can it simply be that this is the first time (or the time of accumulated knowledge) in the history of humanity that we have the experiential ability to tell the story of nature on a planetary scale, that is, once our activities impact nature on a planetary scale? It is in that spirit that the story of water is told. The human species and nature are obviously inseparable. At the same time, the human economy and nature's economy are viewed as divisible; nature serves humanity. Analogous to the division of labor, the mechanistic methodology embraced by modern economics seeks the division of resources, the specialized utilization of our natural resources in the relentless pursuit of growth in isolation from the precepts of ecology. When private and social rates of return diverge, private decision makers will not allocate optimally. The divergence of social and private costs and/or benefits result as much from the "rules" established by institutions as it does from the methodology used to measure such costs.

There is a burgeoning global demand for safe drinking water, environmentally sustainable water use, and industrial process improvement. Yet despite unprecedented economic progress on a global scale, environmental issues have been largely neglected as a critical component of continued growth. For such a basic proposition as clean water, why has the industry dedicated to addressing this need not received more attention? Why is there such a disconnect between the human economy and "nature's economy," as coined by Donald Worster?

The problem is that as economic activity expands, there seems to be an almost cavalier denial of the impact on our natural resources, as if there were no linkage between unbridled expansion and the planet's carrying capacity. It is this fusion of ecology and economics that will reorder the cultural paradigm and facilitate an understanding of our interconnectedness with nature. The assumptions of economic society must be fused with its biological underpinnings. It is time to establish new metaphors that fuse ecology with economics and, in so doing, retell the story of water for the twenty-first century.

Part One

WATER

Chapter 1

Water: Prerequisite for Life and Living

Water is ubiquitous on Planet Earth. As we view our planet from beyond, we are struck by the prevalence of water. It is so much a distinguishing feature on the universal canvas that Earth is commonly referred to as the "Blue Planet." Before we had an interstellar perspective, and before we were even aware of a planetary scheme, the word *earth* took cultural form from the solid footing that was understood—namely, ground, soil, and land. The planet was labeled accordingly. But the reality is that water is a primal driver in shaping the planet and the awareness is that its scarcity is a constraint on its inhabitants. From this modern perspective, it would be more appropriately called Planet Water.

It is believed that large amounts of water have flowed on Earth for 3.8 billion years, most of its existence. There is no coincidence between the abundance of water on Earth and the existence of life. Water is the dominant constituent of virtually all living forms. As Felix Franks of the University of Cambridge puts it, "Without water it's all just chemistry. Add water and you get biology." Water is a prerequisite for life. To understand the intricacies of the water molecule in developing and sustaining life is to understand the economic potential of water in the context of its presence as a prerequisite for living. As humans place burgeoning demands on the substance, water is increasingly recognized for the limitations its distribution places on the socioeconomic well-being of civilizations.

A key requirement for successful investing is a thorough understanding of the business that you are investing in. The fact that we need water to survive, while certainly putting a floor on demand, is not the level of understanding that we are after. Despite the rigors of understanding the many facets of water, it is absolutely critical that investors understand the science. It is the uniqueness of water that governs the technology to maintain its primal purpose, the economics of implementing solutions, and the politics to ensure its sustainable use. All aspects of investing in water are influenced by an understanding of what water represents. One simple fact sets in motion this unprecedented investment opportunity: There is simply no substitute for water.

Prerequisite for Life

The way the water compound is structured, and the resulting interaction with other key biogeochemical cycles, creates an intricate fabric that forms the basis of life on Earth. It is the oft-made statement that life depends on the anomalies of water. It is a critical biomolecule, structuring proteins, nucleic acids, and cells. Remarkably, the behavior and function of water, despite considerable research, is still far from completely understood.

The Life-Enabling Anomalies of Water

The simplicity of the atomic structure of a water (or hydrogen oxide) molecule belies its extraordinarily unique electrochemical properties. The V-shaped water molecule consists of two light hydrogen (H) atoms and a relatively heavier oxygen (O) atom at the vertex. The difference in mass gives rise to the molecule's ease of rotation and the constant movement of the hydrogen nuclei. The way in which the two hydrogen atoms are bonded to the oxygen atom is particularly significant. The electrons are shared between the atoms (covalently bonded) but are not distributed equally. The oxygen atom, therefore, attracts the electrons more strongly than the hydrogen side. The resulting asymmetrical distribution of charge, or dipolarity, creates a net positive charge on the hydrogen side of the molecule and a net negative charge on the opposite oxygen side. Hydrogen bonding causes molecules of water to be attracted to each other, forming strong molecular bonds, and explains many of the anomalous properties of water. The oxygen atom's strong affinity for chemical bonding with other nuclei enables many of life's reactions. Hydrogen bonding also allows water to separate polar solute molecules. The partially negative dipole end of the water molecule is attracted to positively charged components of a solute, while the opposite occurs on the positive dipole end. This polarity explains water's ability to dissolve many "contaminants" (the fact that oil is a nonpolar molecule is the reason that water and oil do not mix). In fact, water is known as the "universal solvent." This seemingly innocuous property accounts for an enormous proportion of the money spent in the water and wastewater industry. All sorts of dissolved substances (some a nuisance, some deadly) must be removed to make water suitable for most end uses, drinking water in particular. Investment applications include all aspects of water and wastewater treatment, nonpoint source surface water (runoff), stormwater, and groundwater. This is why treatment is viewed as such a compelling part of investing in water and why every location has a different treatment challenge.

As essential for life, however, the solvent properties of water are vital in biology, because many biochemical reactions can occur only in aqueous solution and also because this feature enables water to carry solvent nutrients to living organisms. This is also the reason why water seldom has a neutral pH of 7.0. Only pure water is neither acidic nor basic (acid rain, caused by sulfur dioxide and nitrogen oxide emissions from coal-burning power plants and automobiles, can have a pH as low as 2.3—as acidic as lemon juice).

Because of the extensive hydrogen bonding between molecules, water has the second-highest specific heat capacity of any known chemical compound, except ammonia, as well as a high latent heat of vaporization. These two unique properties allow water to moderate the Earth's climate by buffering large fluctuations in temperature. The large heat capacity of the oceans allows them to function as heat reservoirs in this buffering process. These properties have monumental ramifications in the advent of global warming.

The specific heat also helps organisms regulate their body temperature more effectively. Another life-enabling property of water is its high surface tension, the highest among nonmetallic liquids. The stability of water drops is critical in transporting water through the roots and stems of plants via the xylem. It is also responsible for the capillary action that allows water and dissolved substances to move through the blood vessels in our bodies.

In addition, the presence of hydrogen bonds provides another unique behavior for water upon freezing. As water molecules seek to minimize energy when cooled to the freezing point, the hydrogen bonds allow the formation of a hexagonal crystal structure that is more expansive than in the liquid state. Unlike almost all other substances, the solid state of water is, therefore, not as dense as the liquid form; that is, ice floats. This has environmentally significant implications. If water were denser when frozen, susceptible lakes and rivers, and oceans in polar biomes, would freeze solid, preventing thermal stratification from occurring and widely impacting biological systems in the lower aquatic life zones.

There are many additional anomalous properties of water, from the opposite properties of hot and cold water to its unique hydration properties for biological macromolecules that clearly place water in a unique class among the determinants of life on Earth. Interestingly, although the molecular structure of water is assumed stable in molecular thermodynamics, there are studies that have indicated that at the quantum (nanoscale) level, water may behave differently. At very small timescales, the structural permanence of water is more questionable, possibly with nanotechnology implications. The science of water tells us that water is a prerequisite for life and, in this respect, cannot be overemphasized. From an investment perspective, it is an undeniable fact. But the way water is cycled on the planet is the process that determines availability and accessibility from a societal perspective.

The Recycling of Water Energy

The hydrologic cycle is one of the life-sustaining biogeochemical (literally, life-earth-chemical) cycles—natural processes that cycle critical constituents from the abiotic (nonliving) environment to biotic (living) organisms and then back again. As cycles, the assumption is that these systems, for all intents and purposes, are closed, powered by energy from the sun and moving a fixed amount of matter in a continuous process.

Water is the most abundant molecule on the surface of the Earth. It is the only common substance found naturally in all three physical states of matter within the relatively small range of temperatures and pressures encountered on the planet's surface. It composes approximately 75 percent of the Earth's surface in liquid and solid (frozen) states, in addition to being the third most abundant gas in the atmosphere in the form of water vapor. Further, of the atmospheric constituents that vary in concentration both spatially and temporally, water vapor is the most abundant. While the variable components of the atmosphere make up a very small portion of atmospheric gases, they have a much greater influence on both weather (short-term) and climatic (long-term) conditions. Water vapor redistributes heat energy on the Earth through latent heat energy exchange, condenses to create precipitation, and warms the Earth's atmosphere as one of the original greenhouse gases.

The hydrologic cycle is often modeled as having distinct phases; evapotranspiration, condensation, precipitation, and collection. It is viewed as a constant system—water molecules in continuous movement cycling through well-defined states. But that model of uniformity, couched in terms of a human timescale, is increasingly seen, along with other elements of our ecosystem, as a fragile balance between determinism and chaos. While the overall volume of water is not changeable on a human timescale, it is clear that we can, and are, directly and indirectly affecting the spatial and temporal distribution of water on the planet. In other words, we are impacting the hydrologic cycle. This is not only in the obvious sense that we are depleting aquifers, diverting surface water flows, and exacerbating runoff, but we are also impacting the hydrologic cycle by altering the carbon cycle, creating infinite mini–storage units of water in all types of products, and generally mismanaging water in a rapid divergence from sustainability.

The role of water as a prerequisite for life, and its availability as a constraint on the human condition, combine with the natural distribution of water on the planet in a collision course with a rapidly expanding human population driven by economic development. The hydrologic cycle is one of the links between the biosphere (the collection of the earth's ecosystems) and the ascension of civilizations. As human activity approaches globalization, it has a greater ability to alter this global life-support system; that is, an expanding global economy becomes larger relative to the nonexpanding biosphere.

Human activities affect the biogeochemical cycles in vastly different ways. All of these cycles have extraordinarily complex features. The phosphorus cycle, for example, is exceedingly slow. On a human timescale, it can be viewed as a one-way flow from land to oceans. The carbon cycle, on the other hand, is unique in that while carbon-containing fossil fuels take millions of years to form, human activities can relatively quickly change the form, but not the absolute amount, of carbon. The carbon cycle includes carbon dioxide (CO_2) gas that regulates the Earth's thermostat—too little CO_2 in the atmosphere and it will cool; too much and the atmosphere warms. Here, human activities are capable of rapidly altering the mix. Fossil fuels are nonrenewable on a human timescale. In addition, water has now become a limiting factor in economic development: It is a prerequisite for living.

Prerequisite for Living

By "prerequisite for living" it is meant that water is a crucial factor in human well-being and the quality of life. Just behind income, the availability of water ranks as the second most critical factor in a survey of "well-being" among those most burdened in society. Water, through its many consumptive uses, permeates virtually all aspects of the socioeconomic fabric and affects many of our life choices. The lack of water, of acceptable quality and in sufficient quantity, is a major factor in poverty, food insecurity, human disease, economic development, and, ultimately, geopolitical conflict. It is this rapidly accelerating realization that forced water challenges onto the global stage, spotlighting the role of water as a prerequisite for living.

Water and the Quality of Living

If water plays such a vital role in human well-being and economic development, we would expect to face our greatest challenges in areas of the world where water is extremely scarce. And that is certainly the case. As the human population and economy grow, however, it is becoming apparent that hydrocentric constraints are permeating many more activities than would be expected from an obvious imbalance of supply and demand. Accordingly, while water availability is subject to spatial and temporal variations, it is constructive to get some sense of social condition in relation to water resources. The Water Poverty Index (WPI) was developed by the Center for Ecology and Hydrology for just such a purpose. The WPI is designed to be a scalable "evaluation tool for assessing poverty in relation to water resource availability." The composite index is a numerical measure that can be utilized by decision makers in water policy processes. The WPI is one way to produce a standardized framework to capture the complexity of water management issues as they relate to quality-of-life issues. But it is the theoretical basis of the WPI framework that is useful for our current purpose—that of linking water resource availability to, in their words, "the socioeconomic indicators of poverty drivers," or in my words, the quality of living.

Lack of water does not cause poverty, but poverty virtually always includes a lack of water. While *poverty,* like *standard of living,* can be defined in measurable terms, quality of living is a relative condition. It makes sense, then, to focus on a quantifiable level rather than a qualitative notion when viewing water as a prerequisite for living. As such, the long line of advancements that poverty is circumscribed by capability deprivation extends well to the ideal of quality of living encompassed in an ability to make livelihood choices. Having access to adequate water supplies for domestic and productive use clearly falls into the category of capability deprivation. To maintain effective livelihood choices, five capabilities have been identified by Desai (1995):[1]

1. Capability to stay alive/enjoy prolonged life
2. Capability to ensure biological reproduction
3. Capability for healthy living
4. Capability for social interaction

5. Capability to have knowledge and freedom of expression and thought.

Water is linked to all of these capabilities.

Given that water is a prerequisite for life and for living, it bears upon the investment implications going forward to get a sense of the baseline global water condition and to project the likely global water scenarios into the future.

Chapter 2

The Global Water Condition

T he statistics are telling. The World Health Organization (WHO) estimates that 1.1 billion people do not have access to improved drinking water and that 2.6 billion people (40 percent of the world population) live in families with no proper means of sanitation. Half of all hospital beds in the world are filled with people suffering from waterborne and water-related diseases. The health burden also includes the annual expenditure of over 10 million person-years of time and effort by women and children carrying water from distant sources. If the average of one hour per day saved by each household member through the convenience of more proximate safe drinking water were used in a livelihood earning a minimum daily wage, this labor input would be worth $63.5 billion dollars per year.

The proliferation of statistics on the global water condition belies the notion that we have a firm grasp of the extent and depth of the impacts of the shortfall in potable water and sanitation. The impact of water scarcity is devastating: pervasive poverty, food insecurity, conflict, and morbidity. But none are as chilling as the fact that the lack of water and sanitation services kills about 4,500 children per day.

The Human Cost of Waterborne Disease

There are few things more tragic than a resource vital to human life taking life. Yet that is the case every day. Contaminated water causes a wide variety of communicable diseases through ingestion or physical contact. Waterborne disease remains one of the most significant threats to human health worldwide. Strictly speaking, waterborne diseases are caused by the ingestion of water contaminated by human or animal waste containing pathogenic bacteria or viruses including cholera, typhoid, amoebic and bacillary dysentery and other diarrheal diseases. More broadly, water-caused diseases also include water-washed diseases caused by poor personal hygiene and skin or eye contact with contaminated water (scabies; trachoma; and flea, lice, and tick-borne diseases); water-based diseases caused by parasites found in intermediate organisms living in water (dracunculiasis, schistosomiasis, and other intestinal helminths); and water-related diseases caused by insect vectors which breed in water (dengue, filariasis, malaria, onchocerciasis, trypanosomiasis, and yellow fever).

While global mortality figures vary considerably, the human toll from water diseases is clearly unacceptable. An estimated 1.8 million deaths occur annually from diarrheal diseases alone, and 90 percent of those are children under the age of five, mostly in developing countries. According to WHO statistics, there are approximately 4 billion cases of diarrhea each year, caused by a number of different pathogens, including *Shigella, Campylobacter jejuni, Escherichia coli, Salmonella,* and *Vibrio cholerae.* In Bangladesh alone, diarrheal diseases kill over 100,000 children every year. The alarming rate of urbanization, and the crowded condition of Dhaka's slum communities, adds significantly to the morbidity rate. And this scenario is played out in many parts of the world, such as Ethiopia, India, Kenya, Guatemala, Nigeria, and Honduras, to name just a few.

Supply and Demand

On the planetary scale there can be no shortage of water. We have essentially the same amount of water on the planet today that we had millions of years ago. And it is an enormous quantity, about 1.39 billion cubic kilometers (331 million cubic miles or some 3.26×10^{20} gallons). Unfortunately for us, most of that water is unsuitable for human consumption, especially with a global population of 6.7 billion people.

As can be seen in Figure 2.1, 97 percent is saltwater contained in the oceans; leaving only about 3 percent freshwater. And of all the freshwater available only 1 percent is surface freshwater. The rest is locked up in the polar ice caps, glaciers, and permanent snow or comprised of depletable

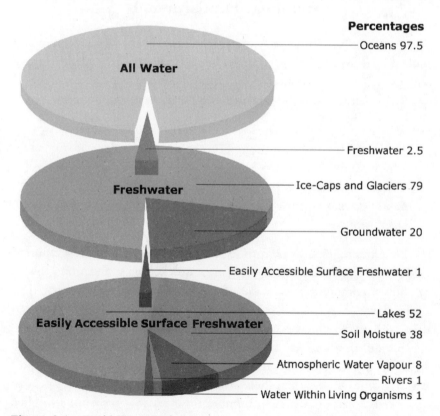

Figure 2.1   Earth's Water Budget

groundwater. All told, only about 0.036 percent of the planet's total water supply is found in rivers and lakes. While estimates of the global water distribution vary among researchers, suffice it to say that only a very small fraction is easily accessible freshwater.

While global water supply has remained constant, global water demand has increased sixfold in the last century, increasing more than twice the growth rate of global population. Right now, nearly three billion people live in water-scarce conditions (40 percent of the world's population), and that proportion is expected to increase to at least 60 percent by 2025. If per-capita consumption of water continues to increase at its current rate, we will be using over 90 percent of all available freshwater by 2025.

Regional Fundamentals

The WHO/UNICEF Joint Monitoring Program for Water Supply and Sanitation revealed glaring contrasts between developed and developing regions, rich and poor countries, and rural and urban populations in regard to access to clean water and sanitation. The challenges identified are:

- To maintain the gains already made in developing countries,
- To extend the reach to the billions of people residing in rural areas who have no services
- To accelerate the efforts in urban areas in order to keep pace with rapid population growth by focusing on low-income and disadvantaged groups.

Despite progress, it's hard to see how the Millennium Development Goals (MDGs) can be met in regions of quickening population growth.

Sub-Saharan Africa remains the region of greatest concern. The *Global Water Supply and Sanitation Assessment* by the WHO reported that, with an 85 percent increase in urban population over the coverage period, the number of people unserved has doubled. In the rural areas, the number of people unserved with improved drinking water was five times higher than their urban counterparts, and with respect to improved sanitation, the rural number unserved was three times higher. The African urban population is expected to double over the next 25 years. In addition to sub-Saharan Africa, the 80 percent unserved global population is concentrated in eastern and southern Asia. Access to drinking water through a household connection is as low as 16 percent in sub-Saharan Africa, 20 percent in southern Asia, and 28 percent in southeastern Asia. The urban population of Latin America and the Caribbean is expected to increase by almost 50 percent by 2025, representing another region of potential shortfall in achieving adequate drinking water and sanitation access.

The sobering nature of the global water condition leads to a horrible and inescapable conclusion: If nothing is done, current death rates traced to water access and water quality will rise dramatically. Millions more will die. What's required to prevent this worst-case scenario is technological, financial, and institutional innovation.

Water Institutions

The term *institution* immediately takes on an unintended connotation with respect to water. It goes beyond the reference to an organization in society or culture although that is obviously a very large, and growing, part of water governance. The WHO, the World Bank, the United Nations Children's Fund (UNICEF), and the International Monetary Fund (IMF) are international institutions that clearly have a large role in defining and addressing global water issues. The regulatory framework is also included within the institutional landscape. National regulatory bodies such as the U.S. Environmental Protection Agency (EPA), the European Commission, the Ministry of Water Resources of the People's Republic of China, and the European Union (EU) Water Framework Directive are institutions linked to specific governments.

Just as significant, and arguably more instrumental to the future of water, is the extension of water "institutions" to more process-oriented meanings. This reference is more to the relational connotation associated with the institution label. While the relationship between markets and governments can take on many traditional institutional forms, regulation in the water industry easily rises to an institutional stature. Water regulations and laws play a key role in driving not only the composite water business but also specific components that can be actionable for an investor.

Regulation is achieved through governance of the water, waste-water, and stormwater utilities and will be discussed more thoroughly in Chapter 9. The key element here is that regulatory frameworks are a major link between the global water condition as it currently exists and what each individual state, society, or culture wants it to be in the future. When it comes to environmental regulation, there is significant difference between developed and developing countries. Developing countries that are rapidly industrializing generally do not have the institutional structure in place to keep up with escalating pollution. And even if rules, regulations, and standards are in place, monitoring and enforcement seldom are, and compliance suffers as a result. Further, while some international agreements have been forged (e.g., the Kyoto Agreement with respect to CO_2 emissions), environmental regulations are generally established based on the sovereign national boundaries. This is problematic with respect to larger regional water resource imperatives because nature's watershed boundaries do not adhere to geopolitical borders and there can be very different regulatory mandates and stringency approaches between countries.

Regulation

Regulation is a key driver of the water industry and therefore in determining the investment potential of specific water companies. A major goal of this book is to provide a guide for investing in water as a thematic strategy. Any discussion of the merits of investing in water must necessarily address the regulatory institutions that touch every aspect of the industry. Unfortunately, rather than detailed analysis of the nexus between regulations and specific investment opportunities, most water analysts totally disregard the regulatory drivers. This is a major omission for a number of reasons:

- The developing countries are, conservatively, two (and, more likely, three) decades behind the United States and other advanced economies with respect to the implementation of regulatory initiatives. This can be surmised from a simple extension of the U.S. timeline relative to the original Clean Water Act (CWA).
- In the United States, many of the water and wastewater systems built in the advent of the CWA are now nearly at the end of their life

cycles. This is yet another factor that perpetuates the positive fundamental outlook of water infrastructure companies well into the future.

- The developed countries are entering advanced treatment phases
  arising from the regulation of ever-emerging contaminants, disinfection by-products, and trace contaminants detected with sophisticated analytical methods.

Accordingly, a detailed analysis of existing, pending, and potential regulations and global regulatory trends will be presented to isolate
specific water investment opportunities. Regulations, and the water institutions that govern their promulgation, are increasingly viewed in concert with market forces as a shaping force in socioeconomic imperatives.

The regulation of water worldwide is a complex interaction of governmental bodies and institutional entities that varies widely from country
to country. At the core, however, is the imposition of water quality standards designed to protect human health and safeguard the environment.

Overview of Water Regulation in the United States

In the United States, with its federalist approach to government, water
policy is shared between national and state (and local) governments.
The mission statement of the EPA, established by President Nixon
in 1970, is to set environmental protection standards consistent with
the country's emerging national environmental goals. The establishment of the EPA was part of a reorganization plan devised to consolidate the federal government's numerous environmental regulations
under the jurisdiction of a single agency. The EPA brought together
15 components from 5 executive departments and independent agencies. While this restructuring occurred almost four decades ago in the
United States, it illustrates the regulatory development currently taking
place in developing and emerging countries.

The Safe Drinking Water Act

In the United States, the EPA administers 10 comprehensive environmental protection laws, several of which pertain exclusively to water.

The Safe Drinking Water Act (SDWA) includes a requirement that the EPA establish and enforce standards (maximum contaminant levels [MCLs], treatment techniques, monitoring) to which public drinking water systems must adhere. States and Indian tribes are given primary enforcement responsibility (i.e., primacy) for public water systems in their state if they meet certain requirements. For example:

- The state must have regulations for contaminants regulated by the national primary drinking water regulations that are no less stringent than the regulations promulgated by the EPA. States have up to two years to develop regulations after new regulations are released by the EPA.
- The state must have a program to ensure that new or modified systems will be capable of complying with state primary drinking water regulations.
- The state must have adequate enforcement authority to compel water systems to comply with National Primary Drinking Water Regulations (NPDWR).
- The state must have adequate variance and exemption requirements as stringent as the EPA's, if the state chooses to allow variances or exemptions.

The EPA coordinates efforts with state and local authorities in the development of drinking water standards. But most states directly oversee the water and wastewater systems within their borders. A critical state function is the adoption and implementation of procedures for the enforcement of state regulations. States must enact the authority to assess administrative penalties for violations of their approved primacy programs.

The SDWA requires the EPA to regulate contaminants that may pose a health risk and that may be present in public drinking water supplies. The EPA sets water quality standards based on physical, chemical, microbial, and radiological parameters. The physical standards include guidelines for solids (total, suspended, and dissolved), turbidity, taste/color/odor, and so on. Accordingly, the measurement of these parameters impacts the analytical sector of the water industry and the companies that provide instrumentation and equipment for measuring, testing, and monitoring. The chemical and microbial standards set

MCLs (and more stringent, nonenforceable maximum contaminant level goals [MCLG]) that drive the treatment sector of the business. This includes not only traditional primary and secondary treatment but also innovative treatment processes and technologies designed for advanced treatment of emerging contaminants. This is one aspect of water regulation that provides a great deal of investment opportunity, as will be discussed at length in Chapter 13 with respect to the growing list of global water quality issues. The 1986 amendments to the SDWA created further business for water treatment companies. A number of landmark regulations were enacted, including the Lead and Copper Rule, the Surface Water Treatment Rule, and the Total Coliform Rule.

The EPA accomplishes its regulation of water resources by integrating research, monitoring, standard-setting, and enforcement activities into a comprehensive framework of institutional oversight. Every state has governing bodies that either implement and enforce the national mandate or promulgate its own set of rules and regulations in accordance with the primacy requirements. States can be very proactive in implementing their own agendas. California, for example, is well known for its forward-looking water advocacy, having adopted requirements for a wide range of contaminants that are more stringent than the national version and even ahead of any federal regulation at all (e.g., perchlorates).

The Clean Water Act

Another major piece of water legislation in the United States is the Clean Water Act of 1972 (CWA), including a host of amendments. The CWA is the cornerstone of surface water quality protection; the act does not directly address groundwater issues. The statute employs a variety of regulatory tools aimed at restoring and maintaining the integrity of the nation's waters through the regulation of point source discharges into receiving water bodies. The main tool in achieving the "integrity" goal is the National Pollutant Discharge Elimination System (NPDES) permit program. Within this institutional framework, the development of a Total Maximum Daily Load (TMDL) determines what level of pollutant load would be consistent with meeting water quality standards. In the early days of implementation, the chemical properties of effluent

discharge was the focus. More recently, physical and biological parameters have expanded the effort in combination with an emphasis on nonpoint sources of pollution and a more holistic, watershed-based strategy.

Global Water Regulations

While the United States' regulatory framework is one of the broadest in the Organisation for Economic Co-operation and Development
(OECD) countries, the size and density of continental Europe has long
dictated that water policy be at the forefront of environmental legislation. Indeed, many advanced technologies, in particular disinfection and
treatment with ozone, preceded widespread adoption in the United
States by many years. EU water regulation, in the form of Drinking
Water Directives (DWDs), has, over time, evolved into an integrated
body of legislation. As in most developed regions, future program
directives include watershed management and protection and sustainable water use.

In many other countries, there is a need to coordinate and consolidate disparate regulations into comprehensive water legislation. It is
believed, for example, that Canada would benefit from a more national
water policy. Beyond the highly integrated regulatory frameworks of
the developed countries there exists a broad spectrum of regulatory
institutions too extensive to document here. Generally speaking, however, centralized governments set water policy at the national level
based on departmentalized responsibilities. So there often exists an
institutional mosaic of rather isolated regulations. In China, for example,
issuers of water laws and regulations can include the State Council, the
State Environmental Protection Administration, the Ministry of Health,
the Ministry of Water Resources, the Standing Committee of the
National People's Congress, and so on.

But by and large, the major developing countries (future dominant economies) are enacting increasingly stringent water regulations,
thereby following the same progression dictated by previously industrializing countries. Fortunately (or hopefully) for the planet, institutional
advancements can be implemented by the newly developing countries
without the need to experience the lessons of the past. For example,

it took many years for the nonpoint source regulations in the United States to evolve in the form of TMDLs, whereas China is already moving toward such watershed specific load requirements; carrying capacity has dire implications for exponentially expanding populations. As compliance enforcement catches up with the standards, all aspects of the water business will benefit. An imposing institutional force in advancing compliance and impacting global water policy is now coming from outside the governmental realm as well.

Nongovernmental Organizations

There are few global causes that are as permeated with nongovernmental organizations (NGOs) as clean water. The existence of so many NGOs in water is testament to the fact that water is indeed the world's most valuable resource. But value is in the eye of the NGO. Water is viewed from as many perspectives as there are agendas among the NGOs. There are NGOs that strongly support privatization and those that are antiprivatization. They can focus on water and poverty, water and economic development, water and human health, water and the environment, and literally any other pairing.

NGOs, typically independent of governments, are a pervasive result of globalization and play an increasingly vital institutional role in water resource management and policy. They often not only provide a fresh source of specific program funding but also serve to bridge national boundaries in addressing water issues. NGOs (also known as civil society organizations) can be community based; national or international; and operational, research oriented, or advocative.

The United Nations (UN), while definitionally not an NGO as a global association of governments, functions in a very similar manner when it comes to international water programs and policy. The UN family of organizations include many water-related programs embedded in the likes of UNICEF, WHO, the United Nations Educational, Scientific, and Cultural Organization (UNESCO), UN-Water and the World Bank, to name a few. In fact, NGOs helped create the UN, and its charter recognizes formal consultation arrangements with NGOs. It is becoming increasingly common for NGOs to be UN system partners.

So while the WHO is a major resource for issuing water quality standards adopted by many developing countries, and even played a role in the EU water directives, the supporting NGOs are very influential. The UN's MDG of reducing by half the number of people worldwide without access to safe drinking water has been a major impetus for international water initiatives.

While NGOs are traditionally more active in democracies, their ability to reach into virtually any forum is becoming quite skillful. NGOs active in water policies are prevalent around the globe. There are country-specific NGOs, such as Water Action in Ethiopia, Newah in Nepal, the Mvula Trust in South Africa, and ProNet in Ghana, that seek a role in guiding water resource management within state borders. There are also many international water research and specialist NGOs that serve as a mechanism for disseminating technical information and expertise in the interest of developing effective water policies. An example is the Water for People NGO that works closely with the American Water Works Association.

NGOs provide an institutional framework that contributes to water policy making in a number of ways. At the community level, they serve to build a consensus around water issues and work closely with political parties as representatives of the local people. They also function as think tanks to transfer innovative ideas and approaches into specific water policy actions. As mentioned, NGOs are often the source of considerable technical expertise that can serve as the foundation for treatment technologies in support of water regulations. And finally, the advocacy role in monitoring the application and enforcement of water laws and regulations is a critical component in the feedback loop that often defines the institutional impact on the expansion of the global water business.

The Institutional Impact on Water Investing

While globalization of capital and labor are driven by economics, it is not inconceivable, given the planetary nature of the water cycle, that standardized global water regulation could ultimately be the first step in a more comprehensive institutional governance of water resources. Unfortunately, the economic value of water is likely to ensure an interim period of sovereignty over water on at least a regional basis if not narrowly confined to political boundaries. This is the presumed basis for the much-anticipated conflicts over water.

The bottom line for investors is that the institutional structures within the water industry, in particular regulation, provide the mechanisms for which technology is transferred to the marketplace, largely in response to the compliance requirements embedded in major water policies. Regulation and innovation, both technological and procedural, form a feedback loop that drives all aspects of the water business. For example, regulations in the United States generally require that the industry use the best available technology (BAT) that is economically achievable to meet the goals. This cost-benefit optimization process is applied to successively more stringent regulations as innovation achieves the policy goal.

What is of interest is that, increasingly, regulation is being influenced by technology. This is truer in the developed countries where technological advancements often precipitate regulatory action. An example is the analytical technology that has enabled the measurement of trace contaminants, that is, concentrations in parts per trillion. This in turn provides the impetus for assessing long-term health effects that may or may not lead to regulatory action. In the emerging countries where the regulatory framework may not be as stringent or where, even if it is on the books, it is subject to less than fruitful enforcement, the treatment technology or the science of resource management is often very well established. Here, there is a lag between the institutional framework and the technology necessary to challenge other than the basics of nontrace contaminants and microbe-free drinking water and rudimentary wastewater sanitation.

The Role of Water in Economic Growth

That water is essential to economic development is unquestionable. The acute interest in water from the investment community is largely based on the premise that water, like energy, is a key input in any country's macroeconomic equation. But, unlike the unbridled exploitation of fossil fuels ushered in by the industrial revolution, the life-enabling nature of water adds an attention-grabbing aspect to the urgency of our global water challenges. This is certainly not to say that water resources have not been exploited (and indeed they have been for far longer than carbon-based resources), but the definition of exploitation takes on a different connotation when the exploited substance is necessary to sustain life.

I am often asked about the timing of the seemingly spontaneous interest in water, rising to almost ecotheist proportions. Aside from my angst over the notion that water resource issues are even remotely new, it is necessary to understand the origins and magnitude of the relatively recent attention from Wall Street. Emanating from the eco-undercurrents associated with global warming/climate change, energy independence, alternative energy, the ethanol craze, and the groundswell of "cleantech" investments, water resources are perceived as even more fundamentally in peril. Ironically, there have been few contamination scares in the United States, other than occasional precautionary "boil water" orders, that have provided an enduring catalyst for investment interest in the water industry. The dangerously high levels of lead leaching into Washington, D.C.'s, drinking water created largely localized concern. And the largest epidemic of waterborne disease ever reported in the United States, the 1993 Milwaukee cryptosporidiosis outbreak, while significantly advancing the knowledge of water treatment, was well before the business of water ever entered collective investment consciousness. The current trend is more concretely anchored in the rapidly increasing economic value of water. This value will inevitably be unlocked as the global population adjusts to the linkages between human health, economic development, and resource sustainability.

Productivity, Economics, and Ecosystems

Investors understand the paramount importance of productivity as a measure of economic efficiency. It measures how effectively economic inputs are converted to output by comparing the amount of goods and services produced with the inputs that were used in production. Gains in productivity, that is, the ability to produce more with less, are a critical source of increased potential income. Productivity performance is the key to improving living standards. For example, China has increased its productivity by an average of 20.4 percent over the past decade. And that productivity growth has been strong enough to off-set not only a rising currency but also higher wages and energy costs. Rising real incomes in China, and other BRIC (Brazil, Russia, India, China) countries, is a key to continued economic success. The only way to sustain increases in per-capita income in the long term is by increasing the amount of output produced per worker, that is, by raising labor productivity.

Labor productivity is often the metric used to represent the notion of productivity and is defined as the ratio of the output of goods and services to the labor hours devoted to the production of that output, that is, output per hour of the labor force. Or, stated another way, it is the rate at which the labor force converts hours worked into output. Under financial analysis, we perceive the human economy as being constrained only in terms of temporal economic conditions: where are we in the business cycle, the impact of declining consumer spending, how interest rates can be used to adjust the business climate, what impact the price of oil has on inflation, when currency values will redistribute global wealth, and so on. The scale of the human economy fluctuates, but it nonetheless expands over time.

The human economy, however, is limited by the flow of resources within the biosphere. The biosphere does not grow. It may fluctuate, but it does not expand in the sense that the global economy grows over time. Consequently, the human economy is getting larger and larger relative to the Earth's ecosystem. This reality is embedded in the notion of carrying capacity (absolute usage) and is central to any attempt at attaining sustainability (relative usage) with respect to any natural resource and, in particular, water. The economy must have an optimal scale relative to the ecosystem.

If we truly want to integrate sustainability into the equation, it is necessary to incorporate a measure of ecological impacts into the measures of the human economy. The eco-counterpart to labor productivity is "primary productivity." This somewhat nondescript label refers to the classification of living organisms on the planet in terms of energy flow through an ecosystem as "producers" (mainly green plants and phytoplankton) that make their own food through the process of photosynthesis, or consumers. By analogy, the producers are the planet's eco-labor force; all other organisms are consumers or decomposers (heterotrophs) that depend directly or indirectly on the food provided by producers.

Carrying Capacity

The gross primary productivity of ecosystems is the rate at which producers convert solar energy into chemical energy, or biomass. Net primary productivity (NPP) is what is left after accounting for the biomass utilized in the process; it is the planet's total food resource. As such, the Earth's NPP is a measure of sustainability and ultimately puts limits on the number of consumers, human or otherwise, that can thrive on the planet. Studies have estimated the potential global NPP that is being appropriated by humans.[1,2] And the results are not encouraging. A detailed, geographic accounting showed large regions of the world where the human appropriation of NPP is between 60 and 100 percent of natural productivity.[3] *Homo sapiens,* being only one of over 2 million known animal species (with many more unknown), exact an immensely disproportionate share of the Earth's resources. Exponential population growth, economic growth, and biomass-based energy sources will only accelerate the impact of human activities. The availability and distribution of water is a key determinant in calculating ecosystem NPP. The human appropriation of water resources (including exploitation, depletion, or degradation) has a staggering impact on the biosphere. The ultimate limitation on carrying capacity is the impetus for many aspects of water resource management and a driving force behind many water investments.

We can learn much on the micro scale by paying more attention to the macro scale. On a planetary scale, the hydrologic cycle is, by definition, always in equilibrium. There is a fixed amount of water on Earth that recycles in a closed system. Left to its own devices, the hydrologic cycle purifies water naturally, maintaining an equilibrium that is capable of sustaining life. Soils filter surface water infiltrating to aquifers of groundwater. In the United States, more than 50 percent of the wetlands that recharge and purify groundwater have been destroyed. Water is also purified as it changes phases. As the surface of saltwater begins to freeze (at 28.6°F for seawater of normal salinity) the salt is frozen out in a process known as brine rejection. But interject accelerated demands on water through population growth, and limit the accessible supply of freshwater through degradation, and the equilibrium quickly disappears. It is at this inflection point that we find ourselves.

Nothing on the planet is untouched by water. There is a massive amount of information being accumulated and reported about the global water condition. Not to be critical, but the vast majority of the information is more productive as data than knowledge. Beyond the molecular level, the basic question that must be addressed is: How exactly should civilizations characterize water?

Chapter 3

Public Good, Commodity, or Resource?

Water is characterized in many ways: "precious resource," "blue gold," "the oil of the twenty-first century," "vital commodity," and so on. While these descriptions may have headline value, they offer little practical guidance for addressing and solving water issues. That is all well and fine with the latitude afforded mainstream journalism, but at best these labels lack nuance and at worst they inhibit market-based solutions to the problem. If water is vital and, as such, a public good, then the implication is that governments must intervene to provide equitable distribution. However, if it is truly a commodity, the implication is that market forces alone can readily provide optimal allocation.

Such a discussion might sound like a preoccupation with semantics. In fact, the proper description of water as a public good, a commodity, or a resource is not only critical to the sustainable management of the planet's water but underlies the fundamental premise from an investment perspective. The reality is that while water is one of the most basic and simplest of molecules essential for life, it is also exceedingly complex—physically, economically, and, certainly, politically.

What *Is* Water?

On a societal level, water must be defined in a way that facilitates water resource management decisions.

Some economists argue simply that water must be defined either as a social (public) good or a private good. It is precisely the language we use to describe water that determines how we address the numerous complex issues. Unbeknownst to most water investors, the distinction is critical. It goes to the very root of the economics associated with the provision of water and the resulting abundance or paucity of market opportunities. Further, the distinction is a common thread that weaves its way through virtually all of the ensuing discussions related to the many facets of the water industry.

The Right to Water versus Water Rights

It is important to address the notion of a human "right" to water. How far should we go in insisting that water, and healthy water in particular, is a basic right for every person on Earth? The issue cannot be summarily addressed and discarded. Nor can it be so preoccupying as to ignore the economic value of water. My view is the human right to water trumps the "invisible hand" of the free market, but, at the same time, elevating water to a human right must not paralyze what needs to be done to achieve water resource sustainability. And the fact is that sustainability requires an element of market influence.

Water Rights

At least in definition, the private ownership of water (namely, water rights) is diametrically opposed to the right to water. Practically speaking, however, the two extremes can, and must, eventually be reconciled.

And, in fact, it is the inevitable reconciliation of these seemingly opposite doctrines that creates one of the potentially most significant investment opportunities of the second half of the twenty-first century and beyond.

Water rights are a highly specialized type of real property. While the holders of water rights include governments, public districts, and mutual companies, it is the private and investor-owned water right holders that most often draw disdain from those focused on the human right to water. Of all the aspects of a market-driven approach to the provision of water, none epitomize the concept as blatantly as water rights. But because the private ownership of water can be made intrinsically less marketable than others due to the legal way in which it is defined, there is a paradoxical imposition of governmental will as dictated by the ideology of lawmakers. In other words, even a private ownership right can contain the trappings of a social good. For example, any restriction on transferability is a restriction on efficiency. The ideal criteria for drafting water rights will be explored in greater detail in the broader context of water marketing. For now, suffice it to say that water marketing is an area with far-reaching investment potential and is a dynamic component of the water business that investors must monitor closely.

Water as a Public (Social) Good

There is no such thing as a list of products or "goods" that fall neatly into the category of social goods. Inclusion is, generally speaking, one of default. If a good cannot be provided through a market system, then it is a social good that must be provided by the public sector. In this context, the word *cannot* refers to either complete market failure or an inefficiently functioning market. Obviously, the determination of any given market "failure" is highly subjective and open to debate. As such, perhaps it's more instructive is to start with the premise that some role of government is a given, with the exact role determined by the prevailing political and/or social ideologies in the relevant community.

When it comes to the provision of water, it is especially easy to extend this macro construct to the micro level, or, stated differently, from the global to the local level. As a budding resource economist designing water rate (tariff) schedules for municipalities, the first thing I learned was that even the most sophisticated econometric models could not overcome a political agenda. To politicians, water rate models are the equivalent of black-box quant funds; they work well when they produce the results that you want, but events at the margin are to be discounted as too many standard deviations from reality. For economists, however, everything happens at the margin. But try explaining the marginal cost of providing water to the local member of a private golf course, for example. All of a sudden, the price of membership is irrelevant and water is a social good.

Historically speaking, much of the fervor associated with water results from a belief that water is somehow unique—so unique that it warrants governmental direction rather than being subjected to the perils of private ownership and the discretion of the "invisible hand." The allocational shortcomings of both the prior appropriations and riparian water rights doctrines in the United States result from the lack of institutional development justified by the uniqueness of water. The prevalence of government in water reflects the notion that decentralized decision making with respect to the allocation of water does not ensure the optimal distribution; that is, water is a public good. From there, political and social ideologies take root. One particular problem with viewing water solely as a public good (and especially a global public good) is that it falls somewhere in between oil and air on the exclusivity spectrum. If I consume a gallon of gasoline, you cannot consume that same gallon. As I breathe air, however, my inhalation does not impact your ability to also do so. Water has characteristics of both rival consumption and nonexcludability. That's a problem, but one that would resolve itself if water were truly a commodity.

Water as a Commodity

When water is analyzed in the context of a commodity, it is important to realize that the current discussion is not focused on water as a commodity *class* but whether water exhibits the economic characteristics of a commodity, particularly in regard to pricing. (Notwithstanding, the asset class issue is very important to investors and deserves a separate discussion after a greater understanding of the water industry.) A commodity is a largely homogenous physical substance that is interchangeable with another product of the same type, traded principally on the basis of a bulk price determined by supply and demand in an open market. Based on that definition, water is nowhere near a commodity. Indeed, at this point in the development of the water industry, it is almost the antithesis of a commodity; treated water is not homogenous (and even raw water is not fungible), there are no substitutes, there are few mechanisms to establish an equilibrium-driven price, and there is no spot market for water. Nonetheless, there are many economic forces at work that are driving water into becoming more and more like a commodity.

As the cost of water rises, water becomes like other economic goods (as opposed to public goods) for which there are supplies, demands, and a pricing and marketing structure to balance the supplies and demands. This transformation is what is referred to as the "commoditization" of water. The market economy serves to efficiently allocate resources in the provision of private goods. Consumers bid for what they want to buy and thus reveal their preferences to producers. The catalyst for change is the inevitable upward adjustment in the cost and price of water.

I am not implying that a much higher (true) cost of water is the panacea of global water issues. If water were a commodity, conventional wisdom would imply that the price would decline as more is provided. This was the premise behind the now antiquated use of declining block rate schedules in charging for water usage. The water utility industry sought to apply the principle of economies of scale in water pricing by charging a lower per-unit (gallon or liter) rate as consumption increased based on the traditional notion that fixed costs were being spread over greater numbers and, therefore, the price should decline in accordance. This is all well and fine if the cost base is adequately calculated, but if it does not include an element of scarcity, or increasing marginal costs of supplies, then the true cost will not be recovered. Such is the position in which water utilities find themselves, having not charged for "replacement" value and, therefore, not accommodating the massive requirement for upgrades to the point where we now have a trillion-dollar infrastructure spending gap.

Water as a commodity also assumes that there is a firmly entrenched market for water that acts in accordance with market forces to achieve equilibrium in supply and demand. The commoditization of water has enormous implications for investors. The market signals contained through a market price impact the entire water industry, from the relative feasibility of desalination to the need for real-time metering, to privatization, to reuse and, ultimately, to sustainable water use. Molecular water may be a commodity but clean water certainly is not. And clean water is the problem. Accordingly, at this stage in the development of the global industry, water, in all of its forms, must be viewed as a resource subject to the principles of resource economics.

The Answer: Water as a Resource

When you look at the schematic of the Earth's water budget, two things become glaringly apparent. First, the amount of easily accessible surface water is only a tiny fraction of the total amount of water available on the planet. And, second, water is not homogenous; it comes in many forms. There is seawater, brackish water, groundwater, surface water, glaciers, and so on. And not even taken into account are "alternative" supplies, such as reclaimed water, conserved water, and "greywater." Each is a resource with its own particular characteristics—depletable, renewable, recyclable, replenishable, or any combination thereof.

Resource Economics

It must be remembered that the classification of water determines how it is allocated to address the global water challenges. Efficiency in allocating water depends on the proper framework. For example, with respect to the allocation of surface water among competing water uses, the dictates of efficiency are clear. As economists explain, surface water should be allocated so that all uses derive an equivalent marginal net benefit.

> If marginal net benefits are not equalized, it is possible to increase net benefits by transferring water from those uses with low net marginal benefits to those with higher net marginal benefits. By transferring the water to the users who value the marginal water most, the net benefits of the water use are increased; those losing water are giving up less than those receiving the additional water are gaining. When the marginal net benefits are equalized, no such transfer is possible.[1]

Tom Tietenberg's theory does not reflect how water is allocated in practice. Instead, allocation is skewed by government definitions of property and by the lack of a market price designed to bring supply and demand into equilibrium.

"Unfortunately, water management and water-related institutions seldom achieve either a separation between fact and value or the assignment of responsibility for making these two different kinds of judgments to those best qualified to make them."[2] This is not the process-oriented enchantment with the free market that it appears to be. Indeed, an overemphasis on prices and markets could contribute more to the preservation of artificial scarcity than to the elimination of supply inefficiencies. This is simply the recognition that the current institutions governing the allocation of water resources are not based firmly on economic principles of efficiency.

The distinction between water as a public good, a commodity, or a resource underlies the framework by which we can properly address the efficient or inefficient *allocation* of water. Military defenses are distributed based on political ideology, oil is allocated based on price, and water is in that transitional stage where allocation and distribution are both required. Water is a resource that must be influenced by market forces within the context of a proper institutional (governmental) framework.

Water Pricing

I alluded to the inherently political nature of the vast majority of municipal water governing institutions. In the water rate design business, we adopted an occupational variation of a familiar tongue-in-cheek expression: "There are two things that you do not want to see being made. One is sausage and the other is water rates." Ideally, a forward-looking water pricing theory provides a class-specific cost-of-service model that charges consumers of a particular class (e.g., residential, multifamily, commercial, industrial, irrigation) in accordance with the particular and unique marginal costs that their consumption imposes on the water system. In reality, the most elaborate cost-of-service econometric models are no match for the subjectivity of an elected municipal water board seeking to appease disparate classes of water users. Whether a golf course, irrigation district, residential user, or small business, the special interests must be appeased in order to get consensus on any water rate hike. The political furor that accompanies the derivation of water rates is something to behold. I highly recommend that readers attend the next hearing by the local water company as it seeks the required public comment on water and wastewater rate hikes.

In my early days as a resource economist, I conducted an empirical study that was designed to estimate the residential demand curve for water. That's economist-speak for determining if the price of water influences demand. In one instance, I concluded that the price of water in a particular location was simply too low to affect consumptive behavior. Judging by the political furor that often accompanies water utility pricing policy, it is often not clear just how economic principles are to be applied to water resource problems. The water rate schedule is not only the price tag for water but also a reflection of broader goals and policies of those involved in rate making. It is this aspect that permeates the view that water is a "public good" that cannot be provided for through the market system. And, as the theory goes, if there is no market mechanism to determine equilibrium, then it generally falls upon the government to dictate optimality.

Equimarginal Value in Use

Economic principles of resource allocation dictate that when costs are incurred in the acquisition and transport of water supplies to customers, the principle of equimarginal value in use is combined with the principle of marginal cost pricing. Additional units of water can always be made available by expending more resources to acquire and transport it at a certain, albeit probably unacceptable, marginal cost. The question of where to stop increasing the supplies made available is then added to the question of how to arrange for the allocation of the supplies in store at any point in time. On efficiency grounds, additional units should be made available as long as any customers are willing to pay the incremental, or marginal, costs incurred. To meet the criterion of equimarginal value in use, however, the price must be made equal to all customers within a class served under identical marginal cost conditions. Marginal cost pricing is widely touted in the water supply industry, but few water utilities actually incorporate it into their rate schedules. Concerns over revenue stability and equity often prevail over the logic of charging for the true cost of service. It is precisely because of practical considerations such as location, use patterns, type of service, and so on, that the marginal costs of serving all customers will not be the same. The consumption characteristics of residential customers indicate that the real price of providing water must increase to reflect the true costs associated with the particular patterns of demand imposed on the system. This concept encourages change in water pricing as a conservation method.

While the regulatory setting indicates that the real cost of providing water will rise, the conservation trend virtually guarantees it. The use of pricing in particular has a dramatic effect because it links the supply and demand for water. As this occurs, the alternatives to the way we traditionally obtain water—from the tap—become attractive. So, in addition to nonprice considerations (quality concerns) that are currently driving the market for tap water substitutes, price will reinforce the shift in demand. The answer, then, to the original question as to who will benefit from the conservation of water is that point-of-use treatment technology will gain. The reason for the reluctance of the water supply industry to implement exactly what they espouse then becomes clear.

The transition to a market solution started as the institutions set up to deal with water as a public good failed to provide an efficient allocation of the resource. As increases in water use depleted easily developable supplies, more costly additional supplies were sought. As the costs of water increased, water resources became more like other economic products for which there are supplies, demands, and a pricing and marketing structure to balance the supplies and demands. Consumers, suppliers, and regulators now are recognizing that water is a complex resource—legally, hydrologically, and economically.

The real price of water is poised to rise significantly after decades of decline due to several factors. First, water is still a highly regulated industry, which imposes significant costs. Second, traditional rate structures that were set artificially low will require a catch-up in rates to adequately replace existing facilities. Third, the scarcity factor inherent in water resources is being incorporated into the supply component of the price of water. And, finally, the increasing importance of water-related technology as a response to water problems will require economic incentives to encourage their adoption. Pricing will provide the mechanism to shift from managing supply to managing change. Water price increases have historically fallen well short of even inflation, let alone true marginal cost increases. And while that is changing across the world as one locality after another has implemented drastic rate increases, especially in wastewater, double-digit increases are likely to become the norm for many years until the funding gap begins to narrow appreciably.

The water industry is like all other industries that must respond to change. Technological, environmental, social, and regulatory changes in the water industry operate to influence the way in which water is provided. As the real price of water rises to reflect the true economic and environmental costs associated with providing it, water utilities will be under substantial political pressure to offset price increases through economic efficiency. As efficiency considerations enter into water pricing, traditional services will be undertaken by new participants seeking to isolate and contain costs. The commoditization of water, then, will facilitate the unbundling of services within the traditional structure of the water industry. Markets (prices) reconcile the difference between what is wanted and what is available. Governments reconcile the difference between what is available and what is needed. The former allocates, the latter distributes.

Accordingly, the water industry likely will be segmented by value added criteria whereby new participants, or existing players in new roles, will provide an unbundled service. One example is privatization. With total annualized water quality costs expected to reach $87 billion by the year 2010, there will be an incentive for cost containment as well as the transfer of new water-related technologies to the marketplace. Water quality expenditures are driven primarily by private spending for the control of industrial effluent discharges and the pretreatment of wastewater, and by local government spending for the construction and operation of treatment facilities. As such, the ways in which economic change translates into investment opportunities are related to the financing mechanisms necessary to fuel the transition.

Just what form will this capital transformation take and what are the investment ramifications? Any time there is a structural change in an industry caused by shifts in the economic fundamentals there is a huge potential for corresponding economic gain. We can look to other industries for guidance. The rationing of health care led to overcapacity in hospital beds and resulted in massive consolidation of the hospital management industry. Commercialization in the biotechnology industry generated substantial growth and investment opportunities. Regulatory upheaval and oversupply in the natural gas industry led to the unbundling of services.

It is accurate to say that scarcity, pollution, or subsidization are not problems in regard to our water resources. The problem is an economic one. It is clear that the institutions sanctioned entirely by operation of government have failed to allocate water in an economically efficient manner. Instead, water should be treated like other private goods for which there are supplies, demands, and a pricing and marketing structure to balance the supplies and demands. As this complete transition will take many decades, the notion of water as a resource takes on an extremely attractive allure, especially for investors desiring to capitalize on the investment potential of water within their lifetime. Moving from the price of water to the cost of providing clean water is a disconnect that must be addressed. Estimates of the global costs associated with meeting demand are staggering and provide a backdrop to the enormous investment potential.

Chapter 4

The Cost of Clean Water

The number of estimates pertaining to the global cost of clean water is as staggering as the actual estimates themselves. International organizations seeking to fulfill their humanitarian or economic mandates, regulatory bodies complying with governing legislation or nongovernmental organizations (NGOs) with their particular agendas, all provide statistics that frame the water industry. The metrics describing the water industry can be couched in terms of funding, costs, needs, market size, or any other descriptor that puts a price on our global water problems. Dollar amounts can be linked to specific regulatory requirements, infrastructure "gaps," emerging country needs, water industry sectors, market size, treatment methodologies, and so on. If there is a way to graphically demonstrate that we are now ascending the exponential slope of monetary resources needed to protect a natural resource, it has been done. The slope keeps getting steeper, the estimates bigger, and the time horizon longer. Just like the world population clock, the aggregate cost of meeting the myriad water demands of the living planet continues to rise.

How Big Is the Universe?

Like many other questions fraught with theoretical perplexity and limited practical application, an estimate of the global cost of clean water does, nevertheless, serve a purpose. In analogous fashion to inquiries into the size of the universe, the sheer scale of the global water industry is the greatest impediment to deriving an answer; it is simply too extensive to be viewed in a composite manner. (Indeed, this is the basis of the notion that the water "industry" is somewhat of a mythological construct.)

So, what *is* the cost of clean water? For our purposes here, clean water refers to the costs associated with the full spectrum of water, wastewater, stormwater, recycled water, and so on, and all related activities and applications. Subsequent discussions will generally differentiate by sector or subsector in order to isolate the costs, needs, spending, or market size and thereby achieve greater precision in the analysis of investment opportunities; for example, spending on desalination, the cost of the arsenic regulations in the United States, the size of the market for ion exchange resins, rehabilitation infrastructure needs, and so on. But from this initial high-level perspective, cost is equivalent to the introductory requirement that water is both a prerequisite for life and for living. And, obviously, costs on one side are revenues to the other. Therein lies the motivation for investing in water.

The Global Cost of Clean Water

The process here reminds me of a project that I was assigned in a high school physics course. The exercise was to calculate the number of grains of sand on Earth. Clearly, the lesson was not in the answer but in the process. And that exercise instilled in me the notion that anything ineffably large can still be estimated. But, of course, the outcome of extrapolation is sensitively dependent on the accuracy of the initial conditions. It must be emphasized, therefore, that the approach used to present the magnitude of the global cost of clean water is not based on independent empirical research but gleaned from a survey of the literature.

The total cost of clean water is derived through the combination of major reports on global water conditions. The Organisation for

Economic Co-operation and Development (OECD) provides cost estimates for global water infrastructure and water-related services in the
update to its *Infrastructure to 2030* report.[1] However, it includes total
projected needs only for the 20 OECD members plus Brazil, Russia,
India, and China (the BRIC countries). The total cost of clean water
in the OECD and BRIC countries for the period 2008 through 2025
is projected to be $14.8 trillion. (Many water industry analysts provide
longer time horizons of questionable worth. The convention for our
purposes will extend to 2025.) As noted, the OECD report intentionally does not include non-OECD countries other than those specifically
added to the calculation. This excludes portions of Latin America, South
America, Central Europe, Asia, and Africa and the Middle East completely. Granted, with the inclusion of the BRIC countries, a significant
gap is filled. But the plight of other developing countries with much
less means is a critical part of the global water equation and cost.

The World Health Organization (WHO) prepared a study[2] that
estimated the costs of attaining the water supply and sanitation target
of the Millennium Development Goals (MDGs). The MDGs are geared
to developing countries where waterborne diseases are epidemic and a
major heath issue. The WHO study provides a phenomenally detailed
baseline of cost estimates that can be added to the OECD numbers.
Target 10 of the MDGs is to achieve, by 2015, a 50 percent reduction
in the proportion of the global population *without* "sustainable access
to safe drinking water and basic sanitation." The two key components of the study contained in that mission statement are the halving
of the proportion and the equivalence of "people without access" to
"developing countries." Thus, the study estimated water and wastewater spending required to meet the target in developing countries, which
WHO summarizes into 11 developing country subregions comprised of
about 160 countries. Another unique feature of this report is that it explic-
itly accounts for the costs of maintaining *existing* coverage levels, thereby
quantifying total costs rather than focusing on marginal costs, incremental
expenditures, or spending gaps, as most clean water cost estimates do.

The OECD and WHO reports have some inherent overlap. The
OECD report includes Russia, India, China, and Brazil, countries that
are non-OECD and subject to the MDG target. The WHO report,
however, is structured by developing country subregions and can

include any country (OECD or non–OECD) in the subregion, whether or not it is currently meeting the MDGs. And it is clear from the WHO numbers that the "big" (BRIC) economies are included in the cost estimates since approximately 90 percent of the projected population of non–OECD regions is represented. Taking these factors into account, adjusting for full attainment of the MDG target, and utilizing a more likely WHO scenario above the base cost case, yields an incremental cost to the OECD study of about $1.1 trillion for the period 2008 through 2025. Adding the two estimates, the magnitude of global water costs beginning with 2008 through 2025 is projected at $16 trillion.

The purpose of the lengthy description of the derivation of the global estimate of aggregate water spending requirements through 2025 is twofold: (1) to convey a sense of the magnitude of our water challenges and the institutional interest in providing quantitative tools to evaluate them as a call to action, and (2) to somewhat desensitize the reader to large numbers such that sector and subsector market size or spending/cost estimates will take on added precision from an investment perspective.

Given the shorter time frame (18 years) and the rigor of the underlying studies in accounting for not only future incremental needs, but also the costs of maintaining existing coverage levels (i.e., the cost of operating, maintaining, monitoring, and replacing existing infrastructure and facilities), the estimate of roughly $16 trillion ratchets the cost of water up further. This figure equates to about $830 billion per year, indicating a significant gap between current water industry revenue estimates and what, at a minimum, must be spent on water. I say minimum because there are significant areas where water cost estimates fall woefully short of reflecting the reality of water in the twenty-first century. These categories could easily add a multiple of 1.15 to the global water cost estimate above. And, ironically, as the emerging dialogue in water, these categories actually represent some of the areas of greatest investment potential, which should become apparent from subsequent discussions. Based on a "developed" versus "developing" country dichotomy, the following are examples of critical omissions in most cost estimates.

Developing Countries
- Marginal cost of new water supplies
- Distribution and storage systems

- Low estimates for the next BRIC countries (i.e., the LAACE regions—Latin America, Africa, and Central Europe)
- Financing costs
- An accumulating spending shortfall

Developed Countries
- Marginal cost of water supply (scarcity)
- Impact of advanced regulatory phase
- Integrated water resource management (sustainability)
- Financing costs
- An accumulating spending shortfall

In addition to critical omissions in many global water cost estimates, and less than robust simplifying assumptions, there is often a great deal of confusion with respect to time horizons. While there is an unavoidable lag in data collection, analyses, and projections, the accuracy of time series data presentation with respect to stationarity assumptions is an increasingly relevant problem, especially in relation to the overlay of climate change realities.

Stationarity refers to a foundational concept in water resource engineering and planning relative to managing the natural variation in hydrologic variables. Critical variables such as annual stream flow, snowpacks, or flood peaks are assigned a probability density function based on historical experience. Anthropogenic impacts on the hydrologic cycle usurp the accuracy of established stationarity assumptions and can radically alter both the cost of all stages of water infrastructure spending and regulatory compliance.

The benefit side totally defies comprehension. While education, income generation, health care savings, and productivity gains are quantifiable, the value of human life (deaths averted), human dignity, and ecological sustainability render objectivity impractical. As a proxy, investors can acknowledge the WHO cost-benefits report[3] that estimates, depending on the region of the world, that economic benefits can be valued in a range from $3 to $34 for each dollar invested in improved drinking water and sanitation. According to the report, the return on investment is highest in developing regions where substantial benefits are derived from the time saving associated with improved access to water supply and sanitation.

From the Whole to the Parts

Given the enormity of the expenditures required to meet the demands placed on water resources, it is constructive to examine the costs associated with individual aspects of the provision of water. Dissecting the costs associated with global water requirements indicates that investors need to take advantage of the dynamics of the water industry. There are four points to be made as the global water costs are dissected:

1. No matter what type of water estimates are involved (global, country, technology, function, product, service, regulation, etc.), there is always some strategic investment information contained therein.
2. It is important for investors to understand the implications of the way that costs are broken down.
3. Assuming that ultrafragmentation of the global water industry is an inherently inefficient structure, the way that costs are unbundled and then consolidated will drive many water investment themes.
4. The presentation of specific cost breakdowns forms the investment framework for judging the relative potential of water companies that operate in various segments of the industry.

Costs by Needs

According to the Environmental Protection Agency (EPA),[4] the documented investment needs of publicly owned treatment works (POTWs) in the United States is $202.5 billion. These needs constitute the capital investment necessary to meet the wastewater treatment, wastewater collection, stormwater management, recycled water distribution requirements, and all related appurtenances of POTWs. A POTW is owned by a state or municipality. The nomenclature is particularly important here. The term *publicly owned* does not equate to *publicly held* in this context.[5]

The delineation of costs in this particular report focuses on the United States, municipal utilities, the wastewater segment, and documented needs. Accordingly, investors can see just how large the costs are based on one very narrowly focused analysis. The requirements outlined in the needs survey are categorized as shown in Table 4.1.

Table 4.1 POTW Spending Needs by Category

Needs Category	Total Needs ($B)	Total Needs (%)
Secondary wastewater treatment	44.6	22.0
Advanced wastewater treatment	24.5	12.1
Infiltration/inflow correction	10.3	5.1
Sewer replacement/rehabilitation	21.0	10.4
New collector sewers	16.8	8.3
New interceptor sewers	17.2	8.5
Combined sewer overflow correction	54.8	27.1
Stormwater management programs	9.0	4.4
Recycled water distribution	4.3	2.1
Total	202.5	100.0

As an example of how these reports are used to drive investment decisions, it should first be noted that spending on wastewater treatment in the United States is increasing faster than drinking water treatment. In addition, while the number of people served by facilities with secondary treatment increased only moderately, the portion of the population provided with advanced wastewater treatment increased dramatically. While somewhat anecdotal, in addition to reinforcing the relative investment weight to be afforded to treatment companies, it further refines the search to wastewater and points out several niche—but growing—markets in stormwater management and combined sewer overflow (CSO). Stormwater expenditures reflect the implementation of the National Pollutant Discharge Elimination System (NPDES) Stormwater program. Further, CSO-documented needs comprised the single largest category at 27.1 percent of the total. CSO expenditures accentuate the additional treatment capacity for handling wet-weather flows, a particularly timely category in the advent of climate change. The new category of recycled water distribution points to the need for greater recycling and reuse in the tool kit of alternative water supplies.

Regulatory Costs

No matter how it is expressed, the regulatory cost of providing clean water is staggering, and the financial ability of water suppliers to comply with stringent standards has created mounting public concerns over water quality. That the cost of providing clean water will rapidly increase is not the issue. The challenge to the water industry is to determine how the economic shifts resulting from increased water prices can be minimized.

The Total Maximum Daily Load Program. An example of the cost of a specific regulation is informative. Because the EPA is very proactive in publishing cost data, this illustration is based on U.S. regulations. The Total Maximum Daily Load (TMDL) program is designed to accelerate the achievement of water quality for the 40 percent of water bodies in the United States that do not meet the standards that have been set for them, even after point sources of pollution have been controlled to the minimum levels required. The EPA indicates that this amounts to over 20,000 individual river segments, lakes, and estuaries. These waters include approximately 300,000 miles of rivers and shorelines and approximately 5 million acres of lakes polluted by sediments, excess nutrients, and harmful microorganisms. According to the EPA, 218 million people reside within 10 miles of these impaired waters. Section 303(d) of the Clean Water Act requires that a comprehensive list of impaired waters along with its pollution limits (TMDLs) be prepared.

A TMDL is an analysis that specifies the maximum amount of a pollutant that a body of water can receive and still meet the applicable water quality standards. Because a TMDL sums contaminant wasteloads from all point sources (industrial and municipal dischargers) as well as nonpoint sources (agricultural and urban runoff), they are increasingly becoming critical watershed planning tools. As such, TMDL regulations dovetail with broader water resource management, source water protection, and stormwater management goals. Further, these calculations enable watershed-based permitting under the NPDES, which governs wastewater discharges.

The TMDL program is an important, yet very specific, part of the Clean Water Act's institutional framework. Even with such a targeted initiative, the EPA estimates that the cost to develop a cleanup plan for all impaired bodies of water will cost $1.04 billion. On top of that, fully implementing the program (installing preventative and treatment measures) will cost up to $4.3 billion annually. These costs will be borne primarily by dischargers. The beneficiaries will be the water resource engineering and consulting firms and wastewater treatment companies that will find in the TMDL program another application for their technologies. As a note, this $4.3 billion is a tiny fraction of the current expenditures for clean water in the United States.

The Transition from Cost to Price

Any time there is a structural change in an industry caused by shifts in the economic fundamentals, there is a huge potential for corresponding economic gain. We can look to other economic transitions for guidance in the future: the rationing of health care, leading to overcapacity in hospital beds, resulted in massive consolidation of the hospital management industry; increasing commercialization in the biotechnology industry has generated substantial promise; regulatory upheaval and oversupply in the natural gas industry led to the unbundling of services; information technology represents the merging of previously distinct technological industries; and more. The inevitable upward adjustment in the cost, and therefore the price, of water is one catalyst for change in the industry. It is this promise of change that creates the unprecedented investment opportunity of the twenty-first century—the business of water.

Part Two

INVESTING IN WATER

Chapter 5

The Business of Water

The water business is the third-largest industry in the world, behind oil and gas production and electricity generation. It is the aggregation of all activities that have water as an output, a defining factor as an input, or in addressing the relationship between the two.

Nonetheless, the water industry is ill defined and ultrafragmented, comprised of companies characterized as cottage businesses to global multibusiness behemoths. The business includes everything from a level transmitter in a sewage pump station to a 250-million-gallon-per-day cogeneration desalination plant.

Water is transitioning to an economic good, but it is also a resource with paramount ecological significance. As such, the water industry not only encompasses all aspects of drinking water and the production of goods (including food) but also, in an increasingly significant context, resource sustainability in ensuring the ecological integrity that allows economic activity to expand in the first place. Providing water that meets the quality parameters of human consumption, ecological integrity, semiconductor manufacturing, and irrigation, to serve a future megacity of a billion people or to maintain the habitat for a single endangered species portends dramatic change.

Once considered static and mature, the water industry is poised for massive structural change. The water industry is realigning itself into strategic groupings based on economic mandates. The combination of need and structure will require expenditures of unprecedented proportions and an investment opportunity that is only beginning to come to fruition. Change will be evidenced by subsector level consolidation, accelerating merger-and-acquisition activity, private equity involvement, and a consistent flow of initial public offerings. The magnitude of the industry transition will be unprecedented, and there clearly will be winners and losers.

Water versus Wastewater

The water business (or industry) has long maintained a distinction between water (drinking water) and wastewater. The two main industry trade associations reflect these distinctions: The American Water Works Association (AWWA), is "dedicated to the improvement of drinking water quality and supply," while the Water Environment Federation (WEF), officially espousing the broader objective of "preserving and enhancing the global water environment," has traditionally focused on wastewater.

Thus, for purposes of edification, we will divide the industry into two segments: the first segment, all activities relative to human consumption (potable water) and to processes where water quality is an important parameter and, the second segment, wastewater, or more precisely, water discharged subsequent to an intended use. In reality, the practical distinction between the two is less than clear cut; somebody's drinking water is somebody else's treated wastewater. Indeed, the notion of greywater creates an intermediate class of water that is increasingly valued in its own right. Water that is not drinkable, yet not environmentally detrimental, is the basis for reuse, recycling, point-of-use-reuse (POUR), irrigation, and recharge applications, to name a few. Contrary to the old industry adage, "dilution is the solution to pollution," the luxury of substantial spatial and temporal intervals between use and discharge is often unavailable. Nonetheless, the categorization of drinking water and wastewater activities will generally remain the convention throughout much of this discussion, largely because of treatment distinctions, plant design characteristics, and differing regional requirements.

Given the narrative being advanced with respect to a holistic approach to the global water challenges, it is unfortunate that a unitary framework is not in place. This is one part of the conversation with respect to the institutional framework that governs water that must evolve along with the reality of a critical resource in transition. An anecdotal advancement of the proposition is illustrated by the suggested merger, albeit with limited political acceptance, between the AWWA and WEF. These are large, well-respected institutions that play a critical role in the future of water, especially with respect to scientific and technical advancements. As such, an integrated dialogue would be invaluable in total water management, watershed initiatives, infrastructure investment, pricing, asset management, and a multitude of operational considerations. For now, greater cooperation is a step in the right direction.

Functional Categories

One way to understand the dimensions of the water industry is to divide it into broad sectors. Following the convention of the Palisades Water Indexes™, which serve as benchmarks for the water industry, the water business can be broken down into five functional sectors plus one to accommodate structures which extend beyond water. The sectors include water utilities, treatment, analytical, infrastructure, resource management, and multibusiness. While the water industry is far from homogenous, categorizing activity by function provides greater cohesion with respect to the particular defining investment characteristics, markets, economics, regulation, and so on. Intersector comparisons, although not perfect, are enhanced by viewing the industry in this way.

Water Utilities

Water utilities are directly responsible for getting water supplies to residential, commercial, and industrial users. The utilities sector also includes wastewater and stormwater utility operations. As public utilities, they are under the jurisdiction of regulatory bodies and must comply with a myriad of federal and state regulatory requirements to ensure the safety of drinking water and the protection of the environment. Foreign water utilities may operate under different regulatory frameworks than U.S. water utilities. Water utilities generally oversee the water and wastewater facilities for a specific geographical region and/or population center or are structured as holding companies comprised of geographically diverse operating divisions.

Treatment

The treatment sector comprises companies that play a key role in the physical, chemical, or biological characteristics of water and wastewater, whether municipal or industrial. *Treatment* refers to the application of technologies and/or processes that alter the composition of water/wastewater to achieve a beneficial objective in its use, reuse, or discharge. The most critical treatment objectives pertain to the global need for safe drinking water and sanitation. Water treatment traditionally refers to the process of converting source water to potable water of sufficient quality to comply with applicable regulations and standards, thereby ensuring the protection of human health. It can also pertain to the treatment of water in the optimization of an industrial process stream. Wastewater treatment, though extricably linked to human health, is differentiated within the treatment category through the additional objective of environmental protection as wastewater streams from municipal or industrial uses are discharged into the environment. While conventional centralized water and wastewater treatment equipment is the core of the treatment group, advanced treatment methods, enabling convergent technologies and innovative treatment systems, are key drivers. Subsectors include chemicals/media/resins, filtration/membrane separation, disinfection alternatives (UV/ozone), desalination, and decentralized technologies such as point-of-use (POU) or POUR applications.

Analytical

The analytical sector includes companies that develop, manufacture, or sell instrumentation or analytical products and/or related supplies and provide services and design systems or develop technologies for the management, analysis, testing, measurement, or monitoring of drinking water, wastewater, and/or process water. Analytical methods are applied, directly or indirectly, to achieve a mandated compliance/regulatory requirement (related to human health or the environment) or a management objective in optimizing the function or safety of water relative to a specific use. Due to the critical need for the detection of a growing number of contaminants at increasingly smaller observation levels, there is a demand for the allocation of manufacturing resources to instrumentation based on advanced analytics. The sector is driven by the convergence of life science technologies, information technologies (protocol algorithms), sensor technologies, and advanced electronics.

Infrastructure

This sector includes the companies that stand to benefit from the extensive construction, replacement, repair, and rehabilitation of water distribution systems, wastewater systems, and stormwater collection systems throughout the world. In the United States alone, the EPA estimates that water and wastewater infrastructure repair costs may be as much as $1 trillion over the next 20 years. The deterioration of a drinking water distribution system, regardless of location, poses significant risks to public health, security, and economic development. International markets for new infrastructure construction in emerging economies add significantly to the magnitude of the potential expenditures. Companies within the sector service and supply the components of the vast interconnected network of pipelines, mains, pumps, storage tanks, lift stations, and smaller appurtenances of a distribution system such as valves and flow meters. The sector also includes the rehabilitation market comprised of "in-situ" technologies and new materials utilized to upgrade, maintain, and restore pipe networks as a cost-effective alternative to new construction.

Resource Management

The resource management sector represents a systems-oriented approach to the integration of the principles of resource sustainability with complex water issues. Companies in this sector emphasize the interrelationships between their water business activities and the "management" of water as a valuable economic and environmental resource. Ultimately, the rationale behind the resource management sector represents the embodiment of a comprehensive, forward-looking, integrated approach to solving water resource issues and ensuring sustainable use for the benefit of future generations. This emerging sector currently includes companies that provide engineering, consulting, construction, operations, and related technical services to public and private customers in virtually all aspects of managing water resources, agricultural irrigation, and privatization activities.

Industry Hybrids: Multibusiness

The multibusiness sector contains companies that contribute significantly to the water industry, but are diversified into other industries or markets such that the financial contribution of water-related activities is relatively small for the company. Conversely, the company may be a worldwide leader in a specific water technology or market. These companies may not be conglomerates in the traditional sense, but may instead apply a particular platform technology, product line, or service capability across several global markets, including water. The multibusiness sector participates in significant water projects worldwide that are likely to be undertaken only by large, international industrial companies.

Table 5.1 provides examples of subsectors included within each functional sector in order to identify the many specific functions within the industry.

Water-Related Applications

One of the more challenging aspects of the water industry from an investor's perspective is the diversity in the number of markets and/or applications associated with water. Once you move beyond drinking water and wastewater treatment, many applications fall into the "water-related" designation. And while not as critical as global drinking water, sanitation, and agricultural applications, water-related activities

Table 5.1 Water Industry Sectors and Subsectors

Sectors	Subsectors
Utilities	Water utilities Wastewater utilities Stormwater utilities
Treatment	Water treatment equipment Wastewater treatment equipment Chemicals/resins/media Filtration/separation/membranes Disinfection Desalination Point-of-use (POU) Point-of-use-reuse (POUR)
Analytical	Instrumentation Testing/monitoring/sensors Supervisory control and data acquisition (SCADA) systems Metering Laboratories Security
Infrastructure	Distribution Pumps/valves/flow control Rehabilitation/repair Pipelines Storage Stormwater/combined sewer overflows (CSOs)
Resource Management	Engineering and consulting Privatization Irrigation Biosolids Reuse/recycling Remediation Management services Water rights/transfers

are mission critical to many industrial processes. In fact, this aspect of the business exhibits many of the characteristics of a free market relative to the economic value of water and thereby drives a significant portion of water company profitability.

It would be convenient if all of the companies in the water investment universe fell neatly into place. But that is not the case and likely never will be. Having said that, it is important to understand the magnitude of water-related activities in addition to the more pure-play applications. In nature's economy there is no such thing as "pure" water, and that extends to the human economy as well. A side-by-side view of the water business categorized by application illustrates the importance of these markets to the water industry and to investors. While the coverage of potable water and wastewater applications is relatively straightforward, water-related (or near water) applications are often neglected by investors. In fact, industrial and manufacturing applications are often a key factor in determining the relative investment merits of water companies.

Industrial and Commercial Processes

The industrial market is often slighted in discussions of the water industry in favor of the more visible and recognizable water themes such as potable water and sanitation. The reality, however, is that industrial and manufacturing activities provide a significant amount of the spending on a broad array of water and water-related goods and services and represent the clearest example of market-driven applications in the water industry. Industrial end users have clear economic motives associated with critical process quality control, operational cost efficiencies, the management of compliance costs, minimization of waste, and so on. Accordingly, industrial end users are proactive in adopting innovative methodologies and have been instrumental in facilitating technology transfers and enabling commercialization of disruptive technologies.

Because industrial markets are more directly influenced by cyclical economic conditions, these applications should be viewed in comparison to other markets served. Water companies that are especially dependent on a particular industry (e.g., energy or oil and gas) are likely to exhibit greater volatility than companies that have not only a municipal/industrial mix but also diversified exposure within the industrial market. Nonetheless, water companies that serve the industrial market often provide critical process-enhancing and -enabling technologies. For example, the need for ultrapure water in many diverse industrial applications is estimated to approach a $6 billion market by 2011. Ultrapure water requires not only ion-exchange resins and membranes to remove contaminants, but also components such as specialized valves, pumps, and piping materials that are able to maintain the integrity of high-purity water in all phases of the process.

Semiconductors. The semiconductor manufacturing process requires ultrapure water at virtually every step, from cleaning to etching. It is estimated that for every dollar of water purchased by a semiconductor producer, it costs $20 to treat it to ultrapure levels and another $10 to pretreat the process wastewater before sending it out into the environment. As such, advanced treatment, recycling, and analytical testing are all water segments utilized by this one industrial process. Ultrapure water is potable municipal water purified on-site to meet the stringent purity requirements of chip manufacturing in reducing the concentration of metals, dissolved solids, and ions. Ultrapure water treatment utilizes membranes with pore sizes down to the hyperfiltration level (reverse osmosis), ozone disinfection, and ion exchange. Analytics require the use of sophisticated mass spectrometry instruments to test for purity levels and controls to constantly monitor the process.

In addition, it takes large amounts of water to fabricate chips. For example, it takes an average of about 2,300 gallons of water to process one six-inch wafer. The larger chip manufacturers can consume as much as 1 billion gallons of water per year at a single location. These quantities not only dictate the need for the efficient use of water and water recycling systems, but also facilitate the need for local and regional water resource management initiatives. Despite the cyclical demand for chips, there is little doubt about the long-term growth of the industry. Much of that growth is centered in China, South Korea, Taiwan, and Japan. The semiconductor business is an application that encompasses both water quality and quantity issues and is one specialized example of the enormous potential associated with industrial applications for water companies that address these specific markets.

Health Care. Water used in health care and hospital settings is another specialized market for filtration, separation, and purification technologies. The quality of tap water used in health care facilities is adversely affected by changes in season, facility renovation and construction activities, and biofilm shedding. Water treatment in this market is not only a microcosm of broader water contaminant issues, but also a unique setting where microbial contamination is an especially problematic situation. Health care–associated infections are a growing and increasingly important industrial application for water treatment technologies. Faucets, showers, ice machines, medical device reprocessing, and wound care are all areas where advanced water treatment is required. Plumbing systems are particularly sensitive breeding environments for contamination (due to temperature and humidity) and result in the formation of biofilms, biological fouling, and microorganism growth.

Cooling Towers. As far as industrial and commercial water markets go, the market for cooling tower water treatment is one of the largest and most competitive of applications. Cooling tower water treatment is akin to the POU markets in its fragmentation, complexity, and confusing array of technological alternatives. In the United States alone, there are an estimated half million water cooling towers used by industry, hotels, hospitals, offices, and commercial buildings. Towers range from small rooftop units to the very large hyperboloid structures that are icons of the industrial landscape.

The basic premise of a cooling tower is the transfer of excess heat from exchangers and air conditioning/refrigeration condensers or waste heat from industrial processes, to the atmosphere. If an industrial plant had only once-through cooling (no tower), it would require a phenomenal amount of water, therefore creating grave ecological consequences from thermal pollution to the receiving water bodies. A typical petroleum refinery processing 300,000 barrels per day circulates about 21 million gallons of water per hour through its cooling tower system. Cooling towers serve to dissipate waste heat more effectively into the atmosphere (remember that anomalous high-latent-heat property of water that enables considerable evaporative cooling). Common industrial applications include cooling the circulating water used in oil refineries, petrochemical plants, natural gas processing, food processing, power plants, and so on. Many water companies supply the water cooling market as an adjunct to other core chemical capabilities or water treatment equipment applications.

Efficiency is critical. Tower tanks and plumbing must be clear of scale and corrosion and free of contaminants such as algae, viruses, and bacteria to operate at optimum efficiency and to protect public health. Cost considerations relate to the significant amount of energy savings that can be achieved through efficiencies in the heat exchange process (scale deposit and corrosion control), while health considerations relate to a microbe-free environment within the systems. For example, Legionnaires' disease (most notably *Legionella pneumophila*) is a now well-known example of bacterial disease caused by aerosol exposure from open recirculating evaporative cooling towers.

As result of the evaporative process, solids will concentrate in cooling water over time, thereby inhibiting the heat transfer process and increasing energy costs. Chemical treatment methods have been the predominant method in the prevention of scaling and the growth of algae, but escalating chemical costs and stringent discharge requirements have led to an increased use of nonchemical methods. Microbiologically influenced corrosion and "white rust" have become particular problems due to an EPA ban on the use of highly toxic heavy metal corrosion inhibitors and the reduction of lead content in the galvanizing process, which raises the pH level and facilitates white rust formation, thereby reducing the effectiveness of biocides and scale-inhibiting chemicals. As a result, the use of nonchemical water treatment methodologies is an emerging trend.

The promoters of many alternatives are somewhat dubious in their assertions, thus the analogy to the POU markets. But investors are safe to assume that proven technologies such as ozonation and ionization to combat scale and bacterial formation will increase dramatically in cooling tower applications. Ultraviolet light has also been used to control bacteria, fungi, and bioslimes. As with many emerging technologies, the higher initial cost is not appropriately weighed against the longer-term return on investment, especially in conjunction with the potentially detrimental environmental and health impacts.

Pharmaceuticals and Biotechnology. Water is a critical reagent in life sciences technologies in confronting challenging human health issues. All life science research starts with the use of pure water. Water purification systems are a critical component in biotechnology and pharmaceutical laboratories where requirements can approach 1,000 gallons per day. Flexible purification systems are needed to produce the water quality needed for a variety of laboratory needs and applications, and, as such, encompass both water filtration and separation (membrane) treatment devices. The pharmaceutical industry uses purified water for injection and cleaning processes typically through distillation or reverse osmosis techniques.

Bottled Water. The reader will note a conspicuous absence of discussion related to bottled water as an investment thesis. There are several reasons for this:

- Bottled water has evolved into a consumer-driven beverage category.
- Except for emergency use, bottled water has little to do with *sustainably solving* global water issues.
- Bottled water does not necessarily ensure quality.
- Bottled water is likely to emerge as part of the aggregate water problem (groundwater depletion and surface water diversion) rather than as a sustainable solution in providing "safe"' and cost-effective drinking water.
- Centralized water treatment, that is, tap water, provides a safe, cost-effective source of drinking water at a much lower cost to a much greater proportion of the population.
- In a decentralized context, resources for POU treatment must focus on a comprehensive distributed strategy rather than on packaging water.

Bottled water is instead viewed as an application for treatment technologies and comprehensive resource management. For investors who cannot resist the attraction of the admittedly rapid growth in bottled water, particularly in developing countries, there are a number of public companies that could be considered.[1]

Heavy Metals. Heavy metals in industrial processes are an especially challenging problem because they generally cannot be degraded or destroyed. Further, while trace amounts of some heavy metals are critical to metabolic function in living things they are very toxic in even low concentrations and accumulate in organisms over time. Unfortunately, the examples of potential contamination from metals are many; antimony

(Sb) used in flame retardants, cadmium (Cd) in batteries and coatings, chromium (Cr) in pigments for paints, lead (Pb) leaching from drinking water pipes, mercury (Hg) in lamps, and so on.

In concert with the number of potentially harmful metallic chemical elements, and the diversity of industrial applications in which they are present, there are numerous specialized treatment processes to remove heavy metals. Because of the differing chemical properties of heavy metals, these treatment technologies are often designed for a very specific metals application, for example, the use of ion exchange in the power and electronics industries, distillation to produce pyrogen-free water for pharmaceuticals, coalescing to separate water from oil, and ozonation to bleach papermaking pulp without chlorine.

Drivers of the Water Industry

The term *market drivers* is investment parlance for the factors that contribute to the growth of a particular market or industry. There are many factors that drive the coalescing water industry: population and demographics, aging infrastructure, global food demand, degradation and contamination of supplies, regulation, technological advancement, economic development, ecological and sustainability considerations, climate change, and institutional reform. The drivers of the global water market encapsulate a complex interaction of economic, strategic, cultural, and political elements. The factors not only represent movement along the supply-and-demand curves, but also positive shifts in the curves themselves, which is indicative of rapidly changing conditions and accelerating growth. But the common thread is that each factor has an explicable link to the growth of some or several aspects of the water business. In totality, these drivers amount to a tsunami of change and create a watershed investment opportunity. Broadly speaking, the drivers can be viewed as exogenous or endogenous (structural).

Exogenous Drivers

The exogenous drivers of the water industry can be viewed in a number of ways. For this purpose, however, exogenous drivers, as those that contribute to the growth of water from outside the industry, are contained within the broad socioeconomic trends of industrialization, urbanization, and globalization. Other, more specific exogenous factors include economic development, water property rights, demographics, culture-based pricing, climate change, and so on. In other words, rather than isolate the discussion of these factors, they are woven throughout the book in the context of a growth driver as it impacts a particular water investment aspect, especially in the context of exogenous institutional factors since they represent potentially significant change in the water industry and reform of water policies. In fact, a World Bank report[2] points out the tremendous impact on water industry "performance" (such as in reducing negative health impacts and poverty levels) that can be achieved through reform of water institutions and policies. This is an argument that is reiterated throughout the many discussions of water pricing, technology transfer mechanisms, regulations, and other institutional structures. At this juncture, it is to be emphasized that the broad macro trends shaping the global economy are very much contributing to the growth of the water industry.

Industrialization. Industrialization is a major driver of growth for the water industry by virtue of the simple fact that large portions of the global population are transitioning to large-scale, mechanized economies characterized by extensive resource utilization. As a result, demand for water across a broad range of consumptive uses is outstripping easily accessible supplies while industrial activity impairs quality. In many of these high-growth, highly populated countries, the water stress threshold ($1,700 \text{ m}^3$ per capita) is rapidly approaching, if not already reached. For example, China has only 8 percent of the world's freshwater to meet the needs of 22 percent of the global population. In India, urban water demand is expected to double, and industrial water demand to triple, by 2025.

Rising real incomes in industrializing countries increases per-capita water consumption as a result of shifts to higher-water-content consumer products and more water-intensive caloric intakes. Industrialization includes agricultural systems. So-called high-input agriculture uses copious amounts of fossil fuel energy, fertilizers, and water. By definition, industrialization entails a shift to a higher-throughput economy in order to sustain economic growth. The law of conservation of matter, and the first law (conservation of energy) and second law (increasing entropy) of thermodynamics, dictate that the high-waste characteristics of industrialized economies lead to constraints on the carrying capacity of the water environment. It is not that water ceases to exist when humans use it, but that it ceases to exist in the previous concentrations (quantity) and purity (quality). Industrialization is closely connected with urbanization.

Urbanization. Urbanization refers to the process in which an increasing proportion of an entire population lives in cities and suburbs. When more and more inanimate sources of energy were used to enhance human productivity (industrialization), surpluses increased in both agriculture and industry. Urbanization is well under way in many developing countries as a result of the immigration from rural areas. Poverty and conflict are often the push factors out of rural areas, while the pull of urban areas is the amenities associated with economic development. Today, about 9 percent of the world's urban population resides in megacities (defined as those with more than 10 million inhabitants). Urbanization is positively correlated with economic growth.

Logically, most of the expected growth in urban areas will be concentrated in developing countries. The 2007 Revision of the UN's *World Urbanization Prospects* reports that by 2050, 50 percent of the population of Africa will live in urban areas. That translates to a threefold increase in the urban population of the continent. And this scenario is based on an assumption of declining fertility rates. China is expected to be 70 percent urban by 2050.

While the Tokyo metropolis is by far the most populous urban city, with 35.7 million people, other areas of Asia and Africa are projected to have their share of megacities. Cities such as Mumbai, Delhi, Dhaka (Bangladesh), Calcutta, Shanghai, Karachi (Pakistan), Manila, Beijing, and Jakarta in Asia and Lagos (Nigeria), and Kinshasa (Democratic Republic of the Congo) in Africa are included in the largest urban agglomerations by 2020 according to the UN Report. The fastest growing urban areas are similarly distributed with the addition of the Middle East. Beihei, in southern China, is forecast to be the world's fastest-growing urban area over the period. Cities with average annual growth of more than 4 percent include Ghaziabad (India), Sana'a (Yemen), Surat (India), Kabul (Afghanistan), Bamako (Mali), and Lagos (Nigeria).

There is the argument that economies of scale associated with higher population density enhance the ability to achieve sustainable use of natural resources, including water. That, however, is a very dim light at the end of a very long tunnel. Further, the experience of water utilities strongly refutes the salvation of economies of scale. Dividing a cost over a larger and larger population works only if the cost is relatively fixed. Water scarcity, compliance, and capital spending gaps virtually guarantee that this will not be the case. The infrastructure to accommodate megacities and urbanization is staggering, as previously outlined. And it is important to reiterate that most global water infrastructure spending estimates do not adequately reflect the urbanization in Africa and Latin America.

Globalization. Classical economic theory, despite the principle of comparative advantage, largely underestimated the integration of global economies by focusing on free trade and somewhat dismissing the circulation of capital and movement of labor based on community attachments. It has become glaringly apparent that economic incentives show little nationalistic loyalty, and capital flows know few boundaries. Even labor is globalizing (outsourcing and immigration are manifestations) despite obviously greater barriers than capital. In another example of the chasm between economics and environmentalism, the metaphor "think globally, but act locally" is at a comparative disadvantage to the economic reality of both thinking and acting globally.

Globalization refers to the process of increasing political, economic, and sociocultural integration and interdependence of countries. The benefits of globalization coincide with the principle of comparative advantage; that is, increased economic productivity through the efficient allocation of resources resulting from specialization and greater political stability derived from economic interdependence.

Institutionally, globalization is the development of rules enforced by organizations such as the World Trade Organization (WTO) to increase efficiency in the production and distribution of goods and services. Among other things, ecological degradation is a concern of globalization because of disproportionate incentives among primary (commodity), secondary (processing), and tertiary (facilitating) markets to establish and enforce environmental standards. Globalization has important implications for both water quantity and quality and is a major driver of efficient irrigation techniques, the implementation of advanced treatment technologies, infrastructure design, privatization, and resource management activities. In addition, transboundary water issues require innovative institutional structures to promote sustainable development.

The pivotal role of comparative advantage in the process of globalization helps to illustrate the emergence of virtual water trade. International food trade can be used as a policy mechanism to mitigate water scarcity and reduce environmental impacts. Countries with a relative abundance of water, that is, a water ratio advantage, can grow food and trade it to water-stressed countries. While globalization can certainly have a detrimental impact on water resources, the commensurate spread of "supraterritoriality" can be a powerful driver in transitioning the water industry toward enlightened interregional solutions rather than conflict.

Structural Drivers

Structural drivers may alternatively be referred to as endogenous factors but the intent is the same. These are growth drivers that investors can relate to by drawing upon analogous situations in their investing experience. These factors may be responses to exogenous variables but they emanate from within the industry and can include the rationalization of any structural or operational inefficiencies, consolidation, competition, privatization, convergent or enabling technologies, and so on.

Rationalization. The process of rationalization is both the most productive of business changes and the most nebulous of concepts. Simply stated, the rationalization of an industry, segment, sector, or market is the transformation to a different way of doing business, presumably for the better, and driven by some economic incentive. Perhaps the best way to apply rationalization to the water industry is to look at what is irrational. Is it rational to charge an artificially low price to a critical resource? Is it rational to exclude ecological considerations in the implementation of water resource sustainability? Is it rational to eliminate competition from the provision of water? Is it rational to apply an institutional structure of governance rather than a market-based approach? The water industry is being rationalized from a delivery-based approach to a solution-based system.

Whereas the provision of water has been viewed as the delivery of a product, clean water as a resource will be viewed as an economic good; that is, the economic pressures generated by the internalization of water pollution costs will no longer permit the inefficiencies of bundled services. The "product" will result from specific processes performed on raw water. There are a number of areas within the water industry that are ripe for rationalization. These areas include some of the most promising dynamics for investors and include monitoring and regulatory compliance, decentralized wastewater treatment, water delivery, resource management, distribution channels, commercialization/technology transfer mechanisms, and demand-side management.

The rationalization of the water industry in general, and niche subsectors specifically, will combine a cost containment scenario as seen in health care reform with the teamed technology approach of the bio- and nanotechnology fields that facilitates commercialization. From the rather philosophical construct of rationalization, we will examine two manifestations of the process: consolidation and privatization. Both are structural drivers of the water industry that illustrate the extraordinary investment opportunity that presents itself as water as a public resource is rationalized as water as an economic good.

Consolidation. The global water purification and wastewater treatment business is highly fragmented and consists of a myriad of companies that design, develop, and manufacture equipment, provide products and services, run treatment facilities, and/or engage in a combination of such services and capabilities. The water industry is still coalescing and rationalizing. Industry consolidation will be the trend as customer demands for comprehensive solutions discourage a segmented structure. In short, the industry is ripe for consolidation. The emerging solutions-based approach to water issues seeks to account for the significant differences in the quality of available water supplies and the varying standards of purity required for different applications. Customer demands for comprehensive, cost-effective solutions discourage a segmented industry structure. Scale efficiencies, technology leveraging, cross-selling opportunities, geographic expansion, and enhanced market concentrations are all necessary in maturing markets.

Historically, the water industry has revolved around regulated utilities that functioned rather autonomously as water providers, aided by engineering consultants and supplied by a highly fragmented network of suppliers. Under this traditional structure, costs are bundled together as a system. But the current focus on the delivery of water as a single finished product has proven inadequate in *efficiently* dealing with the wide variety of water and wastewater problems. While water utilities will retain a pivotal position in the industry, their role will focus on the delivery of a standardized product. The fragmented water and wastewater treatment industry will consolidate to address specific customer needs.

Segments within the water industry that are suitable for consolidation activities include instrumentation, compliance monitoring, membrane manufacturers, pumps, and remediation, to name just a few. And certain commodity-based activities are candidates for horizontal consolidation, such as carbon, bulk treatment chemicals, and ion exchange resins. The water industry is just beginning to fully explore the benefits and opportunities of consolidation.

From an investment point of view, investors should look for companies whose profits are not growing solely from acquisitions but are experiencing earnings growth through successful integration—that is, cutting costs, adding customers, or achieving greater productivity. Consolidation as an economic concept must be distinguished from consolidation as a purely transactional opportunity. While both scenarios have had success in the water industry, the key in the long run is operating integration (strong internal growth) and an above-average return on invested capital, not simply top-line growth in revenue and expanding price-earnings multiples.

Scale economies make it unprofitable for too many firms to coexist in the market. Strategic barriers are more a function of global economics than intentional efforts by incumbents to deter newcomers. For example, the extreme crowding in a number of segments (i.e., chemicals, membranes, carbon, etc.) makes it uneconomic for new competition amid pricing weakness. All this leads to an imperfect oligopoly in that, although there are fewer sellers, they produce similar products.

Privatization. By definition, as promulgated in Executive Order 12803 on Infrastructure Privatization, *privatization* is defined as the disposition or transfer of an infrastructure asset, such as by sale or by long-term lease, from a state or local government to a private party. Infrastructure assets include water supply and wastewater treatment facilities. Privatization elevates each municipality to the same position of power as a manufacturer who can decide whether to make or buy a product component. Early recognition of this trend focused on the privatization of operation and maintenance services at water and wastewater treatment plants. But the ramifications of water as an economic good go well beyond alternative operating approaches.

An Experiment in Competition. No matter how it is expressed, the cost of providing clean water is staggering, and the financial ability of water suppliers to comply with stringent regulations has created mounting public concerns over water quality. One much-touted solution, privatization, is simply an expression of the stronger underlying economic forces at work in the water industry—the economic transition from public governance to market forces.

That the cost of providing clean water will rapidly increase is not the issue. The challenge to the water industry is to determine how to minimize economic shifts due to increased water prices. As the costs of supplying water increase, municipalities will be induced to look for efficiencies through contracting for the financing and management of certain components of the waterworks system. It is true that private industry is well positioned to unbundle the traditional services involved in the provision of water by applying financial capabilities with inherent economic incentives to concentrate on cost efficiencies. Private companies can design, finance, construct, and operate water and wastewater facilities on a long-term basis, thereby partially privatizing the activity. Potential benefits include reduced pressure on local governmental or municipal debt capacity, shorter design and construction periods, and reduced operational and compliance burdens for governmental units.

While governments are responsible for deciding which services are to be paid for by the public, they do not have to produce and deliver the service. And more and more municipalities are relying on private companies to provide water services in a cost-effective manner. These "contract" providers have an economic incentive to contain the costs associated with the construction and maintenance of water facilities. In this context, the institution of privatization can provide the signals and incentives that correctly reflect the scarcity factor in water resources, allowing users to respond to changing supplies and demands.

The Reality of Privatization. The proliferation of privatizing-type transactions, such as operation and maintenance contracts and turnkey services, is pervasive. Ranging from numerous small contracts with local municipalities to large contracts, these "public-private partnerships" were viewed as a convenient financing option for utilities. Yet, after all of the theory, promise, and hype, privatization has more or less failed to achieve its status as a panacea of the water supply business. The main reason was timing, but its day will come because the economics are just too compelling. There was a confluence of factors that proved to be a drag on the widespread acceptance of privatized activities.

First, although privatization is fondly looked upon as an innovative solution engineered by municipalities to alleviate financial burdens, it was often, in reality, a bailout for water systems unable to cope with stringent compliance requirements. Second, the single greatest opposition to privatizing transactions was the perception of a loss of local control. (Indeed, what is the essence of an investor-owned water utility other than a fully privatized municipal waterworks?) And finally, the utility acquisition rampage by the global mega-utilities and private equity groups proved to be based on a failed notion of economies of scale at a time when privatization clients were very skeptical and ultrademanding.

It is little wonder that concurrent with the privatization phenomenon is the trend toward consolidation in the water supply business. What will remain, however, despite privatization and consolidation, are numerous hopelessly burdened small utilities. These systems will not survive; there is virtually no incentive for the private sector to pursue projects that could be investment risks, especially given the cautious environment. Although not consequential from a supply point of view, the structural implications for the water industry are enormous. This structural alteration provides the opportunity that may finally link the micro alternatives (decentralization) to water treatment with the macro notion of water provision (centralization).

Despite some regulatory and tax hurdles that are not compatible with full privatization, the trend is nonetheless in place. And while the water supply business has focused on the financial and operational benefits of privatization, the industry has largely ignored the fundamental reasons for changing the way in which clean water is provided. That degree of change is not privatization; it is the economic transition at work in the water industry.

The privatization trend continues its evolution in the water industry. Refuse collection and solid waste, formerly municipal functions, have largely been privatized, and municipalities see how this approach might also apply to water and wastewater. But the concept is evolving and taking on new meaning for utilities. With the advent of deregulation in the gas and electric utility industries, consumers see competition developing in a market previously characterized by regulated monopolies. As an outgrowth, water utility customers want to see competition and increased efficiency from water and wastewater utilities. The key question now being asked is how water suppliers can incorporate the private sector into their operations. This fundamental shift in focus presents a substantial investment opportunity for the water industry.

The operational response to this notion of privatization was a rather simplistic duopoly referred to as public-private partnerships. But what started out as public-private arrangements is now evolving into competition, outsourcing, and core competencies—buzzwords unheard of in the water business until now. Facing increasing costs, funding limitations, and government pressure, water utilities are not only seeking ways to finance water system improvements and reduce costs but are rethinking the way they do business.

It is true that private industry is well positioned to unbundle the traditional services involved in the provision of water by applying financial capabilities with inherent economic incentives to concentrate on cost efficiencies. The private sector can take the kind of long-term view that municipal governments once took. Private firms need a return on investment for longer than just 5 or 10 years to gain support of the capital markets. This different dynamic supports a change toward heavier involvement by the private sector but not necessarily ownership, as long as municipalities continue to enjoy special tax advantages in this area.

Competition. Now, rather than privatization, the conflict is couched in terms of competition. Public water utilities see themselves as competing with private contract and outsourcing firms. Utilities are looking at the possibility of forgoing privatization in favor of optimizing or restructuring their internal operations. This highlights the new strategies being implemented to create more cost-effective public utilities, a trend with important investment ramifications. For example, a trend in North America is toward unattended, automated facilities, a practice that the private-sector competition has already employed. And outsourcing is not limited to the water and wastewater treatment function. Automation of the meter reading function is a prime area for outsourcing, and one with enormous potential as information technologies are applied.

While the evolution of privatization in the water industry has tended to polarize the public and private sectors, it is likely that in the long run more municipalities will actively seek privatization but in a manner more consistent with competition and the economic concept of outsourcing. As the process evolves, the incentives of both are likely to converge, based on the premise that the ultimate objective is the cost-effective compliance with water quality regulations while maintaining the public trust. In the interest of investing in water, we therefore begin with the regulatory providers of water—that is, water utilities.

Chapter 6

Water Utilities

B y far the largest and most visible component of the water industry is the water utility sector. Water utilities, both municipal and private, are the traditional providers of water. They are directly responsible for delivering water to residential, commercial, and industrial users. Water utilities in the United States, whether government or investor owned, are considered utilities under the jurisdiction of regulatory bodies. Other countries have widely different governing institutions, including governmental edict, concessions, franchises, affermage, and public-private agreements. But the principle of a water utility, as historically structured, is universal: the receipt of monopoly power in return for the near-fiduciary obligation to provide quality, dependable water services.

Despite their fundamental importance, water utilities face considerable obstacles from both regulatory authorities and a rapidly changing environment. The merits of investing in publicly traded water utilities have changed substantially in recent times; a once homogenous investment sector is now anything but. The list of traded water utilities has expanded, contracted, and is expanding again. The components are domestic, established international, and emerging country utilities. Water utilities have morphed into everything from specialized providers to mega-utilities. An investment case can be made for or against categorically investing in water utilities but the days of homogeneity are over. Having said that, water utilities are absolutely critical to the future of water.

Addressing the investment potential of a particular water utility is not always an easy task, but there are clear indications that investors can profit significantly from selective exposure to this sector, which is very much in transition. Numerous acquisitions by European consolidators in recent years, at very favorable multiples, virtually guaranteed that the returns on investing in U.S. water utilities outpaced the returns on many of the major indices. This scenario has led many to point to water utilities as the preferred approach to investing in the water industry. The merit of that proposition, however, requires some background analysis that suggests a different investment stance with respect to water utilities going forward.

A Brief History

It is instructive to frame the current condition of water utilities by examining where the industry has been. Water utilities went through a period of extraordinary consolidation between 1998 and 2001. Significant European acquisitions of major U.S. utilities included Aquarion by Kelda, United Water Resources by Suez, E-Town Water by Thames Water, and American Water Works by RWE. Armed with an unbridled belief in economies of scale, foreign utilities were more focused on acquiring customers than operating water assets. While it is accurate to say that economies of scale exist in the water utility business (i.e., treating a larger volume of water has cost efficiencies), it is more true for a large utility simply selling greater volumes of water to existing customers or for smaller utilities with excess capacity.

The initial wave of acquisitions had its roots in the merger activity in Britain as a result of the privatization of that country's water utilities and spread to the United States in a big way with the acquisition of U.S. Filter by Vivendi in 1999. The match was somewhat of a surprise—not necessarily because Vivendi was into construction, public works, and telecommunications as well as water, but U.S Filter was a hodgepodge of water technologies and equipment. Shortly thereafter, French utilities group Suez Lyonnaise des Eaux purchased United Water Resources, the second-largest water distributor in the United States. The consolidation in the water utility industry continued unabated, limiting the availability of publicly traded vehicles and drawing attention to the "water-as-an-asset" strategy. When Azurix, the public water investment vehicle of Enron, purchased Wessex Water of Britain, it was perhaps a sign that the trend had gone too far.

In addition to foreign water utilities buying other water utilities, electric utilities also entered the fray. Privatization (read "deregulation") was the theme common to water and energy when a cast of global electric utilities decided that water was their next conquest. A prime example of the convergence of water and electricity was the acquisition of American Water Works by RWE AG in late 2001. It was the belief at the time that the water industry was undergoing the same sort of deregulation that the electric industry experienced. And while this convergence lacked economic sense when viewed independently, in theory, a deregulated utility admittedly faces the same economics of competition whether it's gas, electricity, telecommunications, or water. But "one of these things is not like the others"; namely, water privatization does not equate to deregulation. It is this reality that led to the initial public offering (IPO) spin-off of American Water Works (which is again a publicly traded stock) by RWE.

Notably, these major water utility acquisitions came at roughly the peak in the privatization frenzy. Also notably, some utilities, such as Aqua America, deliberately chose to remain independent during this consolidation phase and focus on the benefits of consolidating smaller utilities where their core regulatory experience could be leveraged into operational cost efficiencies. And that proved to be a better strategy as the consolidation phase turned to an equally rapid phase of water utility divestitures. Perhaps caught up in the success of electricity and telecom consolidation resulting from global deregulation and privatization, the advent of the mega-utility was short lived. The destructuring trend now well under way is the next phase in the transformation of the water utility sector, but this time around rationalization will be the strategy and competition will be the mantra.

Regulatory Providers Face Regulatory Burdens

One of the main concerns for water utilities is the mounting regulatory burden, particularly for smaller utilities. Here, consolidation as a regulatory compliance strategy makes sense. Water utilities are subject to increasingly stringent pollution and water quality control rules and regulations issued by state agencies and the Environmental Protection Agency (EPA). In the United States, water utilities must obtain National Pollutant Discharge Elimination System (NPDES) permits for discharges from treatment plants, and compliance with permit restrictions, particularly effluent limitations, is becoming a challenge for smaller water utility systems.

In addition, under the Safe Drinking Water Act (SDWA), water utilities are subject to regulation by the EPA with respect to the quality of water sold and treatment techniques used to make water potable. The EPA promulgates nationally applicable maximum contamination levels (MCLs) for "contaminants" found in drinking water, and has continuing authority to issue additional regulations under the SDWA. Proliferating water quality standards generate costs that are not often adequately reflected in rate increases. Added construction expenditures and related operational expenses, combined with the capital costs necessary to finance these programs, will require frequent requests for rate relief to protect current earnings levels. In short, the number of unfunded regulatory mandates is growing rapidly.

Traditionally, interest rates were viewed as the driving force behind the timing of investments in utilities due to large capital spending requirements and the defensive nature of dividend plays. When it comes to the factors that influence water utilities today, however, interest rates are of secondary importance. In fact, the correlation between water utility stock prices and interest rates declined substantially in the recent rate cycle. Given the dynamics of the environment within which water utilities must operate, the investment quality of a particular utility is more dependent on a variety of other considerations, such as regulatory climate, management capabilities, the cost of water supplies, geographic factors, customer demand characteristics, asset management, competition, and nonregulated activities.

Nonregulated Activities

Many water utilities have created holding companies to separate regulated activities with stable, but often modest, profit potential from nonregulated operations. Nonregulated activities include: laboratory activities, contract operations, Geographic Information System (GIS) services, leak detection, data processing, and remediation activities within the water business. In addition, some water utilities diversified into non-water-related areas, such as real estate development, manufactured housing, telemarketing, and even forest products. At one time, these operations were important to overall profitability, but the trend toward nonregulated activities has all but vanished outside of privatization. Nonetheless, the water utility industry must be analyzed from the point of view of the dynamics affecting traditional water service, as well as the efficacy of diversification strategies, since it is highly likely that this will emerge again in other forms as the water industry adjusts to a rationalized structure.

At this juncture, virtually any diversification effort outside the water industry logically contravenes the investment objective of providing a pure water play, and any water utility that is foolish enough to diversify outside its core expertise should be avoided. While it is not prudent to say that there are no potentially attractive diversifications within the industry, given the current landscape confronting water utilities, only privatizing-type activities would be considered a plus. And even then, it would very much depend on the experience of the utility. As a result, water utilities in emerging regions would not be viewed as a candidate that could successfully leverage operations in this way.

The ability to engage in contract operations, public–private partnerships or any variation on the privatization theme is very dependent upon organizational acuity. Escalating capital requirements and compliance with complex quality standards polarizes water utilities into classification based on size. Generally, the water utilities best suited to deal with the changing dynamics of the industry are the large, well-managed investor-owned companies with some degree of geographic diversity and the major municipal utilities. For these water utilities, privatizing activities are viable but are likely to take on a consolidative feature that makes sense in the context of industry restructuring rather than a purely contractual methodology.

As the cost of providing water increases, many smaller municipalities will be induced to look for efficiencies through contracting for the financing and management of certain components of the waterworks system. Whether investor owned or publicly owned, all water utilities face the same cost pressures that are unlikely to be completely mitigated through rate relief. It is little wonder that concurrent with this phenomenon is the trend toward consolidation in the water supply business.

The Future of Water Utilities

What the water utility of the twenty-first century will look like is perhaps one of the greatest uncertainties in the industry. The fundamentals of the water utility industry present some inherent challenges. The reliable delivery of potable water to end users is an extremely capital intensive proposition. High capital requirements and growing demand theoretically place water utilities structurally on par with other mega-utility operations in energy and telecommunications. Yet the desire for local control keeps the industry unnaturally fragmented. On one level, it can be argued that there is no fundamental conceptual difference between the provision of energy and the provision of water. However, public perception often demands otherwise. When water is viewed as a public good, pricing coincides with the notion of social benefit rather than one of allocational efficiency. And while it is not the intent to presently debate the issue, the rate of return afforded to water utilities is a key driver in the performance of a publicly traded water utility stock.

The water industry in the United States is evolving from a delivery-based system to a solution-based one in order to cost-effectively address expanding regulatory mandates while providing the expected level of service. This trend toward an economics-driven approach with more effective environmental management is the driving force behind dramatic change and will likely result in a substantial consolidation of the water industry. The magnitude of the transition will be unprecedented in an industry.

Historically, the water industry has revolved around regulated utilities that functioned rather autonomously as water providers, aided by engineering consultants and supplied by a highly fragmented network of suppliers. Under this traditional structure, costs are bundled together as a system. But the current focus on the delivery of water as a single finished product has proven inadequate to *efficiently* deal with the wide variety of water and wastewater problems.

Rationalizing the delivery of water is likely to result in an oligopolic system of large national water utility holding companies and a complement of regional water utilities. Numerous smaller water utilities will either be restructured into, or contractually operated by, larger systems. The consolidation in the water utility segment is indicative of maturing markets, burgeoning compliance costs, and the realization that water utilities must focus on growing the core utility business. Horizontal consolidation of water utilities will enhance growth opportunities through greater access to capital, enable geographical diversity, and take advantage of efficiencies arising from economies of scale. The greatest challenge will be finding the most cost-effective method for producing the highest-quality water. Given the regulatory mandate of water utilities, investors may be disappointed by lackluster results in the intermediate term as the industry struggles to define itself within the changing water landscape. Longer term, if the bonds of tradition can be severed in favor of market solutions, key water utilities likely will emerge as industry leaders and may present attractive investment opportunities.

Increasingly stringent regulatory requirements and issues of infrastructure reliability combine to ensure that significant capital investments will be needed over the next several decades, in both distribution and treatment. There are over 50,000 water companies in the United States, 84 percent of which are small systems serving less than 3,300 people. Many of these are undercapitalized and unable to keep up with infrastructure investment requirements. It is this reality that is likely to lead to ongoing consolidation and privatization in the water utility market.

Foreign Water Utilities

Foreign water utilities are one of the more intriguing areas of the water industry in general and the water utility sector in particular. Many of the same factors that facilitated the consistent returns of U.S. water utilities in the 1980s and 1990s are beginning to play out in the more advanced of the emerging countries. These include rising real incomes in a rapidly expanding customer base, less-than-onerous regulatory requirements, increasingly favorable tariff adjustments, and a paucity of public investment vehicles. However, foreign water utilities are subject to unique regulatory frameworks that may hinder an investor's ability to assess associated risk.

As chronicled, changing views on public-private partnerships, privatization activities, and deregulation have opened the way for greater private-sector involvement in utility operations. The scope for expansion is enormous because only a fraction of the market is deregulated. While the percentage of private-sector activity in the water utility sector varies widely by region, the fact remains that the provision of water and wastewater services worldwide is largely provided by public (government-owned) utilities. As such, the local flavor takes on a very significant role. Unlike Europe, of which about 40 percent of water and wastewater services are provided by private and investor-owned utilities, the percentage in the United States is closer to 15 percent. Stated in the converse, a vast percentage of the international water business is controlled by governments. And, simply put, the capital amounts needed to provide service to much of the world population are just too big for the public sector to handle. This is the impetus for privatizing the operations of many of the world's largest public waterworks.

There are many examples of the trend toward publicly traded foreign water utilities. The Bangalore Water Supply and Sewerage Board is the first water utility in India to seek a rating of its financial strength in order to secure public funding. The Water Authority of Fiji is to become a commercial statutory authority as part of the government's plan to "corporatize" the water utility. Malaysia's Water Services Industry Act formalizes the reorganization of the water and wastewater service sector in peninsular Malaysia and Labuan under a single regulator with uniform rules and regulations and rate-setting methodologies. A number of countries are exploring market listings for water and wastewater activities, including Egypt, Bolivia, China, India, and the Philippines. Thai Tap Water Supply PLC (TTW), Thailand's largest private water supply operator, is a recent IPO that further illustrates the trend. TTW has a 30-year contract to supply tap water to the Nakhon Pathom and Samut Sakorn provinces near Bangkok.

Many more countries are motivated to move toward privatizing various operations, although a great deal of controversy follows this global trend, especially in developing countries. The International Monetary Fund (IMF) often requires water privatization and full cost recovery as a condition of its loans, especially in Africa and Latin America. Such conditions govern the IMF's loan policies in countries such as Angola, Niger, and Rwanda. In Latin America, the World Bank and Inter-American Development Bank facilitate the entry of private water companies into the markets, often working cross-conditionally with the IMF. The goal is to provide the capital to increase access to safe drinking water, thereby reducing global poverty. Many recipient countries are small, poor, and debt-ridden. So there is a tenable argument that privatization and full cost recovery tariffs may be manifested in instances of less affordability and, possibly, reduced accessibility. As a result, the large multinational water service companies will benefit.

Herein lies one of the greatest challenges for water utilities. It is critical that the global water utility sector transform itself into a solutions-based system, providing safe drinking water in a cost-effective manner to reliably serve its stakeholders. But it is equally critical that the institutions that govern the provision of water worldwide recognize that the privatization experiment must be allowed to advance in a manner that serves both public and private stakeholders, including investors.

Table 6.1 presents a list of the major publicly traded water utilities worldwide.

Conclusions

The financial performance of water utilities has historically been driven by a combination of weather, interest rates, and regulation. Water utilities hold the purse strings for much of the activity associated with other sectors of the business that cater to the municipal market. But they are also susceptible to the vagaries of public sentiment associated with many of the water challenges that we face. As the regulated purveyors of water, utilities are often forced to balance the provision of a perceived public good with the corporate reality of financial performance.

Table 6.1   Water Utilities

Name	Symbol or SEDOL	Country
Acea SpA	5728125	Italy
Acegas SpA	7057098	Italy
Aguas Andinas SA - A	2311238	Chile
Aguas de Barcelona SA	5729065	Spain
American States Water	AWR	US
American Water Works Co., Inc.	AWK	US
Aqua America, Inc.	WTR	US
Artesian Resources Corp Cl A	ARTNA	US
AS Tallinna Vesi	B09QQT9	Estonia
Athens Water Supply & Sewerage	5860191	Greece
California Water Services	CWT	US
Cascal N.V.	HOO	UK
China Water Affairs Group	6671477	Hong Kong
Cia Saneamento Basico Estada Sao Paula (Sabesp)	SBS	Brazil
Cia Saneamento Minas Gerais (Copasa)	B0YBZJ2	Brazil
Connecticut Water Service Inc	CTWS	US
Consolidated Water Co	CWCO	Cayman Islands
Eastern Water Resources Development	B09C957	Thailand
EVN AG	4295374	Austria
Global Water Resources	GWRI	US
Guangdong Investment Ltd	6913168	Hong Kong
Gruppo Hera	7503980	Italy
Inversiones Aguas Metropolitanas (IAN)	6470522	Chile
Manila Water Company	B0684C7	Philippines
Middlesex Water	MSEX	US
Northumbrian Water Group	3302974	UK
Pennichuck Corp	PNNW	US
Pennon Group	B18V863	UK
Puncak Niaga Holdings	B1SC1H8	Malaysia
Qatar Electric & Water	B124070	Qatar
Ranhill Utilities Berhad	6528692	Malaysia
Severn Trent Plc	B1FH8J7	UK
Shanghai Municipal Raw Water Co	6817367	China
Sociedad General De Aquas de Barcelona	5729065	Spain

Table 6.1   (*Continued*)

Name	Symbol or SEDOL	Country
SJW Corp	SJW	US
Southwest Water Company	SWWC	US
Suez Environnement	B3B8D04	France
Thai Tap Water Supply PCL	B2973Z1	Thailand
Thessaloniki Water & Sewage	7217052	Greece
Tian Jin Capital Enterprises	6908283	China
United Utilities Plc	0646233	UK
Veolia Environnement	VE	France
York Water Company	YORW	US
YTL Power Intl Bhd	B01GQS6	Malaysia

This puts the investor-owned (publicly traded) water utilities in a unique position within the industry. With the experiment of diversification and the first wave of large consolidations largely behind the industry, it's time to reassess the potential of investing in this critical component of the water market.

The salient features of investing in water utilities can be summarized as follows:

• Special situations and domestic consolidators
• Takeover candidates
• Foreign utilities in countries with rising incomes and manageable regulatory burdens
• Water utilities with superior management that are best equipped to manage industry transitional issues

The trend, albeit muted, toward favorable rate increases, especially with respect to wastewater, has benefited water utilities. But it is unrealistic to assume that profitability fueled by rate increases based on the true cost of providing water will continue unabated. Public policy will dictate that rate increases designed to reflect the true cost of water must be mitigated by operational efficiencies in providing water. Water utilities will then be subjected to increasing pressure on profit margins. On the demand side, the customer base only increases through population growth within the communities served or by acquisition of new service territories. In mature markets, rate relief to reflect costs will be limited by the lack of growth or decline in the customer base. These factors do not necessarily foretell a dramatic drop in the segment return on investment, but more likely reflect a stable yet uninspiring business with moderate growth potential.

Several approaches can be taken when looking at individual selections. If an investor is interested in a relatively pure water and wastewater utility play, the multibusiness companies such as Severn Trent, Veolia, and Suez may not be appropriate. Further, the business model of these firms includes large operation and maintenance management contracts that may or may not match the returns of the regulated model. When viewed from the perspective of the consolidation trend in the United States, the large domestic water utilities are positioned to benefit most. Aqua America and American Water Works will usher in the new age of competition between water utilities. It remains to be seen if the water utility sector transitions in a way that would benefit from a merger of the two.

With infrastructure reliability and tightening water quality standards the mandates going forward, the future financial success of water utilities will focus on the ability to manage assets—a competitive advantage for the larger, well-capitalized utilities. Size translates to financial strength (debt ratings will be critical) and higher returns on equity. Asset management, a key component of a competitive strategy for water utilities, will subsequently be discussed at length.

Another facet to investing in water utilities is to look at a particular special situation within the industry that may afford some degree of upside potential over and above the regulated model. This does not imply that investors should seek out water utilities that are diversifying or becoming vertically integrated. Rather, it underscores the potential for water utilities to engage in resource management activities. For example, Consolidated Water is engaged in the development and operation of seawater conversion plants and/or water distribution systems in areas of the world where naturally occurring supplies of potable water are scarce or nonexistent.

The stock performance of water utilities as a sector is likely to be lackluster at best, especially relative to other growth-oriented sectors of the water business such as analytics, treatment, and resource management. To compound the problem, by historical standards they are not cheap. Many sport price-earnings ratios in the mid- to upper 20s or higher, which would have been unheard of at a time when they were valued based largely on interest rate sensitivity, dividend yields, and defensive style. Two decades ago, for example, the average price-earnings ratio of 14 publicly traded U.S. water utilities was 13. Interestingly, the average beta of that same group was 0.7 compared to a beta of 1.2 for Aqua America today. (Beta is a measure of volatility for individual stocks. A stock with a beta over 1.0 is more volatile than the overall market; a stock with a beta of less than 1.0 is less volatile than the market.)

Many equity analysts transitioning to water industry strategists understandably microanalyze the investment merits of water utilities as if the sector is an emerging theme on the green landscape. It is true that water utilities are moving into a phase of dramatic repositioning, but this doesn't necessarily translate into dramatic equity appreciation. With respect to investing in water utilities, there are several common misperceptions:

- Water utilities are often categorically lumped into a broad analytical framework that includes market drivers more associated with other water sectors.
- The magnitude of capital expenditures required does not necessarily equate to the magnitude of the investment opportunity.
- Water rate increases should be viewed as a lack of a negative rather than a positive because of the substantial catch-up required just to narrow the gap in recovering increasing costs.
- Privatization trends are more the result of a shift from delivery to solutions rather than simply a function of unmanageably high capital expenditures. The consolidation of the fragmented water utility market makes more structural sense, *ceteris paribus,* than the mere form of ownership encompassed in privatization. In addition, it remains inconclusive as to whether ownership has a significant impact on efficiency. In other words, privatization is afforded too much financial significance in modeling earnings growth.

Unquestionably, there is no inherent service level differential between the large publicly owned treatment works (defined as those that serve over 100,000) and large investor-owned water utilities. The question is not necessarily whether public water utilities can provide the same level of service, but whether financing transactions can be structured in an equivalently favorable fashion to investor-owned water utilities. And in that respect there is a great deal of uncertainty. Clearly, on the surface, the odds look stacked against public utility funding.

Chapter 7

Centralized Water and Wastewater Treatment

The fundamentals of the treatment sector of the water and wastewater industry are extremely compelling. Virtually all global water quality issues come down to treatment in one form or another, encompassing processes and products such as microbe removal, turbidity, specific contaminant removal, organic chemicals, inorganic chemicals, sedimentation, conventional filtration, wastewater discharge, pretreatment of industrial processes, disinfection, disinfection by-products, and so on. *Treatment* broadly refers to the application of technologies and/or processes that alter the composition of water or wastewater to achieve a beneficial objective in its use, reuse, or discharge. Companies within the treatment sector play a key role in the physical, chemical, or biological characteristics of water and wastewater, whether municipal, agricultural, commercial, or industrial.

Water and wastewater treatment is one of the most confusing sectors for investors. This is because there are many treatment methodologies of varying technical complexity serving a myriad of applications. There is no one treatment solution because there is no one prototypical water quality challenge. The number of treatment technologies and processes are almost as diverse as the characteristics of the source water. Further, the adoption of technological innovation within the water industry is slow because the ramifications of inadequate water treatment can be dire and water industry professionals are not, nor should they be, technological risk takers. Having said that, treatment methodologies are expanding in concert with cost and efficiency considerations and represent an area of investment exposure that cannot be denied.

The challenge for the investor is determining the best approach for gaining exposure to the treatment sector. Several points must be considered, the first being technological risk. Given the critical function achieved by treatment, it is not prudent, or even practical, to speculate on emerging treatment technologies. The toolbox of basic treatment methods is somewhat fixed. Accordingly, the criteria that investors should use to gain exposure to the treatment sector include market leadership in a particular area, diversity of treatment methodologies, application to a number of large markets, and industry acceptance. What should be avoided is treatment technology looking for a market, unproven innovation, processes premised on proprietary claims, and ultraniche applications. The second point is regulatory risk. Despite the perceived efficacy of any treatment method, the reality is that some form of compliance is the objective. Here, regulatory authorities often identify a best available technology (BAT) with respect to a specific compliance goal. Third is the obviously important execution risk. The best water treatment technology is of little benefit if company management is ineffective in transferring it to the marketplace or effectively commercializing its application.

Investors in the treatment sector need to understand both the widely accepted treatment methods that are likely to experience above-average growth and the potential applications of these technologies going forward. Examples where the identification of new markets for existing treatment technology have proven very profitable include the application of UV radiation to wastewater streams, membrane bioreactors in multibarrier systems, activated sludge variations in ammonia removal, ozone in disinfection, reverse osmosis (RO) in desalination,

ion exchange in specific contaminant removal, engineered resins in arsenic removal, and ozone inactivation of *Crytosporidium* oocysts, to name just a few.

The Basics

The most critical treatment objectives pertain to the global need for safe drinking water and sanitation. Water treatment traditionally refers to the process of converting source water to potable water of sufficient quality to comply with applicable regulations and standards, thereby ensuring the protection of human health. It can also pertain to the treatment of water in the optimization of an industrial process. Wastewater treatment, though extricably linked to human health, is differentiated within the treatment category through the additional objective of environmental protection as wastewater streams from municipal or industrial uses are discharged into the environment.

While water and wastewater treatment equipment used in primary and secondary systems are the core of the centralized treatment sector, advanced methods used in tertiary treatment, enabling and convergent treatment technologies that address emerging contaminant issues and innovative multibarrier treatment systems, are key areas of growth. Because of this, the line of demarcation within the treatment sector can become blurred. For example, desalination may be considered an advanced treatment process but given its significance in the overall investment theme associated with developing alternative water supplies it is better addressed on its own merits. Desalination is discussed in Chapter 12. Here, the emphasis is on specific types of water and wastewater treatment technologies.

In the United States alone, the potential use of advanced technologies is enormous. According to the *WaterWorld* Directory of Municipal Water & Wastewater Systems, 97 percent of drinking water systems surveyed use chlorine/chlorine dioxide/chloramines as a disinfection process, with only 3 percent utilizing pressure membrane filtration processes. On the wastewater side, less than 1 percent of primary treatment in wastewater plants use UV radiation. Secondary treatment methods still largely utilize conventional activated sludge. Of course, there are differences in the global percentages (e.g., in Europe, ozone is used more) but the opportunity for growth in the treatment sector is significant.

One of the most arduous tasks for investors in water is not only having a working knowledge of water and wastewater treatment processes and the associated technologies, but understanding the dynamics wherein a particular treatment technique may have a relative advantage or where industry trends are likely to favor one process, method, or alternative over another. For example, there is a trend toward alternative disinfection methods that involve the expanding use of membranes over conventional filtration, convergent, enabling, and disruptive technologies, and a trend toward using the BAT associated with regulatory mandates. And there are many broader issues that impact the specific treatment applications such as economics, sustainability, technology transfers, and structural considerations.

One of the more intriguing aspects is the difference between centralized and decentralized delivery mechanisms. This chapter will focus on the treatment technologies associated with centralized treatment; Chapter 8 will focus on decentralized. From a treatment technology perspective, the overlap is substantial, but it is a way not only to educate the reader on the relative investment merits of each but to lay the foundation for potentially significant changes to the industry and to describe how such transformations could change the investment mix.

Nontraditional water and wastewater treatment techniques are poised for explosive growth. Many countries—particularly emerging economies—are free to choose the most cost-effective means of providing clean drinking water and treating wastewater. And, because the cost curve is coming down on advanced technologies such as nanofiltration, desalination, UV radiation, and ozone oxidation, the utilization of these techniques is on the rise.

Centralized Treatment

The treatment of water is taken for granted in developed countries. Most of us are unfamiliar with the physical, chemical, or biological processes by which raw water is brought up to the standards required for human consumption, as well as the challenges faced by those charged with the responsibility for ensuring a reliable, healthful supply of potable water. We are hardly aware of the large, centralized treatment plants that provide us with clean tap water.

Conventional Treatment

Conventional water treatment comprises both primary and secondary treatment. Technologies involved include sedimentation, coagulation, filtration, and disinfection. Sedimentation is removal of dissolved or suspended impurities through the force of gravity. Settling tanks or clarifiers allow particles (under minimal flow velocities) that are denser than water to settle to the bottom of a tank. Since suspended particles cannot be completely removed from water even given long detention times, chemical coagulants are used to neutralize the effects of colloidal charges and agglomerate particles into larger and heavier flocs (clumps of solid matter) that are settleable and can be more easily removed. The most common coagulant is aluminum sulfate, $Al_2(SO_4)_3$, also referred to as alum. Alum is a water treatment chemical supplied by a number of chemical manufacturers. In order to reduce turbidity and expose microorganisms to greater disinfection efficacy, the physical process of filtration is employed. Filtration involves the removal of suspended particles in water by passing the water through layers of porous granular material, such as green sand.

Companies engaged in conventional primary and secondary centralized water treatment (such as makers of clarifier equipment and filtration media) are experiencing growth in emerging markets, but are not doing as well in developed countries. Increasingly, in developed countries, regulatory mandates require tertiary treatment. Investors are well advised to focus on companies that are active in advanced treatment technologies or multiple barrier systems.

Membrane Separation

Technically, there is a fundamental distinction between filtration and separation. While the filtration of drinking water covers a broad spectrum of materials and processes, the basic function remains the same: to remove particles from water. The increasingly minute levels of contaminants required to be separated from water under varying scenarios is changing. The refinement in form and function of the filtration process has been crucial in meeting this challenge and has facilitated the expansion of a number of markets with extraordinary potential. The reason is that a relatively small adaptation of a given filtration process can pay large dividends in terms of removing difficult contaminants. Membrane separation is capable of many such adaptations. As a result, membrane processes continue to capture a larger share of the water treatment marketplace.

Except for applications such as desalination and point-of-use (POU) treatment, membrane filtration technology is a process that has not been widely used in potable water treatment. As stated earlier, only 3 percent of drinking water systems surveyed utilize pressure membrane filtration processes. But that is changing as decreasing costs and increasing membrane durability provide a cost-effective means for municipalities to meet tighter regulatory mandates and ensure public health. In addition to helping utilities meet more demanding regulations, membranes allow for the use of secondary water resources, such as brackish groundwater, and have been extensively applied in the production of high-purity industrial water and domestic bottled water.

Generally speaking, filtration is a process used for separating solids from a liquid by means of a porous substance, such as a permeable fabric, layers of inert media (sand/gravel), or a membrane. The types of filtration are often characterized by the degree to which solids are separated from the liquid phase being treated. Membranes, which are highly engineered polymer films containing a controlled distribution of pores, are capable of separating the smallest materials from water. They serve as a barrier, permitting the passage of materials only up to a certain size, shape, or character.

Membranes are used as the separation mechanism in the processes of hyperfiltration or reverse osmosis (RO), nanofiltration (NF), ultra-filtration (UF), and microfiltration (MF). The primary difference between the types of membranes is the size of the pores in the membrane material. The removal or rejection characteristics of a membrane are usually rated on the basis of the nominal pore size in microns or the molecular weight cutoff of the membrane, summarized in Table 7.1.

Table 7.1   Separation Spectrum

Process for Separation	Removal Range
Particle filtration	5–75 microns
Microfiltration (MF)	0.1–2 or 3 microns
Ultrafiltration (UF)	0.001–0.2 microns
Nanofiltration (NF)	300–1,000 molecular weight
Hyperfiltration (RO)	Down to 150 molecular weight

The nominal rating refers to an approximate particle size—the vast majority of which will not pass through the filter. In other words, a small amount of particles this size or larger may pass through. The absolute rating, however, indicates that all particles larger than that specified will be trapped within or on the filter and will not pass through. Absolute rating establishes a level of filter performance throughout its useful life, thereby guaranteeing consistent performance.

The pore size of media used in membrane systems can vary from reverse osmosis, which rejects everything but water, to microporous membranes with pores from 0.01 micron to 10 microns. (Particle filtration covers filtration in the range of 5 to 75 microns and is typically handled by cartridge filters.) Reverse osmosis removes undesirable materials from water by using pressure to force the water molecules through a semipermeable membrane. The process is called "reverse" osmosis because the pressure forces the water to flow in the reverse direction, from the concentrated solution to the dilute solution, than that occurring in natural osmosis. RO removes ion-sized material such as sodium, chloride, calcium, and sulfate as well as small organic molecules down to a molecular weight of 100 to 150.

Nanofiltration (NF) and ultrafiltration (UF) are other methods of cross-flow filtration that are similar to RO but use lower pressures. NF removes selected salts and most organics. The UF process falls between nanofiltration and microfiltration (MF) in terms of the size of particle removed, typically rejecting organics over 1,000 molecular weight while passing ions and smaller organics. UF is often used for removal of macromolecules, colloids, viruses, and proteins in the biomedical and pharmaceutical industry. UF is sometimes applied to surface or groundwater treatment for potable use when the source water is consistently low in turbidity. MF, another in the family of membranes, is best suited for removal of particulates, turbidity, suspended solids, and pathogens such as *Cryptosporidium* and *Giardia*. A typical *Cryptosporidium* oocyst is approximately 3 to 5 microns in size, which is 15 to 25 times larger than the pores in a typical 0.2 micron MF membrane.

While much of the focus for emerging membrane technologies has centered on residential and low-volume POU installations, the vast majority of benefits will accrue from growth in large-scale municipal applications and high-purity commercial water treatment systems. Although membrane processes have been used in water treatment for several decades, primarily for desalination, they are not yet part of standard treatment. Water suppliers have long been eager to apply membrane technologies to complex treatment situations, but cost has been a barrier. As the price comes down and durability increases, the potential of membrane filtration is becoming reality. The advantages include a smaller footprint than conventional treatment plants, the ability to capture pathogens and natural organic matter, and the potential to keep utilities ahead of tighter regulatory limits for surface water quality and disinfection by-products.

There is considerable interest in comparing the costs of emerging membrane technologies with costs for alternative potable water treatment processes. For example, based on pilot studies, the cost of particle removal by UF is estimated to be less than or comparable to that using conventional treatment for capacities of approximately 5 million gallons per day. That is to say that it can be a cost-effective option for small facilities. Further, many industries, from pharmaceuticals to electronics to beverages, rely on treated water to produce products. The development of new or refined high-technology and biotechnology products that require ultrapure water as part of manufacturing will also facilitate the rapid growth of membrane technology.

Membrane technologies are used increasingly where high-purity water is a necessity. Ultrapure water, which has been purified by a series of processes to the degree that remaining impurities are measured in parts per billion or trillion, is required by the semiconductor industry and other specialized industrial users. The demand for technologically advanced ultrapure water equipment and systems has increased as the industries that use ultrapure water have become more knowledgeable about their quality requirements. The semiconductor industry, in particular, has continued to demand higher-purity water as the circuits on silicon wafers have become more densely packed.

In addition, membrane technologies are rapidly emerging as a viable water treatment option for municipalities confronted with complex regulatory issues. Membranes can be used as the primary means to remove materials from water, but they can also be used in conjunction with other physical, chemical, or biological processes to separate phases or isolate organisms. Pressure-driven processes of barrier separation are also finding dramatic growth in the provision of high-purity water in an expanding number of industries. All told, yearly sales of membrane technology are predicted to top $5 billion by 2010. Judging by the fundamentals as well as the merger-and-acquisition activity in the membrane filtration business, this segment represents an area in the water industry with above-average growth and investment potential.

Treatment Chemicals

Chemicals have long been a basic component of water and wastewater treatment methods. Corresponding to the surge of technology-driven research in the water industry, however, chemicals are recognized as having a growing role in an increasingly complex technical and regulatory environment. Chemicals can be engineered to achieve a greater range of treatment applications or used in a multibarrier approach. Either way, the cost advantage of chemicals makes them an attractive alternative to many physical or mechanical treatment options. Few segments within the water industry have undergone the number of ownership changes that the chemicals segment has experienced. While there is a dwindling supply of pure-play public companies in water treatment chemicals, there are a number of companies that stand to gain from specialty market positions or the addition of chemicals to their business mix.

According to the American Chemical Society, the demand for water treatment chemicals in the United States is expected to rise at an annual rate of 5 to 6 percent. Much of the opportunity, however, results from worldwide demand. For example, China's demand for water treatment chemicals is projected to grow at an annual rate of approximately

13 percent. By the end of the decade, the global business is estimated to be at over $7 billion. Driving the global growth is worldwide population growth, enforcement of regulatory mandates, innovation in industrial water treatment, and multibarrier approaches in drinking water treatment. The major applications of chemicals in water treatment include:

- Coagulants and flocculants
- Biocides and disinfecting chemicals
- Corrosion- and scale-inhibiting chemicals
- Filter media and adsorbent chemicals
- Softeners and pH adjusters
- Antifoaming agents
- Fluoridation agents

The most common types of treatment for surface water used for drinking supplies are clarification and disinfection. Clarification is usually accomplished by a combination of coagulation, flocculation, sedimentation, and filtration. Coagulation and flocculation are two liquid/solid separation processes that are heavily dependent on the use of chemical additives. Suspended particles cannot be completely removed from water by plain settling, even when they are given very long detention times and low overflow rates. One of the properties of very small turbidity-causing colloidal particles that keep them in suspension is the small electrostatic charge they each carry. Coagulation takes place when the energy barrier between suspended particles is lowered and effectively eliminated. Coagulant chemicals neutralize the effect of the colloidal charges.

Flocculation refers to the successful collisions that occur when the destabilized particles are driven toward each other. Agglomerates of a few very tiny colloidal particles then quickly bridge together to form larger and heavier particles or flocs. After the initial flash mix of the coagulant with the water, a gentle agitation caused by slow stirring further enhances the growth of flocs by increasing the number of particle collisions and enabling removal in a sedimentation tank.

Coagulation or flocculation is enhanced by the addition of chemicals to wastewater to aid gravity settling of suspended or colloidal materials. There are several different chemicals that can be used for coagulation. The most common coagulant is aluminum sulfate (alum); it has become the major coagulant for treating surface water. At the same time, aluminum compounds produce an aluminum hydroxide sludge that is difficult to dewater. The mounting regulation of biosolids (sludge) has led to the greater use of polymeric compounds. Polymeric flocculants (synthetic organic chemicals) are long-chain, high-molecular-weight compounds that help the formation of larger, heavier floc particles.

There are several reasons for the increased demand for water-soluble polymers, including regulations and various environmental concerns regarding volatile organic compounds in paints, adhesives, and cosmetics; the phosphate components in detergents and municipal and industrial water treatment; and the need for paper recycling. Other factors include the growth of the processed food market, changes in paper processing technology, and the highly versatile nature of these compounds in terms of end uses and applications. Worldwide trends toward water reuse, waste minimization, stricter discharge regulations, equipment life extension, and productivity improvement place a high demand on industrial water and process treatment chemicals. The current market breakdown for the United States shows manufacturing industries accounting for about 50 percent of shipments, followed by municipalities, electricity generators, and commercial and residential users.

In addition to the burgeoning industrial applications for wastewater treatment, chemicals used in clarifying drinking water have been found to be effective solutions for a growing list of contamination problems. In potable water treatment, slightly over two thirds of polymer consumption goes for clarification. Enhanced coagulation, proposed as a BAT in Stage 1 of the Disinfectants/Disinfection By-Products (D/DBP) Rule, is capable of controlling disinfection by-products by removing natural organic matter precursors. The D/DBP Rule regulates total trihalomethanes, a carcinogenic by-product of the disinfection process. The list of complex issues mitigated by water treatment chemicals in conventional unit processes continues to expand as research progresses: arsenic removal, reduction of hazardous sludge, enhanced filter performance, improved dewatering of sludges, and increased effluent quality.

It is for precisely these reasons that the specialty chemicals business of the water and wastewater treatment industry holds so much promise for investors. Chemical companies are following the lead set by the large water purification and wastewater treatment systems suppliers in

providing integrated solutions that maximize performance and minimize costs. This integrated approach is an established trend in the water
industry but for water chemical marketers it is just unfolding. Because
of the specificity of this concept and the fact that extensive knowledge of
the industry is required to implement the strategy, several large players
dominate the market for engineered water treatment chemicals.

The water and wastewater chemical treatment business has undergone a tumultuous restructuring over the past decade. This is likely
due to the consolidative nature of a commodity business in combination with one of the most traditional of water industry components
that exhibits a fairly straightforward business model. General Electric
acquired BetzDearborn from Hercules in 2002. About the same time, a
consortium of private equity firms purchased Ondeo Nalco (renamed
Nalco Company) from Suez. In 2004, Nalco returned to the public
arena with an IPO at $15 per share and remains the preeminent pub-
licly held water treatment chemical company in the world.

The water treatment chemicals business has historically been a fragmented, undercapitalized industry, vying to solve treatment problems
with competing methodologies. That changed with the consolidation
of key water treatment chemical technologies and the emergence of
integrated service chemical providers. The common characteristics of
the companies that signify substantial opportunity are a global reach,
engineered chemical treatment, on-site innovation, and in-depth technical service and support.

Many water treatment chemical companies are minor parts of
much larger companies or are private. Table 7.2 presents the prominent
global water treatment stocks.

Disinfection: The Chlorine Controversy

Chlorine has been making our drinking water safe for almost 100 years.
It is the most commonly used substance for disinfection in the United
States. After chlorine's introduction into the public water supply, U.S.
typhoid deaths dropped from 25,000 in 1900 to less than 20 in 1960
to virtually none today, not to mention its role in preventing the spread
of other waterborne diseases. Chlorine and chlorine-based compounds
are used to disinfect 98 percent of the publicly supplied drinking water

Table 7.2 Water Treatment Chemicals

Name	Symbol or SEDOL	Water Segments or Brands	Water Activity
Nalco Holding Company	NLC	Leading global provider of water treatment chemicals	Integrated water treatment applications; raw water treatment, wastewater treatment, cooling and boiler programs, process improvement
Arch Chemicals	ARJ	HTH Water Treatment Products	Municipal (drinking water), residential (pools) and industrial (disinfection) biocides
Ashland Corp.	ASH	Drew Industrial	Municipal and industrial water and wastewater treatment chemicals
Chemtura	CEM	Great Lakes	Industrial water treatment; desalination; pool/spa
Kemira	4513612	Municipal and industrial; Cytec	Global leader in coagulants; also flocculants, corrosion/scale inhibitors, biocides, ion exchange, activated carbon, pH adjusters.
Dow Chemical	DOW	Rohm & Haas, DOWEX	Ion exchange resins, scale inhibitors, biocides
Met-Pro Corp.	MPR	Pristine Water Solutions, Inc.	Proprietary chemicals for municipal drinking water and cooling towers; lead/copper reduction, corrosion/scale inhibitors, etc.

in the United States. At the same time, the use of elemental chlorine in water purification is the subject of a broader controversy that shows no sign of disappearing.

In drinking water treatment, clarification (comprised of the unit processes of coagulation, sedimentation, and filtration) is followed by chlorination to remove pathogenic bacteria or viruses. In gaseous form, molecular chlorine (Cl_2) is very toxic. But when the chlorine is dissolved in low concentrations in clean water, it is not harmful. It reacts with the H^+ ions and the OH^- radicals in the water to produce hypochlorous acid, $HOCl$, and the hypochlorite radical, OCl^-. These are the actual disinfecting agents. If microorganisms are present in the water, the HOCl and the OCl⁻ penetrate the microbe cells and react with certain enzymes. This reaction disrupts the organisms' metabolism and kills them.

What is a growing concern, however, are the so-called "by-products" of the disinfection process (the growing list of so-called disinfection by-products or DBPs). Source waters often contain trace amounts of organic compounds, primarily from natural sources such as decaying vegetation. These substances can react with the chlorine to form trihalomethanes (THMs), which are suspected of causing cancer in humans. Chloroform is an example of a THM compound. It is for this reason that the Environmental Protection Agency (EPA) regulates disinfection by-products by setting maximum contaminant levels for total THMs and the sum of five haloacetic acids. The levels of these substances formed upon chlorination of natural waters depend on several operational conditions, such as chlorine dosage and free chlorine contact time, as well as water quality conditions, such as organic content, bromide, temperature, and pH.

As the debate over the health risks associated with chlorine disinfection by-products intensifies, the water industry continues to take a critical look at alternative disinfection processes. And while ozone and ultraviolet disinfection, among other methods, have benefited from the scrutiny of chlorine, it is unlikely that a change based solely on the chlorine controversy will occur overnight. First, other chlorine-based disinfectants such as chlorine dioxide, bromine chloride, and hypochlorites (solid and liquid chlorine compounds) do not lead to toxicity problems as often. For instance, chlorine dioxide does not produce chlorinated or brominated organics, THMs, dioxins, or other haloforms. Second, alternative disinfection methods also have potentially harmful by-products under certain conditions. And third, adjustments to the treatment process prior to chlorination, such as enhanced coagulation, can remove natural organic matter and reduce by-product formation.

Chlorine Dioxide

Chlorine dioxide (ClO_2) manufacturers may achieve some near-term gains in market share as a result of demand for chlorine-based disinfection methods other than the commonly used chlorine gas process. In addition, there are special situations that present an opportunity as the chlorine controversy heightens. For example, enhanced coagulation for the purpose of removing natural organic matter, which is the primary precursor of disinfection by-products, should help the coagulants business of water treatment chemical companies.

Ozone: Good Up High, Bad Nearby

While much is said about the potential for alternative disinfection methods to chlorine, little is written about the ways in which these technologies are actually being transferred to the marketplace. Ozone, however, is one segment that is relatively well established and developing in a rather deliberate manner. Major industrial gas producers are aligning themselves with leading ozone technology producers to create formidable alliances designed to take advantage of ozone's potential in the water industry.

Ozone (O_3), which is an unstable gas comprised of three oxygen atoms, is an extremely powerful oxidant, second only to the hydroxyl free radical. It is capable of oxidizing many organic and inorganic compounds in water. Reactions with organic and inorganic compounds cause an ozone demand in the treated water that must be satisfied during ozonation prior to developing a measurable residual. Ozone gas readily degrades back to oxygen, and during this transition a free oxygen atom (free radical) is formed.

In the United States, ozone is gaining a foothold in the arsenal of water treatment technologies. Fueled by the ongoing regulation of disinfection by-products specifically and the efficacy of disinfection technologies generally, ozone treatment should be a segment of investor interest. Ozone treatment is utilized in a wide variety of applications in the water industry. It is used in treating landfill leachate and industrial wastewater, where it improves biodegradability, disinfects, and oxidizes nitrogen compounds. In drinking water, it replaces chlorine as the primary oxidant/disinfectant; eliminates pesticides and chlorinated hydrocarbons, removes iron and manganese; and improves odor, taste, and color. In combination with UV radiation or H_2O_2 (hydrogen peroxide), ozone is used to reduce chlorinated hydrocarbons and nitroaromatics in the remediation of contaminated groundwater. Ozonation is also growing in its use in the oxidation and disinfection of industrial process water for the food and beverage, semiconductor, and pharmaceutical industries. Most of the larger ozone equipment manufacturers make all components: ozone generators; ozone introduction equipment such as diffusers, injectors, or mixers; and destruction units.

The traditional way of producing ozone is by means of dielectric barrier discharge or silent electrical discharge. Because ozone is an unstable molecule, it is generated at the point of application. It is generally formed by combining an oxygen atom with an oxygen molecule in an endothermic reaction that requires a considerable input of energy. Dry feed gas (either oxygen or filtered ambient air) is pumped to ozone generators where it is passed over hundreds of glass tubes individually fused with an electrical filament. The gas is subjected to a corona (lightning-like) discharge at up to 15,000 volts causing an electron flow across the discharge gap. These electrons provide the energy to disassociate the oxygen molecules, leading to the formation of ozone.

Ozone generation does not form halogenated disinfection by-products (TTHMs and HAA5s) when used in oxidation/reduction reactions, but it does form a variety of organic and inorganic by-products. However, if bromide ions are present in the raw water, halogenated DBPs may be formed. These brominated DBPs pose a greater health risk than nonbrominated DBPs. Further, although ozone is an effective oxidant and disinfectant, it cannot be relied upon as a secondary disinfectant to maintain a residual in the distribution system. The advantages and disadvantages of ozone disinfection can be summarized as follows:

Advantages
- Ozone is more effective than chlorine, chloramines, and chlorine dioxide for inactivation of viruses, *Crytosporidium*, and *Giardia*.
- Ozone oxidizes iron, manganese, and sulfides.
- Ozone controls odor, taste, and color.
- Ozone can enhance the clarification process and turbidity removal.
- Ozone requires a very short contact time.
- In the absence of bromide, halogen-substitutes (DBPs) are not formed.

Disadvantages
- Ozone provides no residual.
- The initial cost of ozonation equipment is high.
- The generation of ozone requires high energy input.
- DBPs are formed in the presence of bromide.
- Ozone is highly corrosive and toxic.

Ozone technology is being transferred to the marketplace through a rapidly developing mechanism of alliances between global powerhouses. Major joint ventures are seeking to take advantage of the explosive growth in ozone-based environmental technologies. Praxair, Inc. bought Henkel Corporation's 50 percent share of its joint venture with Trailigaz Ozone, forming a global alliance bringing together its expertise in vacuum pressure swing adsorption (VPSA) oxygen generation systems with Trailigaz ozone production systems. Praxair is the largest industrial gas company in North and South America, and one of the largest worldwide. Trailigaz, the third-largest ozone water treatment technology company in the world, was a wholly owned subsidiary of Veoolia Environnement, until purchased by Wedeco AG, which itself was purchased by ITT Corporation. PCI-Wedeco has a strategic marketing and research-and-development alliance with British giant BOC Gases.

In another ozone consortium, Air Liquide S.A. (France) joined with Degremont S.A. (a subsidiary of Suez) to form a joint venture called Ozonia International, which took over the activities of Switzerland-based ABB AG (Asea Brown Boveri). The combination of Degremont's water technology and the industrial application technology of Air Liquide make Ozonia a leading manufacturer of ozone generation equipment and ozone plants. The joint venture is also moving into UV applications. Suez has rebranded its water operations under the ONDEO brand. The ONDEO water business is the world's second largest, behind the water unit of Veolia Environnement. Ozonia has grown into a group of five companies in Switzerland, the United States, Russia, South Korea, and Scotland, with the holding company, Ozonia International, in France. The worldwide ozone generation equipment market is segmented into municipal water treatment (70 percent) and industrial applications (30 percent).

Ultraviolet (UV) Disinfection

Ultraviolet energy is increasingly being used to disinfect wastewater, process water, sewage effluent, combined sewage runoff, and even drinking water. With UV's efficiency in reducing *Cryptosporidium* established, ultraviolet light irradiation is positioned to become another option as best available technology for surface water treatment. With the added potential of UV light for inactivating *C. parvum* oocysts efficiently and cost-effectively, ultraviolet technologies promise to be a powerful tool for water suppliers as a viable disinfection alternative.

Ultraviolet irradiation is nature's own disinfection method. The sun generates large quantities of ultraviolet energy that is naturally filtered by the ozone layer and does not occur in large quantities in the atmosphere. Ultraviolet energy is the photonic energy that lies just outside the visible violet end of the electromagnetic spectrum and is defined as light between the wavelengths of 100 and 400 nanometers (nm). This light has longer wavelengths than x-rays and shorter wavelengths than the light visible to the human eye.

Ultraviolet C (UVC) is part of the broad ultraviolet waveband. The portion of the UV spectrum that is important for the disinfection of water is the range absorbed by DNA (RNA in the case of some viruses). The "germicidal range" is approximately 200 to 300 nm, with a peak germicidal effectiveness at about 260 nm. This band of the UVC spectrum is highly destructive to microorganisms and is used for ultraviolet disinfection. The mechanism involves absorption of a UV photon by pyrimidine bases where two are positioned next to each other on the DNA chain. The photochemistry involves formation of a molecule that links the two bases together. This causes a disruption in the DNA chain, such that when the cell undergoes mitosis (cell division), the replication of DNA is inhibited. When water or wastewater is exposed to a special light source that produces this radiation, the cells of microorganisms are altered in a way that inhibits their ability to propagate.

The germicidal properties of UV lamps are a function of intensity, duration of exposure, and radiation wavelength. UV intensity dissipates with distance from a lamp so that a primary objective of UV disinfection system design is to maintain as close contact as possible between the UV lamps and the water being treated. In the past, the problem with this method of disinfecting wastewater, process water, or sewage streams has been the vast number of UV energy lamp sources needed at locations with poor effluent quality. However, recent versions of low-mercury, vapor pressure, ultraviolet-producing lamps have improved the electrical power to UV energy conversion efficiency without generating unwanted heat or other energy or light wavelengths. Lamps have been developed that continuously vary the UV energy output to match the effluent flow and clarity conditions. This has greatly extended the range of effluent streams that can be effectively treated while retaining the inherent benefits of UV irradiation.

The UVC germicidal waveband can treat liquid streams containing microbiological contaminants that cause infections, such as bacteria, viruses, and spores—and disinfect the streams without the use of chemicals and without producing changes in the fluid. This makes the technique extremely suitable for treating wastewater and effluent streams that empty into large bodies of water such as lakes, rivers, and oceans. Quality parameters such as biochemical oxygen demand (BOD) and chemical oxygen demand (COD) remain unaffected. In cases where discharge regulations severely limit the impact on receiving waters, UV technology can provide an effective solution.

Other advantages of UV disinfection include the elimination of the potential hazards of handling gaseous chlorine, alleviation of concerns about disinfection by-products, elimination of a dechlorination requirement, reduction in taste or odor problems and acceleration of treatment times. The disadvantages of UV disinfection include its sensitivity to water quality characteristics; dosage inflexibility; exposure risks; the lack of a residual; and the fouling of UV lamp tubes by oil, grease, mineral salts, and the like.

The disinfection process is used for different purposes in water and wastewater treatment plants. However, the types of devices used to inject disinfectant into the water or wastewater stream are similar. UV disinfection equipment is currently available in two configurations, enclosed systems and open-channel systems. Until the mid- to late 1980s, UV disinfection was accomplished in expensive, enclosed stainless steel tanks that were subject to fouling and troublesome to operate. Since that time, significant improvements to the equipment have been made. The advent of open-channel contactors with drop-in bulb assemblies has revolutionized the technology. The more recently developed open-channel systems are now the predominant UV system in wastewater treatment. Open-channel units are generally able to maximize use of the entire space around the lamps, since flow enters and leaves the lamp array without changing direction.

The application of UV radiation for primary disinfection is often limited by the turbidity (suspended particles) associated with many water supplies. This limits the transmittance, and hence the effectiveness, of the UV light. In addition, UV disinfection lacks a measurable residual as required in the distribution system. Although the use of UV radiation still lacks widespread application in the primary disinfection of drinking water, there is significant growth potential in large-scale installations and expanding specialized niche applications such as POU, wastewater reuse, industrial process water, and wastewater effluent disinfection.

Mixed Oxidants

The disinfection of drinking water is an area of continuous research to find more efficient disinfectants against presently known microorganisms for the protection of public health. The use of mixed oxidants, an emerging technology, while not new, is receiving a growing amount of interest. The general concept is that of an electrolytic cell and electrolyte used to generate amounts of anolyte and catholyte, believed to contain a variety of oxidants, the mixture of which is referred to as "mixed oxidants." The oxidants are purported to include chlorine, chlorine dioxide, hydrogen peroxide, ozone, and hydroxyl radicals. This technology is thought to present a number of advantages over present disinfection methods. For one, the efficiency of the oxidants produced is, by mass, higher than that of chlorine. Second, a residual may be maintained in product water. Third, the oxidant concentration and composition may be adjusted according to specific needs. And, finally, the oxidant mixtures can be produced on-site using only electricity and sodium chloride.

In its application, mixed oxidant treatment is similar to chlorination. Rather than applying commercially available gaseous, solid, or liquid forms of chlorine, the process produces a strong disinfectant solution on-site. On-site oxidant generation (also known as anodic oxidation and salt brine electrolysis) is accomplished by an electrolytic process that generates a concentrated solution of oxidants, mainly free chlorine. This process involves passage of an electric current through a continuous-flow brine (salt) solution within a cell. The electrolyzed brine solution containing the concentrated disinfectant is injected into water for treatment. The concentrated solution is diluted approximately 100-fold in drinking water treatment. Although there is no record of the large-scale application of mixed oxidants in water disinfection, the technology can be a means of primary disinfection on small water treatment plants and to augment depleted disinfectant concentrations in distribution systems. In remote areas, mixed oxidants may be appealing because the application of chlorine can be problematic due to distance from the place of chlorine manufacture, the unreliability of delivery schedules, and the lack of sufficient expertise in chlorine dosing.

The chemistry of mixed oxidants is complex in the sense that while there are clearly constituents other than chlorine present in the reactions, the identity of these other components is not fully known. Although the chemistry is not completely understood, the other active oxidant components are limited to combinations of the oxygen and chlorine generated electrolytically in the saltwater brine used. Theoretically, due to the electrochemical processes within the cell, $HOCl$, ClO_2, O_3, and H_2O_2 could be formed.

Interestingly, the application of mixed oxidants in the disinfection of drinking water has been used for some time in eastern Europe. It is because of the chemical uncertainties that mixed oxidants have not yet been widely adopted in the United States. At the same time, the known benefits of mixed oxidants are enough to garner support by the EPA for certain applications and to continue promising research into lesser known, but theoretical, benefits. Mixed oxidants have been demonstrated through actual installations to have superior characteristics when compared to conventional chlorine, whether in the gas, liquid (sodium hypochlorite), or solid (calcium hypochlorite) form.

A number of scientific studies, some peer reviewed and some funded by manufacturers, have shown significant benefits of mixed oxidant disinfection. Mixed oxidants typically demonstrate lower THM production when compared to chlorine. Manufacturers report that THM formation can be reduced by 30 to 50 percent when compared to chlorine. Again, the chemistry is not completely understood, but the belief is that the oxidants in the mixed oxidant solution (apart from chlorine) react more rapidly with THM precursors. These oxidants are not prone to produce large amounts of THMs. Thus, most THM reduction observed in actual practice may be explained by the other oxidants of the mixed oxidant solution satisfying a major portion of the oxidant demand of the raw water, allowing satisfactory disinfection and residual maintenance at lower free available chlorine doses than would be required using chlorine alone. Reduced doses lead immediately to lower THM formation. There is also promise in the ability of mixed oxidants to inactivate *Cryptosporidium parvum* oocysts and other hard-to-kill microorganisms at free available chlorine doses that are normally used. Chlorine is unable to inactivate these microorganisms at practical doses.

Mixed oxidants enhance coagulation and flocculation processes in a manner similar or superior to ozone. The process creates a micro-flocculation effect following the same patterns generated by ozone pretreatment. The results are substantially lower alum and polymer requirements, reduced finished water turbidity, reduced sludge handling, and faster reaction times that allow for increased throughput and filter runs. Another key factor in the use of mixed oxidants as an alternative disinfection method is that the chlorine residual in the distribution system is much more stable and persistent in the distribution system. Mixed oxidants have been reported to have other beneficial characteristics. These include safety advantages over chlorine gas; biofilm removal and prevention of regrowth; improved taste and odor; oxidation of iron, manganese, and hydrogen sulfide; ammonia oxidation at subbreakpoint doses; and minimal increases in total dissolved solids (salt).

There are a number of regulations that support the benefits of mixed oxidants as an alternative disinfection method. The interim Enhanced Surface Water Treatment Rule (ESWTR) requires that large filtered surface water systems improve their reliability to remove at least 99% of *Cryptosporidium* through a dual-barrier approach. In the guidance document in support of the Surface Water Treatment Rule (SWTR), the EPA lists mixed oxidants as a small system compliance technology for disinfection. In addition, water systems serving more than 10,000 people must implement treatment strategies to achieve compliance with the Stage 1 D/DBP Rule, which lowers maximum levels for total THMs from 100 ppb to 80 ppb. Haloacetic acids, previously unregulated, will now be regulated at 60 ppb. Many systems will not be able to achieve compliance without making significant capital improvements. Nonetheless, the market for mixed oxidant technology is relatively small, and the investment potential is limited to the companies that sell on-site hypochlorite generators.

Carbon

Carbon is the sixth most abundant element in the universe, appearing in 94 percent of all known compounds. It is the only element on Earth capable of forming the complex and varied compounds essential for living organisms. Yet what is so ubiquitous in nature is also a material used extensively in the water industry. When treated at high temperature, carbon-based materials are transformed into products essential in purifying the water we drink.

Granular activated carbon (GAC), derived from naturally occurring materials like coal, wood, and coconut shell, has two unique properties that make it useful for water purification. First, it is a very porous material. In the activation process, high-temperature heat treatment creates an intricate network of microscopic pores and pathways within each carbon granule. GAC has an extremely high ratio of surface area to unit weight—up to 100 acres of area per pound. Second, the surface of activated carbon attracts and holds many of the impurities in water through the adsorption process. As a result, contaminants—which are highly concentrated in the liquid stream—move to the solid phase where the concentration is lower.

Adsorption on activated carbon is an effective method for removing dissolved organic substances that cause taste and odor problems in drinking water and has been sanctioned by the EPA as the BAT for organics removal. It is also effective in removing the organic precursors that react with chlorine to form harmful THM compounds after disinfection. In special applications, GAC can remove synthetic organic chemicals (SOCs) or volatile organic chemicals (VOCs) from contaminated water. As such, GAC is useful in complying with the D/DBP Rule established under the Safe Drinking Water Act amendments.

Carbon treatment can be used for both secondary and tertiary treatment directly in large, centralized physical/chemical treatment plants or to polish effluent from biological treatment systems. Powdered carbon is mixed with the water by a special dry-feeder device, at a point in the treatment plant that precedes the filtration process. It is then removed from the water by the filters. Granular carbon is sometimes used in the filter bed itself, combining both filtration and adsorption in one treatment unit. Similar treatment processes, on a miniaturized basis, are widely used in decentralized point-of-use filtration devices.

Environmental applications of activated carbon in wastewater and sewage treatment, groundwater remediation, and water purification offer enormous potential. In addition, substantial new opportunities are emerging within the process industries as environmental and process applications converge. Trends toward pretreatment and waste minimization as process improvement and cost reduction steps are also creating significant demand for GAC. Part of the reason is the physical nature of carbon. When the carbon surface becomes saturated with adsorbed impurities, it can be cleaned or reactivated by heating to a high temperature in a special thermal reactivation furnace or removed chemically in a regeneration process and then reused. On-site reactivation, rather than complete replacement with fresh carbon, is economical for large municipal water treatment plants. The ability to reuse granular carbon over and over makes it financially attractive as a treatment option but has also contributed to the past oversupply of carbon worldwide. In addition, activated carbon is used in manufacturing a variety of products from decaffeinated coffee to automobiles to magazines. In the food and beverage, oil and gas, chemical, pharmaceutical, and other industries, there are more than 700 different applications of activated carbon. This helps to explain why, with all the promise carbon holds for the water industry, manufacturers are sensitive to worldwide economic conditions.

The industry is dominated by several large manufacturers. Calgon Carbon Corporation is the world's largest producer and marketer of

GAC, related services, equipment, and systems for both environmental and industrial applications. Calgon's share of the global market for GAC is estimated at approximately 30 percent, and its volume of sales is three times that of its closest competitor, Norit N.V. There are also many smaller manufacturers that comprise a fragmented component to the business and create competitive pressures. While the amount of Chinese carbon imported has slowed, it is still disrupting the industry's pricing structure. In response, several major producers have diversified into other businesses.

Even though end-market improvement is still the key for an overall improvement in the carbon industry, the prospects for applications in the water industry are phenomenal. Product innovations such as extruded activated carbon blocks, catalytic carbons, and biological activated carbon offer opportunities in process applications and the growing POU market. As the industry works off excess capacity and pricing pressure subsides, there is tremendous potential for leverage and a return to the historically high growth rates to which the carbon industry is accustomed. With so many uses for activated carbon in the removal of contaminants, the overcapacity of the past is not likely to remerge. At the same time, carbon is a commodity and manufacturers face a great deal of competition; there is limited value added that can differentiate suppliers.

Resins: Ion Exchange

While physical treatment methods such as RO, adsorption, mechanical filtration and even ultraviolet light receive much of the attention in water treatment, the chemical treatment process of ion exchange is increasingly being utilized in a variety of treatment applications. After an extended period of overcapacity, the ion exchange segment has experienced substantial global growth, reflecting increased demand from Asian economies. While resin price increases have taken some competitive luster off the ion exchange process, the segment is developing into an effective option within the overall treatment scheme.

Ion exchange is a chemical treatment process in which undesired ions in water are replaced with less objectionable ones (the contaminant must therefore be present as an ion). An ion is an atom or molecule that has lost or gained one or more electrons, thereby acquiring a net electric charge. Ions are preferentially adsorbed from a solution by equivalently charged ions attached to small solid structures known as resins. Ion exchange is an equilibrium phenomenon. As untreated water passes through the device, the undesired ions are exchanged for ions on the exchange material and the process continues until equilibrium is reached.

The efficiency of the exchange depends on the concentration of ions in the water, the attraction between the ion exchange resin and the unwanted ions, and the contact time between untreated water and the resin. The exchange occurs in a fiberglass tank or plastic-lined steel tank filled with a special ion exchange material—either a commercial resin, which is a petrochemical compound shaped into beads, or a synthetic zeolite, which is a crystalline formulation of aluminates and silicates. The appropriate exchange material depends on the untreated water quality and the desired water quality. The two types of ion exchange units are cation and anion exchange devices. Water softeners remove cations (positively charged minerals such as calcium and magnesium) and replace them with sodium. Anion exchange devices remove anions (negatively charged ions such as arsenic and nitrate) and replace them with chloride.

The primary applications for ion exchange technology are water softening, industrial water treatment, dealkalization and demineralization. Water softeners (or water conditioners) are the most widely used point-of-entry (POE) home water treatment devices. Water softeners consist of a corrosion-resistant brine tank that is filled with resin beads saturated with sodium. The resin prefers calcium and magnesium (the principle components of hardness) over sodium so as water passes over the resin, sodium is released and calcium and magnesium are adsorbed. Softeners remove hardness minerals that form scale on water heaters and pipes. These devices can also remove barium, radium, small amounts of dissolved iron and manganese, and, in many cases, soluble iron (ferrous). Contrary to industry claims, water used for drinking generally does not need to be softened, nor should softened water be used for irrigation.

While there have been many improvements in home and commercial water softeners in recent years, the basic cation resin used has remained the same. The thrust for operating efficiencies and soft water quality has focused on obtaining higher salt efficiency and automatic regeneration. Other factors influencing design changes have been the effort to conserve water and minimize saltwater discharge to the wastewater system. These changes have spurred the demand for residential water softeners and have greatly contributed to the success of water softening equipment manufacturers. The end market is mature and overcrowded, limiting the value of the residential water softener segment as an investment play. This theme is discussed in greater detail in the context of decentralized treatment.

Where ion exchange is gaining momentum is in the industrial, municipal, and restoration markets. Variations of ion exchange technology such as deionization, demineralization, and complex mixed-bed ion exchange technologies are increasingly being used in specific applications. Ion exchange deionizers (DIs) use synthetic resins similar to those used in water softeners. Typically used on water that has already been prefiltered, DIs use a two-stage process to remove virtually all ionic material remaining in water. Two types of synthetic resins are used: cations to remove positively charged ions, and anions to remove negatively charged ions. Cation deionization resins exchange hydrogen (H^+) ions with cations, such as calcium, magnesium, and sodium. Anion exchange operates on the same principle as cation exchange. The only difference is that anion exchange devices adsorb anions such as nitrate and sulfate instead of cations such as calcium and magnesium. Anion deionization resins exchange hydroxide (OH^-) ions for anions such as chloride, sulfate, and bicarbonate. The displaced H^+ and OH^- combine to form H_2O.

Deionization can produce extremely high quality water in terms of dissolved ions or minerals. Deionization holds promise in the desalination of seawater, the extraction of harmful contaminants from wastewater, and the removal of inorganics associated with the application of agricultural fertilizers. Deionization is also used as a water purification method in bottling plants, electroplating operations, and pharmaceuticals, as well as in high-purity applications such as low-pressure boilers and power generators.

Much of the expansion in the use of ion exchange technology results from advances in the exchange materials. Resins give preferential treatment to certain ions and, by engineering special resins, consideration can be given to innovative applications. For example, resins typically

Table 7.3 Water Treatment Companies

Name	Symbol or SEDOL	Country	Water Segments or Brands	Water Activity
Hyflux Ltd.	6320058	Singapore	Treatment	Broad pure play
Hyflux Water Trust	B29HL02	Singapore	Plant Ownership	Invests in water, wastewater and recycling plants in PRC, India, Middle East and North Africa
BioteQ Environmental	2504083	Canada	Treatment and Remediation (Turn-Key plants)	Industrial wastewater treatment applications; sulphate reduction, lime sludge processing, metals
Bio-Treat Technology	6740407	Singapore	Treatment	Wastewater treatment
BWT AG Group	4119054	Austria	Treatment	Residential/industrial
Amiad Filtration Systems	B0P0D83	Israel	Treatment	Filters and filtration systems
General Electric	GE	US	GE Water & Process Technologies: Ionics, Osmonics, GE Betz, Zenon, Sievers, Autotrol	Membranes, POU, filtration, chemicals, instrumentation, EFR, desalination; broad range of treatment services and equipment
Calgon Carbon	CCC	US	Treatment	Activated carbon, UV, ion exchange
Nalco Holding	NLC	US	Treatment	Chemicals
Halma Plc	0405207	UK	Aquionics, Berson, Hanovia	UV disinfection drinking water, wastewater, process water; municipal and industrial
Kemira Oyj	4513612	Finland	Cytec	Municipal chemicals
Keppel Corporation	B1VQ5C0		Keppel Seghers	MBR, biosolids, biological wastewater treatment
Layne Christensen	LAYN	US	Reynolds	Water and wastewater treatment plants and systems

Company	Code	Country	Segment	Description
GLV Inc. Cl.A	B23Y0V3	Canada	Water Treatment Group (Eimco, Enviroquip, Brackett Green, Copa, AJM)	Treatment/recycling of municipal/industrial water and wastewater; membranes, biological treatment, filtration systems and equipment
Organo Corp	6470522	Japan	Treatment	Full range of municipal and industrial water treatment systems
Nitto Denko Corp	6641801	Japan	Hydranautics	RO membrane applications; MBR
Mitsubishi Rayon Engineering Co Ltd	6597164	Japan	Treatment	RO membrane applications; MBR
Kurita Water Industries Ltd	6497963	Japan	Treatment	Industrial treatment, desalination, membrane
Doosan Heavy Ind.	6294670	South Korea	Desalination	Multi stage flash (40% global market share)
Impregilo Group SpA	B09MRX8	Italy	Fisia Italimpianti (desal)	Integrated water cycle activities and desalination
Ion Exchange India	6324931	India	Treatment	Ion exchange
Christ Water Technology	B0P0KL5	Austria	Treatment	Municipal/industrial process water treatment
Pall Corp	PLL	US	Treatment (Aria Filtration Systems)	Diverse filtration, separation, and purification; municipal water and wastewater membrane treatment, desalination, POU devices, MBR, industrial applications.
Veolia Environnement	VE	France	Environmental Services	Comprehensive
Basin Water Inc.	BWTR	US	Treatment	Ion exchange
Siemens AG	SI	Germany	US Filter	Comprehensive
Severn Trent Plc	B1FH8J7	UK	Water Purification; Operating Services; Analytical Services	Water and wastewater treatment; disinfection, filtration, arsenic removal, contract operations, leak detection, sampling and analytical services.

prefer sulfate over nitrate (the order of adsorption depends on the characteristics and concentration of each ion in the water). Most resins are ineffective in removing nitrate if sulfate is also present in the water. Nitrate-selective resins have been designed to rearrange the preference order; nitrate is adsorbed first, then sulfate, then chloride, then bicarbonate. Nitrate-selective resins push sulfate off the exchange material if the two ions are competing but do not dump nitrate when the resin capacity is exhausted.

The market for ion exchange technology is evolving from the more saturated water conditioning applications to complex industrial, remediation, high-purity, and even organic applications. At the same time, growth rates within the industrial segment are mixed. Generally, demineralization by ion exchange has been declining as the usage of reverse osmosis membranes has increased. Other contaminant-specific applications for ion exchange such as removal of radionuclides, nitrates and arsenic are showing significant growth. While much of the innovative technology still remains to be commercialized, breakthroughs in operating efficiencies and resin materials are creating exciting opportunities that investors should monitor.

Table 7.3 summarizes a diverse array of water treatment companies.

Centralized water and wastewater treatment evolved as the logical extension of increasing urbanization and the application of the economic model of economies of scale. At the same time, if we are to foretell the future of water, latitude must be given to the theorem that centralized treatment may not necessarily hold the answer to sustainability. Especially with respect to "bottom-of-pyramid" markets and the reverse flow of technological innovation, decentralized (distributed) treatment has a disruptive story to tell and a potentially compelling investment premise.

Chapter 8

Decentralized Water and Wastewater Treatment

D ecentralized water and wastewater treatment holds a rather distinct place in the water industry. This is partly because it encompasses a broad array of activities that are not neatly packaged within traditional centralized treatment (such as remote sites, point of use (POU), point of entry (POE), and on-site "packaged" plants) but also because it potentially represents a radically different approach to treating and reusing water resources (point-of-use-reuse, or POUR). An interesting aspect of the discussion about decentralized water and wastewater treatment is not just the parallels to distributed energy and the logical economic transition to a distributed model but whether a decentralized structure for the water industry may be a better approach in the first place. The developing countries are likely to be the experimental ground for this determination. It ultimately comes down to the question of whether decentralization as a treatment mechanism will facilitate or impede the protection of human health and sustainable water resource management.

Decentralized Treatment

Disruptive Decentralized Development (DDD)

The markets are replete with examples of a seemingly contradictive technological approach's radical transformation of an existing structural paradigm. The reverse flow of technological innovation for bottom-of-pyramid (BOP) markets is a phenomenon that can be seen in a number of industries. In telecommunications it involves the buildout of a network of telephone wires to remote regions when a more advanced mobile network could be implemented at a fraction of the cost. With respect to electricity generation, the notion of distributed energy produced with solar or biomass alternatives may be an obvious preference to centralized fossil fuel consumption. By extension, why build massive conventional, centralized water treatment plants when the science behind biomembrane reactors, for example, might represent a more sustainable approach through a decentralized framework? The notion of DDD is an issue of great potential importance to investors in the water industry. Not only does it portend a global macrotrend to a dedicated water industry in emerging economies, but it also provides a fertile ground for institutional change and the commercialization of enabling technologies that are gaining momentum in developed countries.

Decentralized or Distributed Treatment: Which Is It?

A dominant feature of the wastewater treatment infrastructure in the United States is the large, centralized wastewater treatment facility. At the same time, the Environmental Protection Agency (EPA) has long recognized the significant contribution of decentralized systems to the nation's wastewater landscape. Decentralized wastewater treatment has traditionally been considered analogous to septic systems. But as the water industry seeks to provide solutions to a broad range of wastewater treatment challenges, decentralization has grown to encompass an expanding definition. Thus, decentralized wastewater treatment collectively includes not only conventional individual on-site wastewater systems but also cluster or common systems and packaged wastewater treatment facilities. Yet to go much beyond this description, as many do by extending the necessity of decentralized wastewater treatment to the notion of "distributed" wastewater treatment, is currently counterproductive.

Decentralized systems serve 25 percent of the U.S. population, are used in about one third of all new housing and commercial development, and are utilized extensively in rural areas. While decentralized systems that are properly sited, designed, installed, operated, and maintained protect human health and water quality, the reality is that these systems have the enormous potential for creating water resource problems, either for our health or for our environment. The U.S. Department of Commerce estimates that between 10 and 20 percent of all on-site systems are not adequately treating waste.[1] Greater than 50 percent are more than 30 years old and more likely to malfunction. Finally, septic systems are the second-greatest threat to groundwater quality, second only to leakage from underground storage tanks. It is against this backdrop that a comparison between distributed electricity generation and distributed wastewater treatment begins.

Comparative Characteristics. It is in vogue to extend the reality of distributed energy generation to the evolution of decentralized wastewater treatment, that is, distributed wastewater treatment. Distributed generation is a market-driven trend contributing to a restructuring of the electricity industry. The extension of this phenomenon to wastewater treatment is intended to be predictive of the future of the increasingly dynamic wastewater industry. While energy generation and water provision share a history of centralization, the emergence of a "distributed" model in wastewater treatment does not necessarily follow. Many commentators draw their vision from a rather superficial application of overly broad definitions. Distributed generation encompasses many technologies and is subject to a seemingly endless number of definitions. One definitional grouping focuses on scale, and, at least on the surface, this is where comparisons are made with the emergence of distributed wastewater treatment. The reason for concern is that there is growing acceptance that this is a new market with investment potential comparable to the rationalization of the electricity grid.

Distributed generation is often defined as small-scale electricity generation, that is, the production of electricity at or near the point of consumption (use). Size is considered a defining characteristic of distributed generation, used primarily to meet on-site requirements for individual homes or businesses or small clusters of customers. Rather than having one central, high-capacity plant that provides power for a large area with long transmission distances, potentially dangerous electromagnetic fields, and a high risk of catastrophic blackouts, small plants offer communities independence from a wide-area grid, boosting resilience.

But, aside from scale, the technological innovations and the changing economic and regulatory environment that drive distributed electricity generation are vastly different than the necessity of decentralized wastewater treatment. The International Energy Agency cites five factors that have contributed to the evolution of distributed generation:

1. Developments in distributed generation technologies
2. Constraints on the construction of new transmission lines
3. Increased customer demand for highly reliable electricity
4. Electricity market liberalization
5. Concerns about climate change

The bottom line is that the benefits of distributed energy generation are the result of efficiency and reliability considerations within the framework of a commoditized market for electricity and the transformation of global energy.

Wastewater Treatment

As with large-scale electricity production, centralized wastewater treatment developed initially in response to a belief in economies of scale. The bigger the plant, the more customers served, the lower the average cost. Centralized wastewater treatment was considered the most cost-effective method to manage the process to ensure human health and environmental protection. As funding for centralized wastewater collection and treatment has diminished, there has been a dramatic shift in interest among professionals and the public toward decentralized wastewater technologies, which can be environmentally compatible and cost effective. Decentralized wastewater treatment, while a necessity under various conditions, differs from the deliberate application of a distributed wastewater treatment structure.

Some of the key advantages of distributed generation include improving the level of power quality and reliability, reducing the amount of electricity purchased during peak price periods, serving niche applications, lowering of energy costs through effective demand reduction, cost savings in transmission and distribution, and environmental benefits. It cannot be said that distributed wastewater treatment shares these beneficial characteristics. For example, wastewater treatment does not exhibit peak load characteristics like electricity consumption. Generator installations relieve congestion in power lines during periods of peak demand, helping to defer investments in additional transmissions and distribution capacity. If anything, drinking water treatment is more amenable to the distributed resource management concept than wastewater treatment, but not when a POU system is receiving potable water from a centralized treatment plant; that is, the enabling technologies that give rise to distributed generation have no analogy in drinking water "generation."

Distributed generation technologies are widely available. Gas turbines, microturbines, fuel cells, photovoltaic cells, and renewable fuels enable the distribution of electricity generation. In wastewater treatment, decentralized technologies are critically dependent on the characteristics of the wastewater stream and the sensitivity of the environment into which the effluent is discharged. One of the main problems associated with making the leap from decentralized to distributed wastewater treatment is the concern over human health and effluent water quality. Accordingly, management of these systems is of great concern.

Emerging Decentralized Regulatory Framework. The EPA defines five basic management models, ranging from basic regulatory oversight to full-scale utility ownership, operation, and management of on-site and clustered wastewater systems. The Level 1 model entails a basic regulatory framework consisting of issuing permits, performing construction inspections, and maintaining records. At the other end of the spectrum, the management model calls for creating a private utility corporation or responsible management entity that would own, operate, and maintain all of the systems within its service area. This removes the property owner from responsibility and is analogous to a micro–centralized wastewater treatment system. This level of management provides the greatest assurance of system performance in the most sensitive of environments.

The problem is that the regulatory scheme has not yet effectively developed centralized management to ensure care of on-site and decentralized wastewater treatment facilities. Clearly, the technology exists to maintain on-site systems to work in perpetuity, but they must have the proper oversight. In this respect, decentralized wastewater treatment is far from the distributed generation model, which, other than the reliability issue, is not subject to the same management challenges.

The bottom line here is this: Wastewater systems have enormous implications for the quality of surface and groundwaters. If the discharge is to surface water, effluent limitations will be specified within a National Pollutant Discharge Elimination System (NPDES) permit to protect water quality standards and the designated uses of the waters. If the discharge is to groundwater, the permit applicant will be required to meet drinking water standards at the property boundary. In both cases, the permit will include monitoring of the effluent to ensure that standards are being met and to demonstrate that the system is operating efficiently.

As technology, regulations, and public perceptions change, so must the level of oversight for wastewater treatment and disposal. Decentralized wastewater treatment systems can be an effective option for protecting public health and the environment if properly designed, installed, and managed. Otherwise, they can be a significant threat to public health and the environment.

The reality of decentralized wastewater treatment (as opposed to drinking water treatment) has attracted the attention of distributed model advocates because of the clear need for on-site solutions, the overriding concern over the health issues associated with decentralized potable water treatment and the relative ease of on-site wastewater discharge. But the economic and regulatory forces that are driving the move to distributed generation are simply not yet present in the structure of wastewater treatment. If anything, a hybrid system of drinking water and wastewater treatment may be the optimal model for a distributed structure. I choose to refer to this as a POUR system rather than the less appealing "toilet-to-tap" label often used in obvious rebuttal to the concept.

Drinking Water

The necessity of decentralized wastewater treatment is acknowledged as an alternative to large centralized facilities. Decentralized wastewater treatment is vastly more expansive than traditional septic systems; it includes not only conventional individual on-site wastewater systems but also cluster or common systems and packaged wastewater treatment facilities. The point, however, is that to characterize decentralized wastewater treatment as a distributed concept similar to that used in electricity generation is counterproductive. The question now is whether drinking water treatment can fulfill the promise of distributed resource management.

The clear alternative to centralized drinking water treatment is embedded in POU treatment. By and large, POU treatment uses centrally treated water as the source water. And while there are clearly localized needs and aesthetic reasons to "treat" already-treated drinking water, this certainly does not rise to the stature of the benefits associated with distributed energy management. If anything, a hybrid system of drinking water and wastewater treatment may be the optimal model for a distributed structure such as POUR.

To reiterate, some of the key advantages of distributed generation include improving the level of power quality and reliability, reducing the amount of electricity purchased during peak price periods, serving niche applications, lowering energy costs through effective demand reduction, cost savings in transmission and distribution, and significant environmental benefits. Therefore, drinking water treatment is more amenable to the distributed resource management concept than wastewater treatment, but not when a POU system is receiving potable water from a centralized treatment plant.

Despite an understandable lack of public acceptance about drinking treated household wastewater, the fact is that all water is eventually reused; the hydrologic cycle is a closed system of continuous water circulation. The notion of water reuse can take on a variety of applications, from groundwater recharge to industrial recycling to irrigation and even direct decentralized potable reuse. The common thread is economics; different uses and reuses can be addressed with differing water-quality levels. It is the necessity of differentiating water supply needs that will inevitably govern the growth of POUR.

Water Reuse

On a macro scale, water is thought of as a renewable resource because it can be replenished fairly rapidly (on a human time scale) through natural processes. But the accumulated degradation of water supplies and burgeoning demand beyond the sustainable yield has modified its status on a micro level. Because of the imbalance of supply and demand, and the lack of a workable structure to achieve local equilibrium, water reuse presents a mechanism to efficiently allocate water, that is, replenishing a locally depletable resource through "recycling." But one of the areas with great potential, yet significant cultural resistance, is the residential reuse of wastewater.

Water reuse generally refers to the use of wastewater following some level of treatment. Water reuse can be inadvertent, indirect, or direct. Inadvertent reuse of water results when water is withdrawn, used, treated, and returned to the environment without specific plans for further withdrawals and use. Indirect water reuse is a planned endeavor, one example of which is using reclaimed wastewater to recharge groundwater supplies. Artificial recharge of depleted aquifers using treated municipal wastewater is increasingly common. Direct water reuse refers to treated water that is piped directly to the next consumer or back to the same user. In most cases, the "consumer" is industry or agricultural activity. But indirect and even direct potable reuse remain viable options in residential applications and is increasingly being discussed as a water resource alternative in the age of sustainable utility practices. It is POUR that has the greatest chance of delivering the true benefits of distributed water resource management.

Nationally and internationally, pressure is increasing to introduce nutrient-reducing, water-conserving, and recycling measures for sustainable residential, commercial, and small community water/wastewater systems. There is a growing debate over the limitations of centralized treatment and the ability of municipalities to accommodate increasingly varied contaminant loads and volumes. The utilization of on-site rainwater collection, wastewater separation and treatment, and water recycling provides a proven, decentralized, economical, and sustainable alternative to the traditional drilled wells, piped water infrastructures, and commingled septic or sewer wastewater treatment systems.

POUR applications have the potential to alleviate many of the problems associated with septic systems. Septic tanks receive a commingled waste stream comprised of greywater and toilet wastes moved with substantial amounts of drinking-quality water; an average of 75 to 125 gallons of water per person per day. Approximately 25 percent of the estimated 109 million housing units in the United States are served with septic tanks, receiving and discharging 175 billion gallons of wastewater per year. The need to develop alternative water supplies, especially in drought conditions, is driving the demand for water reuse and recycling. In addition, over 10 percent of septic systems malfunction or fail completely at least once per year. The contamination of groundwater sources from failed septic systems represents a significant source of pathogens that can be alleviated with advanced on-site wastewater treatment systems.

The major sources of wastewater pollution in conventional septic and sewer systems are the toilet and garbage disposal. POUR wastewater systems can separate and treat those wastes at the source, reducing residential water consumption by at least 40 percent and commercial consumption by up to 80 percent while reducing BOD and fecal coliform by 99.9 percent, and nitrates and phosphorus by 99 percent. Because of the emerging trend in decentralized treatment in the context of water reuse, on-site treatment is likely to be one of the fastest-growing specialty segments in the wastewater industry. The study projects that almost 9 million homes will be served by on-site wastewater systems between now and 2015 and that a significant percentage of new installations will utilize alternatives to conventional septic systems. For example, mandatory hookups to central sewer systems, as currently required in Florida, are not seen as economically sustainable in the future. The opportunity for POUR systems is obvious.

The EPA promotes on-site treatment systems as a sustainable treatment and water recycling option. As they report in "Decentralized Wastewater Treatment Systems: A Program Strategy," on-site systems "offer several advantages over centralized wastewater treatment facilities. In many communities, on-site systems are the most appropriate, least costly treatment option, and they allow maximum flexibility in planning future growth."[2] The existing and future financial burdens of maintaining existing sewer collection and treatment systems is enormous compared to on-site options. But the EPA is far from blessing the decentralized treatment of wastewater for consumption as drinking water.

As the regulations that govern effluent discharged to receiving waters become increasingly stringent, municipalities have an economic incentive to reuse or recycle process water and wastewater. While irrigation and industrial, urban, and indirect nonpotable reuse are developing applications for reclaimed water, the challenge is public acceptance, and protection, in the application of reclaimed water to potable uses. Relative to drinking water regulations, standards were developed piecemeal to address problems in traditional water sources. They do not fully address the problems of converting reclaimed water into drinking water in the areas of virus control and organic matter. As such, significant progress must be made in legislating additional criteria for controlling contaminants in the water reuse process. While the dual distribution system (which distributes both potable and reclaimed grades of water to the same service area) is practiced under strict state guidelines, a next step in the evolution of reuse is likely to be POUR.

Convergent Technologies

Critical to this evolution, and a major opportunity, are membrane technologies and multiple-barrier methodologies that will drive the expansion of water reclamation—an analogy to the technologies that enable distributed electricity generation, such as gas turbines, micro-turbines, fuel cells, photovoltaic cells, and renewable fuels enable the distribution of electricity generation. These bioreactor systems biologically convert 90 to 95 percent of all toilet and kitchen garbage disposal wastes into odorless carbon dioxide and water vapor. Oxygen-consuming (aerobic) organisms thrive in the systems, converting the remaining portion into a beneficial soil amendment. Utilizing blackwater separation and greywater treatment, filtration and disinfection technologies for partial or total reuse represent a cost-effective option for reducing and eliminating water supply pressures while improving and protecting national security.

It is clear that water reuse is an economic proposition that is inevitable in the future of the provision of water. As a general category, it has yet to fully emerge as an industry segment of the water industry capable of defined investing. At the same time, there is a great deal of private investment interest in the residential application of reuse technologies due to the "large-market" potential; substantial opportunities exist for early entrants in the field with demonstrated technologies and products. Residential POUR has broad implications for existing segments such as privatization, distribution systems, infrastructure components, disinfection technologies, and membrane utilization. And as the public accepts reclaimed water as part of the recycling ethic, POUR will secure a permanent position in the scheme of efficiently providing water for residential consumptive uses.

Why does it even matter whether we call noncentralized water and/or wastewater treatment decentralized or distributed? The reason is that if the industry improperly develops the notion of distributed resource management with respect to water, the likelihood of reaching sustainable solutions will only be delayed. The investment potential inherent in the water industry critically depends on the right choices.

The Roots of Decentralized Treatment

Residential POU Market

There is a groundswell of activity in residential water treatment equipment that represents a mature but changing subculture within the broadly defined water industry. In contrast to municipal and industrial water treatment markets, which are currently influenced largely by direct government regulation, the residential markets are driven by economics. As a result of deteriorating municipal water quality, both perceived and real, end users are taking control of their own water by purchasing home water treatment equipment. The market here is obviously enormous, comprising nearly every household, condominium, and apartment in the country.

The market for residential water treatment equipment is a billion-dollar-plus industry and is expected to grow significantly over the next decade. And these figures could pale in comparison to the actual market numbers upon full realization. At the same time, the next five years represent a good transition period and can probably be estimated with reasonable clarity. Beyond that time horizon, however, the landscape of what constitutes residential water treatment is likely to look dramatically different, that is, whole-house units as commonplace as an air conditioner or a standard kitchen appliance in white, black, or whatever color is the trend at the time.

For these reasons, it is useful to delineate certain segments within the market for home water treatment equipment. For instance, water softeners, probably the most traditional and established home water treatment product, should experience rather staid growth. And sediment filters, another segment, are also expected to remain at a stable growth rate. But product segments that involve more recent and innovative water treatment technologies will grow at a much more rapid rate through the end of the decade. These technologies include reverse osmosis (RO), ozone, ultraviolet (UV) radiation, and microfiltration (MF). Residential end users have been slower to accept these newer technologies, but are beginning to do so. None of the segments in the residential water treatment market have been saturated and are either in growth or development stages.

Water Conditioning

Water softeners represent a mature but stable segment. *Softening* refers to the removal of calcium and magnesium ions that react with soap to form curds and create water that is "hard" for washing. Softened water used in the home enhances bathing, washing, cleaning, and heating. Other ions that are removed by softener resins include aluminum, lead, ammonia, cadmium, barium, copper, iron, manganese, zinc, and naturally occurring radium. Resins in home water treatment units can successfully reduce a wide range of contaminants and are experiencing renewed interest as selective applications expand. Specialty chemical companies that produce ion exchange resins should benefit from this activity as pricing pressures subside. And while the basic technology has not changed much, certain component innovations have altered the performance of these systems. Demand-initiated regeneration in water softeners, provided by advances in controls and valves, is enabling many residential softeners to use much less salt and water and discharge less brine. Other mature segments, such as carbon and sediment, are also benefiting from new technology. Advanced media technology in carbon block filters and molded sediment filters is producing greater mechanical filtration, allowing these filters to treat water for both aesthetic and health problems.

At the same time that established home water treatment technologies are being boosted by innovations, newer technologies are also beginning to significantly impact the market. Although the market for UV, MF, and RO are all in the intermediate to later stage of development, they are becoming accepted by residential end users. Improvements in these technologies are progressing and are expected to increase popularity of these products within the market. For example, advances in thin film membrane technology have increased the retentive capacities of RO systems in addition to making them more space efficient. Chlorine-resistant thin film membranes are gaining favor in the residential market where chlorine degradation is a problem for membranes.

Technology is not the only factor that has spurred the dramatic growth of the home water treatment market. Major trends in marketing these products have also had a role. Health issues have led to wider distribution of products and created awareness. And microbiological contamination aside, other less threatening parameters such as taste and odor have taken on greater significance to households. For one thing, these measures are relatively easy to apply by using two of the senses. And for another, they are simple to cure with even the most basic water treatment equipment. The temptation to exploit such appeal by those who serve the home market is probably the greatest problem facing the industry. But it also the catalyst for the onslaught of a hugely powerful marketing trend, namely, retail sales.

The growth in home water treatment equipment is very much a function of expanded distribution channels. In a market traditionally controlled by water treatment dealers, the movement to mass merchandisers and retailers will not take place overnight. A number of manufacturers or assemblers boldly state that they will not "destroy" the industry by selling directly to mass retailers or wholesale clubs. This logic is more than vaguely similar to the water supply industry's reluctance to face the reality of the home treatment market itself.

While service and credibility are key concerns in the emerging market for home water treatment, consumer-driven market forces will simply not allow such archaic stands to survive. Standardization is rapidly developing. Collaboration on standards by the National Sanitation Foundation (NSF) and the Water Quality Association will begin to solidify the impact that standardization has among both consumers and retailers and marks the beginning of the large-scale production, characteristic of new markets that can stand on their own.

Branded® Consumer Water Products: Part 1

The retail market for water filtration products continues to grow and evolve in response to concerns over the quality of tap water. That consumers perceive a blanket need to filter municipally treated water is, in part, the by-product of a burdensome regulatory system and a complacent water supply industry. Without arguing the merit of consumer perceptions, the reality is that this concern has created a huge demand for residential water treatment devices, a demand that is now being addressed by some of the biggest players in branded consumer products. While it is difficult to predict just what brands will be successful in the retail market, let alone find a pure play in which to invest, the magnitude of the payoff warrants an updated look at the current status of the field.

As predicted, many of the early entrants to the residential filtration market have fallen by the wayside, an inevitable result of the diseconomies of a "cottage" industry. Large retailers have added marketing prowess to an industry that was not only unskilled in the vagaries of volume pricing but was also characterized by a product-push attitude with me-too products. The entrance by large consumer-driven companies into this category has opened up the traditional housewares retail channels and has fostered differentiated designs, colors, and features that are appropriate to housewares merchandising.

Much like the growth in home water treatment equipment, the market for drinking water filtration products is very much a function of expanded distribution channels. The bulk of housewares-type POU sales are concentrated in two low-cost product categories: faucet-mount filters and pour-through pitchers. The largest increase in sales was registered by faucet-mount filters, followed by pour-through pitcher sales. And innovation is finally creeping into an otherwise traditional business with devices such as "filtering faucets" with filter cartridges built in.

While it is difficult to estimate potential market size, there is almost certainly going to be a number of years of very rapid growth. The market itself is expanding as the industry caters to an increasingly knowledgeable consumer. The marketing of water filtration products has drawn extensively from other retail consumer products. Lower prices and greater health claims have accompanied the strategy of creating brands. There is "Water by Culligan," "Desal inside" (GE/Osmonics), GE SmartWater™ (GE), and PūR™ (Proctor & Gamble), to name a few. A strong brand, however, is no assurance of success in this increasingly crowded market. While the end-of-faucet category is becoming more crowded with a variety of products, the similarities are apparent— low cost and focus on the household. Another category is countertop water filters, which represent a small fraction of industry sales.

As mentioned, the growth in home water treatment equipment is dependent upon an expanded distribution structure. While service and credibility are key concerns in the emerging market for home water treatment, consumer-driven market forces will simply not allow such archaic stands to survive. Standardization is rapidly developing. Collaboration on standards by the NSF and the Water Quality Association will begin to solidify the impact that standardization has among both consumers and retailers and marks the beginning of the large-scale production, characteristic of new markets that can stand on their own.

Branded® Consumer Water Products: Part 2

The previous section focused on the status of faucet-mount and flow-through pitcher devices as branded consumer water filtration products. That segment is characterized by an abundance of low-volume, small-appliance offerings at an impulse-buy price point. While the level of health claims on these products is rising, there is a noticeable reluctance on the part of consumers to address their water quality concerns with what may be perceived as a partial solution. It was reported that among U.S. consumers considering water filtration, a large number want under-the-counter (POU) or whole-house (POE) methods. This is a vastly different market and one with far greater long-term implications.

Faucet mounts and filter pitchers are clearly an intermediate step in the evolution of consumer water products. As consumers become aware of the technologies available and demand more comprehensive solutions, residential water devices will take on a different functionality. At this juncture, "home treatment" (as opposed to lower-priced filtration products) can be generally defined as either POE (whole-house) units or POU treatment that consists of multiple devices (i.e., a "system"). According to this criterion, more comprehensive and complex water quality problems can be addressed. This is why it is said that decentralized treatment is embedded in the concept of treated water at the place where it is to be used.

The Ultimate Tap-Water Substitute: POU Filtration

By definition, POU units can utilize virtually any treatment method, but are currently dominated by RO, ion exchange, and/or filtration technologies. Certain components of this segment are mature, such as softeners (ion exchange) and basic RO units. Others are developing, such as ozone, pulsed UV, automated RO, combination systems, and package units. At this relatively early stage in the evolution of the home treatment market, there is a substantial divergence between what is technologically possible and what is widely available to homeowners.

The opportunity in residential water treatment is, therefore, more one of what is likely to develop than what is currently offered. The marketplace is glutted with softeners and me-too RO units with ghastly product designs and almost nonexistent service. That said, what was historically a smallish market crowded by water treatment dealers and direct sales organizations is yielding to the economics of volume pricing and retail merchandising. Because consumers do not know how to solve the water quality issues that they perceive, the notion of branding is a way to tap into broader consumer appeal. Retail branding is a trend that promises to open up the category, and it is for this reason that the current state of the industry, while not overwhelming, is important to monitor.

The added appeal of POU treatment systems and whole-house units is that these methods offer a cost-effective solution to more complex water quality issues. This equipment can be an alternative to centralized treatment technology for individual and small systems. While the current focus is on the branding of devices sold to residential end users, it is likely that small systems will increasingly use POE treatment as an acceptable technology for complying with drinking water regulations under certain circumstances.

If the consumer is concerned only with taste, odor, and color, water treatment is largely a matter of personal preference satisfied by many off-the-shelf products. But to solve specific contamination problems, such as nitrates, pesticides, volatile organic chemicals (VOCs), lead, arsenic, and the like, requires technical adaptations. Water treatment is rarely simple; a systems approach is crucial to designing effective treatment schemes. Pretreatment and posttreatment devices are often necessary. To this end, the EPA is currently operating and evaluating several small package plants and POU/POE units. Regulatory hurdles must be overcome. Neither POU nor POE is designated as a best available technology (BAT) by the EPA because of the difficulty in monitoring the reliability of treatment performance and controlling performance in a manner comparable to central treatment. Home water treatment manufacturers are cognizant of this concern; the base of "smart" faucets integrates an electronic monitoring device that indicates when the filters or membranes need to be replaced. Regardless, increasingly stringent state requirements will overshadow the self-regulating rhetoric of the home treatment industry and pave the way for more advanced products accepted by the EPA.

Residential Treatment

The home water treatment industry is a potentially vast, yet ill-defined, opportunity for many companies in the water industry. Product certification and, especially, monitoring are key to the advancement of the industry. The EPA is evaluating telemetry as an option for monitoring and controlling maintenance and operation of remote treatment units. It is conceivable that, in the age of information, home treatment units will be monitored much like security systems. As the home treatment industry responds to the tough issues in protecting public health, consumer water products will become commonplace appliances in the home.

The residential POU market encompasses the filtration and/or purification of tap water by advanced treatment methods to ensure the removal of potentially harmful or unhealthful contaminants. The very nature of water "treated" in the home begs the question of what is effective treatment for each water quality problem. This confusion did not escape the less scrupulous players in the early days of the POU market. Rather than recount the nefarious history of the multilevel marketing phase of the POU market, the focus should be on the new entrants and the positive contribution that this form of decentralized treatment can ultimately provide.

Once the bastion of water treatment dealers, POU distribution channels now include mass merchandisers such as department stores, discount warehouses, catalogs, hardware and building supply stores, and plumbing supply companies. The "do-it-yourself" market will continue to grow as consumers respond to increasing reports of pathogens and other contaminants by demanding higher-quality water at the tap. The POU market is dominated by manufacturing companies and value-added assemblers. The filtration-related residential business of a number of companies offers tremendous investment potential. Perhaps the greatest growth is in the area of value-added resellers, where there are few barriers to entry and the technology is firmly established. An example of this strategy is the Watts Water acquisition of Topway Global.

Given the large numbers actively involved in the POU industry, consolidation is inevitable. Competition domestically will encourage horizontal mergers, and prospects internationally will send smaller firms looking for greater resources. It is likely that new entrants, in the form of large-appliance, consumer or water-related technology companies, will appear on the scene. This would expand the market significantly and bring with it product innovation and retailing expertise. Product innovation will likely take the form of new POU designs, increased efficiencies (ultrafiltration) and decreased purchase and operating costs. In addition, the POU market is likely to gain market share from other alternatives to tap water. Consumers of bottled water, for instance, are likely converts to POU water treatment. Bottled-water consumers are already convinced of the need for a substitute to their tap water and are beginning to recognize the cost and convenience components of water treated in the home.

When the enormous regulatory costs of a centralized water treatment and distribution system succumb to the economics of site-specific treatment, POU will become actualized. From a standard feature in new construction to the next appliance in the kitchen, water treatment devices will move from convenience to necessity in the quest for quality water.

Retail Perspective: The Water Filtration Category

The POU industry, though still the renegade by-product of a failed regulatory system and complacent water supply industry, has come of age. The entrance by large consumer products companies into this category has opened up the traditional housewares retail channels and has fostered designs that are appropriate to housewares merchandising. Such an interest belies the enormous potential for residential water filtration products when marketed properly.

Retailers have added marketing prowess to an industry that is not only unskilled in the vagaries of volume marketing but is too self-consumed to learn. This "aquacentricity" has allowed the "big-box" retailers to take over the market. The POU industry, as the name implies, relies on the "thousand points of light" at the end of the water supply system for its prosperity. And no other channel reaches the masses like the large brand-name consumer products retailers. They have entered the POU market with a vengeance, driven by consumer demand for better tasting, healthful water.

Manufacturers offer a wide variety of water filtration systems, from pitchers in a range of sizes and, most recently, colors, to faucet attachments and countertop units in various designs. In the mass merchandise channel, pour-through units represent the bulk of the sales to consumers, at 78 percent; followed by faucet mounts, with 17 percent of the market; in-line units, at 4 percent; and countertops, at 1 percent.[3] Retailers often carry at least one of each type to satisfy the preferences of a diverse customer base.

The POU market is littered with casualties, from traditional housewares companies to small-appliance manufacturers, to home environmental controls divisions of major companies. And then there are those companies whose orientation is decidedly water filtration technology. As the number of large consumer products companies entering the water filtration category increases, the proliferation of water industry–based filtration companies will slow drastically. In fact, it will contract significantly as their me-too products sold directly are overshadowed by the branded products sold through housewares retail channels at lower price points. While it would be difficult to justify an investment in many of these diversified housewares companies based solely on the potential for the water filtration category, the power of the demand for these products should lead to consolidation in the segment. As that occurs, the emerging dominant players would certainly merit a look.

State of the Residential POU Market

The success of many technology products today is heavily dependent on the ability to plug into the broad-based appeal of a consumer culture. Purpose, functionality, and value (cost) all must come together at the right time and in the right proportions. In reality, more so than in theory, the residential POU and POE water markets should be no different. On the surface, the logic is simple: (1) consumers want to drink water at home or work that is healthful and tasty, and (2) there are many residences and workplaces, so (3) there is a huge market for additional water treatment at the point that it is consumed. So why has a sub-sector with such seemingly compelling fundamentals failed to live up to expectations? The answer is elusive, but several observations can be made to add clarity to the current state of the residential POU market.

Two conditions are implicit in the logic. First, even though tap water is considered safe, there must be a perception that POU treatment is "better" yet, whether aesthetically or healthfully. And second, POU treatment must be more cost effective or efficient than bottled water in the quantities consumed. To be clear, the focus here is strictly single, residential-type POU/POE, not small community, commercial, or industrial. There is clearly enormous potential in these other applications, a reality that the water quality treatment business should embrace, both technically and professionally. For example, POU (activated alumina and RO technologies) is recognized as an acceptable treatment for arsenic removal in small systems.

Now back to the residential market. Why does this conceptually sound, clean-tech-driven, health-conscious-motivated segment of the water business continue to languish, morphing from one misdirected strategy to another? Several current observations from within the residential POU business will be presented as anecdotal evidence of a continuation of the lack of identity. Then some opinions will be expressed to provide investors in this market with an actionable plan.

Part of the long-standing problem with residential consumer water treatment products is a monumental lack of definition and consumer understanding. Are water treatment dealers selling a process or a product? And if they are selling a product, it's not clear where such devices would fall in the category of retail merchandise. The residential home water treatment industry would be well served to learn from the lessons of the consumer electronics business, for example, in applying market-driven innovation to consumers anxious to improve the taste and quality of the water that they drink. Whether a necessary appliance or a home improvement product, the POU water treatment industry must come to grips with the fact that they compete in a marketing-driven retail business. To date, the way in which the water industry has served this market remains a confusing blend of distribution channels, from direct sales to retail marketing and everything in between.

One of the most interesting aspects of the residential POU market is how the product is sold into the marketplace. By far the largest share of water treatment devices is sold to consumers through sales-driven dealerships that operate in limited geographic locations. These dealerships are supplied largely by a very specialized group of distributors, some value added but most just passing through the tanks, faucets, filters, valves, and casings that can be assembled by anyone wanting to sell to consumers. While substantially better than the multilevel sales organizations of times past, the current dealership approach for home water treatment products resembles an antiquated adaptation of a cottage industry. There is no end to the number of assemblers, dealers, and distributors that comprise the hugely fragmented residential POU market. The problem is that the dealer approach is not even closely scalable to the enormity of the consumer market.

Continued change in the residential POU market is inevitable. There are variables on all sides of the home treatment equation that are changing. Suppliers have been actively seeking new distribution channels. A number of industrial companies are seeking new distribution channels for their consumer water treatment products. As a result, there is an ongoing consolidation in wholesale distribution. New international manufacturers are also supplying the markets. On the distribution side, "big-box" retailers continue to take market share and are increasingly open to the low-cost manufacturers from abroad. Dealerships are finding it very difficult to compete on price and will be forced to reevaluate their traditional business models. In principle, however, they have much to offer in the value chain.

Though the water filter and pitcher business is profitable, top-line growth is declining as convenience-focused consumers turn to bottled water. Any gains in water treatment products will be driven in part by the development of more efficient and user-friendly systems with innovations such as faster operation, filter performance indicators, and higher-value purification technologies that can eliminate a broader range of contaminants. Above all, the residential POU market has to compete with the nondifferentiating (commodity) pricing of the oversaturated beverage industry. The intrusion of the beverage mentality continues, however, as evidenced by water filtration systems that allow consumers to add fruit flavors to filtered water. Can performance-enhancing additives be far off?

So who stands to benefit in the residential consumer water treatment market? In the end, it is likely that one particular distribution method will prevail, but for now the market is large enough to accommodate several approaches: local dealers and distributors, plumbing wholesalers, contractors, and mass merchandisers or do-it-yourself (DIY) centers. Watts Water's strategy illustrates the dilemma. The company does sell to the big-box retailers (some actually refuse to) but recognizes that many POU products are sold by installers that do not go through traditional wholesale channels. Instead, they purchase components from the specialized distributors of water treatment products. The purchase of Flowmatic was to gain a key distribution channel into the consumer POU market. And, more recently, Watts acquired privately owned Topway Global Inc., to further extend its distribution network to independent water quality dealers, particularly in the Southwest. Topway Global manufactures (assembles) a wide variety of water softeners, POE filter units, and POU drinking water systems and sells its products to independent water treatment dealers, distributors, and original equipment manufacturers. At the same time, Watts is gaining shelf space in Home Depot and Lowe's. Other early POU companies have made it their mantra that they will not sell products through mass merchandisers or DIY home-improvement centers. Clearly, the residential POU market is having trouble figuring out an effective way to reach residential consumers. Is it any wonder that the residential water treatment business has not fulfilled its retail potential?

Before the realignment of Home Depot, the company was very aggressively pursuing a move into the professional distribution market itself, seeking to acquire POU water treatment and distribution companies. The company had already made several large acquisitions of water product wholesalers to expand beyond its core DIY business (e.g., National Waterworks Holdings). The idea was to create an installation services business in the residential POU market. But a fall-off in base sales derailed the expansion effort, and they finally sold the wholesale distribution business to a private equity group for about $1.8 billion less than originally proposed.

It is also interesting to note the activities of the large consumer products companies that are increasingly active in the consumer water treatment market. Procter & Gamble is a case in point. After the acquisition of Recovery Engineering (PūR brand) many years ago, this preeminent consumer products company continues to sell its home water filtration products only through retail channels, including Wal-Mart, and manufactures filters that fit a variety of competing POU/POE products such as Ametek, Culligan, CUNO, and Teledyne. And now, after years of research, P&G is test-marketing a home water purification kit to be sold across the developing world. Under the PūR brand, the kit sells for only 10 cents and can reportedly provide safe drinking water in 20 minutes. P&G is currently focused on relief agencies. While the company is confident in the science, the business model is still uncertain. But as the product is designed specifically for developing countries, it is an experiment in basic decentralized water treatment. Investors should watch the progress very carefully.

Perhaps a telling example of consumer behavior can be seen in the contamination scare in Washington, D.C. After the D.C. Water and Sewer Authority reported that thousands of city homes had high levels of lead in their drinking water, consumers rushed to purchase home filtration products. And where did they turn? While many filtration businesses experienced an increase in volume, one big-box retailer in particular, Home Depot, was the source to which many consumers turned.

The emergence of water treatment products for the residential consumer market is clearly an area with *potentially* above-average growth prospects. But the retail market is easier to define for electronic equipment than for water devices. While the business model that attempts to crack the retail market for water treatment products is compelling, no one has succeeded on a large scale. For those in the water treatment business who believe that service alone can justify higher product prices, much can be learned from other retail markets. Despite the lack of clarity, the consumer market for water treatment products remains one to watch. The joint venture between Pentair and GE's Water and Process Technologies segment, combining the companies' water softener and residential filtration businesses, is perhaps yet another strategic restructuring of the POU market. All the confusion, however, plays into the simple appeal of tap water. After all, as the municipal water supply slogan states, "Only tap water delivers."

Water Softeners and Salinity

With the enactment of a California law designed to restrict or ban water softeners, the issue of salinity is gaining recognition as a growing problem for many cities. Salinity (also referred to as total dissolved solids or salts) has long been a concern for irrigated agriculture but is emerging as a significant urban water quality issue as well, particularly for the arid southwestern United States and the West. While the magnitude of the release of sodium from water softeners is still being researched, it is clear that the contribution impacts the environment. The home treatment industry lobbied that restrictions are unnecessary. Municipalities argued that softeners jeopardize discharge limits. In the end, manufacturers will adapt to the regulatory framework just as in other segments of the water industry. The water softener issue is more an illustration of the trends in home water treatment than an example of imposing regulations.

Decentralized Desalination

Nearly a fifth of monitored surface waters in the United States with high withdrawals for municipal use have salinity levels greater than 500 mg/L, the EPA's secondary drinking water standard (which equates to about a quarter teaspoon of mineral content per gallon). Because of the difficulties faced by many municipalities to comply with the standard for total dissolved solids (TDS), and the growing importance of reuse as a water source, the contribution of water softeners to the salt balance is increasingly under scrutiny. Water softeners (or water conditioners) are the most widely used POE home water treatment devices. Water softeners remove cations (positively charged minerals such as calcium and magnesium) and replace them with sodium. They consist of a corrosion-resistant brine tank that is filled with resin beads saturated with sodium. The resin prefers calcium and magnesium (the principle components of hardness) over sodium. As water passes over the resin, calcium and magnesium are adsorbed and sodium is released. The discharge from a softener occurs during regeneration and includes a salt solution (sodium or potassium chloride).

The salt balance is surprisingly complex. Salinity is inherently an ecosystem (watershed) level problem that requires a holistic management approach that integrates source water management, drinking water treatment, wastewater treatment and disposal, and irrigation management. Conventional water treatment methods do not reduce TDS content in source water supplies, so it is critical that the salt balance be maintained. As water softeners are manufactured to assist in mitigating the TDS problem, as opposed to contributing to it, it is likely that widespread acceptance of POE units will be encouraged. Otherwise, the growing trend toward water reuse and recycling is likely to lead to more restrictions on the continued growth of water softeners nationwide. Units that demonstrate greater salt efficiency, portable exchange units that are regenerated off-site, and innovative technologies that rely less on the ion exchange process are all possibilities that create growth opportunities for the home water treatment industry.

Clearly, water softeners are not the only, or even most significant, source of salinity problems. Salts are concentrated by evaporation during the irrigation of lawns or crops, leaving them behind to accumulate in soils and aquifers. And the predominant sources of salts are natural, particularly evaporite minerals, which leach large quantities of salts rapidly. But salts imported by humans are becoming increasingly important as urbanization continues. For the Central Arizona–Phoenix ecosystem, for example, at least 70 percent of the salt that enters the system via surface water accumulates within the system.[4] High salinity in water supplies forces municipalities to turn to alternative water sources and dramatically increases treatment and maintenance costs. In Southern California it is estimated that for every 100 mg/L TDS increase over the standard, entities are spending $95 million to repair damage to utility infrastructure, agriculture, and industrial facilities, not to mention the impact on wastewater treatment costs and the impairment of recycled supplies. It is because of this that municipalities are looking at all sources of salinity, and water softeners are one source that is suitable for regulatory control.

The controversy in California is particularly interesting because it involves a statewide ban. Assembly Bill 334 became law in 2003 after years of controversy. Earlier legislation modified a softener industry–sponsored state preemption of local control of softeners. However, under pressure from the water softener industry, the bill was amended to allow the option for local control. SB 1006 required a local agency to already be out of compliance with their discharge requirements before being able to ban self-regenerating water softeners and thereby did little to address the salt-loading problem that led to noncompliance in the first place.

Shortly after SB 1006 took effect, the WateReuse Association and the Association of California Water Agencies introduced AB 334, which did not require utilities to actually be in violation of their discharge permits before placing restrictions on automatic water softeners. This bill was designed to implement one of the recommendations of the Recycled Water Task Force and arose out of concerns that water softening was contributing to chloride levels. Higher chloride levels through the release of sodium in the ion exchange process of water softeners was believed to be a detriment to water reuse and added to wastewater treatment costs.

AB 334 authorizes a local agency in California to regulate the use and availability of self-regenerative water-softening appliances that discharge to the community sewer system. However, the softener law maintains provisions that all sources of salt must be defined, quantified, and controlled, and that restrictions on softeners must be "necessary" for a utility to achieve compliance. The ban was supported by a number of water districts, including Irvine Ranch Water District, the Los Angeles Water Districts, and the Inland Empire Water District. Opposition to restrictions came from those affected by a potential loss of softener sales, including the Water Quality Association, the regional Pacific Water Quality Association, and the California Pipe Fitters.

The home treatment industry lobbied hard to avoid restrictions as if the outcome would have created a bad precedent. In reality, however, the restriction on water softeners is an established means of controlling high TDS levels. Currently, communities in over 30 states, and some states themselves, have enacted bans on certain types of water softener discharge. Among them are Texas, Connecticut, Massachusetts, Michigan, New Jersey, and virtually all other states in the Northeast and Southeast. Salinity is increasingly becoming a key consideration in municipal water supply and infrastructure planning.

Higher concentrations of TDS are progressively accumulating in the soil and water. The collective impact of irrigation, urban growth, low rainfall, and the high mineral content of geologic features exacerbate the problem. To maintain or improve the quality of water with respect to salinity, several areas must be advanced. First, the efficiency of salinity treatment processes must be increased to achieve higher levels of brine concentration, thereby reducing source water losses. Second, the disposal or use of the brine concentrate must improve. And third, conditions or practices that result in salt accumulation must be modified (e.g., the widespread use of regenerative water softeners).

The focus on the softener/salinity issue is presented in detail because it symbolizes the main problem with residential POU devices: decentralized treatment without centralized control.

The home water treatment industry must understand that it is part of a number of comprehensive solutions to water quality issues rather than narrowly focus on self-interest. Whereas POU/POE dealers and distributors may feel the economic pressure of shifting regulations, the manufacturers are likely to adjust. Thus, the equipment manufacturers continue to have a bright future as long as they adapt to a changing regulatory climate and seek to become part of a larger water quality picture. In fact, the opportunity for the home water treatment segment lies in its ability to work with the municipal water industry in serving customers. The large, branded manufacturers will have a distinct advantage in technology, service, and acceptance. All have acquired technical expertise: GE/Osmonics and Ionics, MMM/CUNO, Watts Water/Topway Global, Pentair/Everpure and Omni, Procter & Gamble/PūR, Axel Johnson/Kinetico, and the Marmon Water/KX Industries. The residential water filtration market is the Schrödinger's cat of the POU market—is the market dead or alive?

Groundwater Treatment

Groundwater is the source of potable water for approximately 40 percent of the population of the United States. Of a total of about 200,000 public water systems in the United States, 93 percent rely on groundwater as their primary source of water. Ninety-five percent of the rural population is dependent on groundwater for drinking purposes, and fully three fourths of the major cities in the United States are totally or partially dependent on groundwater.[5] Groundwater is a vital natural resource that is gaining increasing attention as the extent of degradation unfolds. Of all types of water pollution, this is perhaps the most insidious because at low concentrations the contaminants rarely impart any taste or odor to drinking water.

The quantity of groundwater underlying the continental United States is immense. The amount that can be retrieved with current technologies is at least six times greater than all the water stored in surface lakes and reservoirs. But unlike many surface water environmental problems, the magnitude and complexity of groundwater contamination requires more than market forces to correct. Although hidden from sight, groundwater is not hidden from sources of contamination. Eventually, water becomes the ultimate repository of all substances released into the environment. Once contaminated, groundwater may remain so for hundreds or even thousands of years. Lack of sunlight, oxygen, and significant water movement inhibits the process of degradation. Groundwater is one of the more perplexing challenges in the water industry; every aspect of groundwater management is directly driven, defined, and in some cases created, by legislation and regulations.

Numerous and often complex federal, state, and local laws have been enacted for the purpose of investigating and remediating pollution of underground aquifers as well as controlling or preventing the potential environmental hazards caused by groundwater contamination. The Comprehensive Environmental Response, Compensation, and Liability Act of 1980 (Superfund); the Resource Conservation and Recovery Act of 1976 (RCRA); the Underground Storage Tank (UST) law; and the Safe Drinking Water Act (SDWA) all have provisions for groundwater within the context of their particular regulatory objectives. Each law addresses a particular source of groundwater contamination (i.e., municipal landfills, hazardous waste sites, septic tanks, underground storage tanks, injection wells, agriculture, and other nonpoint sources of contamination). And each law supports a growing level of business activity to service the regulation.

Remediation of contaminated groundwater is probably the most elusive portion of the otherwise promising investment potential in groundwater management. Most environmental engineering and consulting firms have activities in groundwater remediation. But this industry is beset by problems independent of the growing need to clean up and manage groundwater. Negative trends in the environmental consulting area, such as maturing markets for site assessment and underground storage tank cleanup, blur the overall prospects for these firms.

Another component of the groundwater segment of the water industry is the physical drilling of wells, both in support of the actual infrastructure needed to access groundwater for drinking water, irrigation, and industrial use, and as a means of remediating groundwater contamination. The demand for water well–drilling services is primarily driven by population movements and expansions, deteriorating water quality, and limited availability of surface water. The demand for environmental drilling services is driven principally by heightened public concern over groundwater contamination and the resulting regulatory requirements to investigate and remediate contaminated sites and aquifers.

Groundwater contamination prevention also offers long-term investment potential to patient investors. Substantial regulations have been enacted relative to the protection of groundwater from waste materials. For example, Subtitle D of the RCRA legislation imposes strict standards with regard to groundwater protection and requires, among other things, that all new hazardous waste landfills use lining systems. Further, the use of liners is a "presumptive remedy" prescribed by the EPA to alleviate the tremendous costs associated with Superfund cleanups. At the same time, the synthetic liner business is very competitive and suffers from overcapacity.

The greatest impediment to investing in the groundwater theme is the lack of an industry definition and the complexity of the regulatory environment. While it is true that, from an economic point of view, the marketplace will not properly protect groundwater resources, the regulations designed to intercede have also failed. Groundwater has many unique characteristics that make it a particularly difficult resource to manage. But because of the sheer number of people who depend on groundwater for drinking, the pattern of neglect is gradually yielding to one of proper development. As this occurs, the economics inherent in protecting groundwater supplies will channel technology into this arena and provide a substantial investment opportunity.

Table 8.1 provides a compilation of POU and "decentralized" treatment companies. It is important for investors to realize that this is currently one of the more elusive water investment strategies.

Membrane Bioreactors: The Future of Decentralized Treatment

The concept of "sustainability" is used as a blanket expression for describing the ultimate objective of water use practices. While the phrase is used loosely, and often without specific performance metrics in mind, it encompasses the notion that themes such as reuse and decentralization are essential for meeting current needs for clean water without worsening the situation for future generations. Membrane bioreactors (MBRs) are emerging as a key technology in advancing water sustainability because they facilitate water reuse and are highly suited for decentralized wastewater treatment.

Biological processes alone can successfully remove organic contaminants, nitrogen, and phosphorous from wastewater. The main operational and design challenge associated with traditional biological treatment,

Table 8.1 Decentralized Treatment and Point-of-Use

Name	Symbol or SEDOL	Country	Water Segments or Brands	Water Activity
Pall Corp	PLL	US	Healthcare POU	Faucet, shower, tap, in-line filtration in healthcare facilities
Millipore	MIL	US	Healthcare	Faucet, shower, tap, in-line filtration in healthcare facilities
BWT Group	4119054	Austria	Residential/Industrial	Softeners, membrane filters
Pentair	PNR	US	SHURflo, Everpure, Fleck, OMNIFILTER	POU/POE filtration products; valves, tanks, cartridges, pressure vessels.
Woong Jin Coway Co	6173401	South Korea	POU	POU water filtration devices
Sinomem Technology	6648880	China	Pharmaceutical	Membrane technology in waste reduction
United Envirotech	B00VGB5	Singapore	Wastewater	MBR technology; industrial waste-water treatment and reclamation
Layne Christenson	LAYN	US	On-site treatment	Package plants; removal of radium, arsenic, iron, manganese, VOCs, nitrate, turbidity, suspended solids, organics, microbes
MMM	MMM	US	Cuno	POE/POU devices
Proctor & Gamble	PG	US	PuR	Faucet mount POU
Watts Water Technologies	WTS	US	Topway Global and Watts Premier	RO Systems; POU and commercial purification systems
Basin Water Inc	BWTR	US	On-site treatment	Package plants; perchlorate removal

however, is the reliable separation of sludge (biomass) and water in the clarification process. The membrane bioreactor is an innovative system for the treatment of wastewater that combines an activated sludge process with membrane separation. Instead of gravity settlement, biomass retention is achieved by a cross-flow filtration process. MBRs eliminate the clarification settling process by immersing membrane modules directly into the bioreactor and separating water and biomass by passing water through the membranes, which reject the biomass and all other minute particles.

With the substitution of the settling tank by a cross-flow filtration unit, and the commensurate increase in total biomass retention, even slow-growing microorganisms can be enriched efficiently. The biological breakdown of many contaminants, especially xenobiotic compounds, is accomplished by bacteria having long generation times. Because of this, the membrane bioreactor offers an improved degradation capacity for persistent chemicals. So, in addition to removing biodegradable organics, suspended solids, and inorganic nutrients (such as nitrogen and phosphorus), MBRs retain slow-growing organisms. This enables the treatment of more slowly biodegraded organics. For example, the higher biomass concentrations of MBRs have been shown to be suitable for the degradation of particularly stubborn polyaromatic hydrocarbons such as phenanthrene. MBRs also remove a very high percentage of pathogens, thereby reducing chemical disinfection requirements.

The high-effluent quality associated with MBRs is a significant advantage over other wastewater treatment methods, particularly with respect to reuse options. In addition, MBRs require less space than traditional activated sludge systems because less hydraulic residence time is needed to achieve a given solid's retention time, and they create the possibility for a flexible and phased extension of existing wastewater treatment plants. MBRs are suited for decentralized treatment because they have fewer unit processes and are more automated and thereby simpler to operate.

Despite the benefits of MBR wastewater treatment, concerns over higher costs have historically dominated discussions of its widespread use. As Table 8.1 illustrates, although MBR technology ranks high according to the sustainability criteria used, sociocultural factors are the main impediment to embracing the technology. As is characteristic of the U.S. municipal water industry, innovative technologies (even if not new) are slow to be accepted and implemented. In addition to a relative lack of expertise in the technology, marginally higher costs have yet to be adequately compared with the economic benefits associated with future regulatory compliance and indirect operational efficiencies. It is anticipated that the growing field of research in the area will facilitate the transfer of technology to the marketplace and continue the rapid emergence of MBR technology, particularly in U.S. industrial applications.

MBR technology has already seen rapid development and penetration in the European market in the past five years and is arguably dominated by Japanese manufacturers. The ability to invest in MBR technology is somewhat limited because the technology is still early in gaining widespread acceptance. However, in recent years, MBRs have seen significant growth as the technology has been redesigned and greatly refined by manufacturers.

There are several reasons to believe that MBR technology will continue to gain institutional acceptance in wastewater treatment:

- The underlying technology is solidly based in engineering principles. There is a significant research effort under way to apply activated sludge–related biology to MBRs.
- There is a growing installed base of municipal and industrial MBRs available to verify performance and identify critical design and operating factors.
- Membrane manufacturing capacity expansion is driving down unit costs, which will likely spur further demand.
- Current water shortages in many parts of the United States are making water reuse and recycling critical.

Due to recent technical innovations and significant cost reductions, the applicability for the MBR technology in municipal and industrial wastewater treatment has sharply increased. Especially in areas where urban and industrialized areas are located near sensitive surface water, the MBR technology offers a number of advantages compared to the traditional activated sludge processes. While the international market for MBRs is sufficiently large for all of the technology leaders to realize significant growth, the landscape is likely to become very competitive over the next three to five years. Price will certainly be one aspect of that competition but product depth, service/maintenance, and technological innovation will also play a large part in shifting market shares. From an investment perspective, the potential of MBR technology can be best realized through the centralized treatment companies (presented in Chapter 7) as opposed to the fledging decentralized activities presented in the company listing in Table 8.1.

Chapter 9

Water Infrastructure

The importance of the water and wastewater infrastructure in safeguarding health, supporting economic growth, and protecting the environment cannot be overemphasized. But despite widespread agreement on the severity of the symptoms, little consensus has been achieved on the prescription for a cure. Funding is at the center of the controversy due to the staggering estimates extended well into the future and the accumulating gap resulting from current inaction.

Water supply infrastructure is made up of the components constructed to move water to the consumer through transmission, distribution and lateral lines, pump stations, storage, and all appurtenances necessary to facilitate the delivery of water or the discharge of wastewater. These components are collectively referred to as the distribution system. For practical reasons, the collection networks associated with sewers, sanitary sewers, and stormwater are also included within this category. Wall Street generally adopts a much broader definition of infrastructure along the lines of the National Council on Public Works Improvement as "the physical framework that supports and sustains virtually all economic activity." In that context, public supply infra-structure needs generally arise from three factors:

- The maintenance and/or replacement of existing facilities
- The construction of new facilities due to increased demand
- Compliance with regulatory requirements

The reason why a much narrower definition of water, wastewater, and stormwater infrastructure is adopted centers on the unique attributes of disparate water assets and facilitates the formulation of an investment premise. The water infrastructure, as a subset of the all-inclusive defini-tion, has traditionally referred to distribution and collection systems as their *infrastructure*. An overly broad definition of infrastructure from an investment perspective obscures the critical functional distinctions asso-ciated with other physical facilities such as treatment and supply and service components like engineering, construction, and analytics. Each sector has very different capital and operational characteristics including asset life cycles, regulatory backdrop, and water quality considerations. The distribution system is not subject to nearly the same regulatory oversight associated with treatment and compliance. Nonetheless, the distribution system is receiving increasing attention due to aging net-works and water quality issues. Most often, it is the cost associated with the replacement, repair, and rehabilitation of pipelines that is referred to as the *infrastructure gap* and, accordingly, infrastructure and distribution and/or collection will be used interchangeably.

The Distribution System

The Pipe Network

The staggering estimates presented earlier with respect to the global cost of water are based on the broadest definition of water infrastruc-ture. While there are few quantitatively determined estimates of the cost to specifically construct, replace, or repair the extensive global network of water, sewer, and stormwater pipelines, the ability of water utilities to afford necessary improvements is demonstrated by endless anecdotal evidence in the United States alone.

Urban areas commonly face problems of deterioration of aging distribution systems that have outlived their useful service lives. For example, at one time Boston could account for only 50 percent of its water after distribution. A metering program was adopted and the city spent $64 million to replace or reline all water mains over 100 years of age, or approximately 15 percent of its 1,000-mile distribution system. Parts of St. Louis's sewer system predate the Civil War. In Los Angeles, about half of the 6,500 miles of sewer pipe is 50 years old or older. While aged pipes are not inherently a problem, many need in-place cleaning and lining, and others must be replaced completely. Old pipes frequently leak, which can result in strained supplies, inadequate pressure for fire protection, and degradation of water quality.

In addition, shifts in population strand water and wastewater assets in urban cities with few ways to pay for needed improvements. Stranded assets are those network components that become obsolete or irreparably inefficient in advance of full depreciation. And stranded assets mean stranded costs to the water utility. Funding increases (including higher water rates) are urgently needed to help close a rapidly accumulating annual gap between pipeline needs and current spending. One transfer mechanism is through the capitalization of state Water and Wastewater Infrastructure Financing Authorities, which are characterized as the "next generation" of Drinking Water State Revolving Funds (DWSRF).

The country's aging water and wastewater infrastructure has yet to see dramatic improvement as state and local budgets are spent in compliance with other federal mandates, and water rates fail to recover the cost of replacement. Regardless of federal spending support, it is apparent that most water suppliers across the United States have significant needs to expand, upgrade, and rehabilitate large portions of their systems. While new infrastructure construction is sure to accelerate as politicians come to some consensus, the rehabilitation market is growing in the interim and promises to become a significant factor in the ultimate approach. As technological advances continue, rehabilitation methods are rapidly gaining acceptance. This specific segment of the infrastructure theme is discussed subsequently. An even higher priority would logically seem to be prevention of loss with respect to the existing network.

Leak Detection

It is surprising that with all of the concern about dwindling water supplies, there is relatively little effort on the part of water utilities to reduce
the amount of water "lost" within their own systems. A significant
amount of finished water is lost to leakage in the distribution system.
Leaks not only impact production capacity and reduce operational
efficiency, but also have a significant impact on costs. Many utilities
recognize the need to recover supplies through leak detection but are
faced with a market that is underserved by water technologies. While
leak detection has been historically low tech, technological innovation is
increasingly viewed as a cost-effective solution. Advanced leak detection
methods and integrated monitoring systems have the potential to generate a high-growth subsector within the water industry.

Water utilities spend a great deal of time monitoring water production records, pumping station throughput, the flow in and out of
reservoirs and tanks, and the amount of water used in the treatment
process. But from points forward there is a real disconnect in accounting for water quantities. Most utilities simply create a line item in their
budgets for "unaccounted-for" water, chalking up the lost revenue to
the inevitable loss of a certain percentage of production.

Unaccounted-for water is the difference between the amount of
water a utility purchases or produces and the amount of water that is
metered and billed to customers. In the United States, unaccounted-for
water averages about 15 percent of production. Globally, the percentage
is much higher; the International Water Supply Association estimates a
figure typically in the 20 to 30 percent range. And while unaccounted-
for water is attributed to several causes other than leakage, such as
unmetered uses, water theft, and reservoir overflow, leakage is the major
cause, representing, on average, over half of all unaccounted-for water.

It is not hard to see why. Underground leakage is becoming a
greater and greater problem in tandem with the aging and deterioration
of our water infrastructure. A water leak just one-fourth inch in diam-
eter can result in a loss of almost 15,000 gallons per day. If undetected
for a month, over a half million gallons can be lost. Even a pinhole leak
can mean an average loss of 18,000 gallons of water per quarter, equal-
ing the average demand from a residential customer. And many leaks are

substantially larger, leading to the regrettable loss of much valued potable water.

While most municipalities still price their water at a fraction of the true economic cost of providing it, water has a greater value than ever before. Because water has been relatively cheap and readily available, many water utilities have not considered leak reduction as a cost-effective way to lower operating costs and increase revenues. Reducing leakage is effective because it is under the utility's direct control and saving water translates directly to saving costs. Not only is it a significant source of "additional" water adding to strained supplies, but reducing leaks is a cost-effective way to lower operating costs, from energy to chemicals. After all, the lost water is treated, just like the water that makes it to the consumer's tap. In addition to environmental and economic losses caused by leakage, leaky pipes pose a health risk, as leaks are potential entry points for contaminants.

There is currently no good measure of the size of the leak detection marketplace—a testimony to the fact that it is underserved. While flow meters play an important part in detecting potential problems within a distribution zone, the leak detection market also directly refers to the equipment used to isolate and confirm the existence of a leak. The methods for detecting leaks have traditionally been relatively low tech, consisting of listening surveys, visual observation, and geophones (or ground microphones). Acoustic equipment can detect the sound or vibration induced by water as it escapes from pipes under pressure. More advanced electronic leak detectors coming into use have the advantage of filtering out extraneous noises as well as metering devices to show the strength of the noise being investigated. Even more advanced are the leak noise correlators. These are computer-based field instruments that work by measuring leak signals at two points that bracket a suspected leak. The position of the leak is then determined automatically based on the time shift between leak signals calculated using cross-correlation.

Because of the potential of the market, there is a growing interest in incorporating technological innovations into leak detection equipment. These improvements include the revision of automatic mode algorithms, use of higher sensitivity sensors (accelerometers), very-low-frequency wireless transmission, and verification of propagation velocities for various pipe types. The latter is a positive event in view of the increasing use of plastic pipes in water distribution systems worldwide. Emerging technologies in leak detection include ultrasonic transducers, cable-based sensors, digital signal processing, ground-penetrating radar, thermography, and advanced software tools.

Eliminating leaks in effect recovers production capacity allowing a utility to defer construction expenditures for new water supplies and system expansion. With mounting infrastructure costs and growing constraints on water resources, utilities must strive to account for all of the water that travels from the source to end users. Technological innovations have the potential to rapidly transform the leak detection business into a large market opportunity. Given the political and budgetary obstacles in solving the nation's infrastructure problems, solutions such as leak detection should represent an obvious objective. Despite the imperatives of reducing water leakage, the market is underserved. But enabling technologies are converging, creating an area of specialized investment interest.

There are no known undiluted water leak detection stocks. As is so often the case, divisions of large, diversified companies serve many of the underlying themes within the water industry. Yet many of these companies have other water-related activities that must be aggregated in order for an investor to determine if the exposure is substantial enough to quench their thirst. Absent a public company that concentrates primarily on leak detection, a favorable alternative is to invest in emerging solutions. A representative example is the combination of leak noise loggers with radio frequency meter interface units. Halma Plc is a leader in the detection of leaks in water networks. Its Fluid Conservation Systems business, part of Halma Water Management, is partnering with a number of meter manufacturers (one is Neptune/Roper) to provide water utilities with distribution-side leak monitoring capabilities that can integrate with automatic meter reading (AMR) systems. This is a good example of the growing trend in utility operations toward the application of enabling information technologies for monitoring water networks. Many of the innovations in water leak detection satisfy the increasing demand by utilities for "real-time" data on system conditions. Another example is the integration of leak detection methods in advanced supervisory control and data acquisition (SCADA) systems, which is also seen as a critical management tool of the future.

For reference purposes, a prominent private, international company in leak detection is Gutermann International Ltd., based in the United Kingdom.

The Importance of Distribution Systems in Water Quality

While the concern over deteriorating transmission and distribution networks is normally couched in terms of the associated quantity issues (reliability and leakage), it is also rapidly becoming a serious quality problem. Rarely, if ever, is the drinking water released from the treatment plant the same water that flows from the consumer's tap. The latter bears the scars of its journey through pipes, pumps, reservoirs, and storage tanks.

The majority of regulations in the water industry have historically focused on enforcing treatment concentrations at the plant. But recent regulations, and those emerging as a result of the growing concern by consumers regarding the integrity of the nation's drinking water systems, mandate that water suppliers also ensure that the distributed water is safe. Many of these standards must be met at the consumer's tap. Of principal concern is the maintenance of treated water quality in the extensive maze of drinking water distribution systems. The significance of forcing inclusion of the entire distribution system into compliance decisions has led to some unique investment opportunities within the water industry.

Water suppliers have traditionally relied on the distribution system to deliver finished drinking water and provide reliable fire protection. Sustaining system reliability was more a function of hydraulic considerations, such as maintaining pressure, balancing capacity requirements, and building excess storage for peak demands. But the benefit of optimizing the distribution system has a downside that is becoming increasingly problematic.

Maintaining equilibrium in these conditions often results in the water's remaining in the system for a longer period of time, thereby reducing the disinfectant residual, supporting bacterial growth, promoting nitrification, increasing disinfection by-product concentrations, and causing aesthetic degradation (taste, odor, and appearance). Recent research has increased the body of knowledge on reactions within the network and has expanded distribution concerns to include maintaining the quality of the treated water as it flows through the system to the customer's tap.

The utilization of online SCADA systems addresses many of the hydraulic aspects associated with operating the distribution system, thereby freeing municipalities to address the water quality issues that are subject to increasing regulation. Impaired water quality is caused by actions and reactions of the physical, chemical, and biological properties of the distribution network and the water itself. That distribution lines can compromise quality is nothing new; corrosion has been a fact of operational life for water suppliers since the industry began to use materials other than wood to transport water. What is new is the complexity in determining precisely what does happen to water as it moves through the system in combination with restrictive regulations that strike at the basics of distribution operations.

Distribution System Regulation. The Total Coliform Rule, the Lead and Copper Rule, the trihalomethane (THM) regulation, the Disinfectants/Disinfection By-Products (D/DBP) Rule, and the Surface Water Treatment Rule (SWTR) are all oriented toward water quality and monitoring in the distribution system. The SWTR requires that a detectable disinfectant residual be maintained at representative locations in the distribution system to protect against microbial contamination. The lack of a disinfectant residual, the presence of coliform bacteria, and high levels of THMs or haloacetic acids in distributed water can result in serious violations of regulations and subsequent public notifications. The Total Coliform Rule regulates coliform bacteria, which are used as surrogate organisms to indicate whether treatment has been adequate or whether the system is subject to contamination. Monitoring for compliance with the Lead and Copper Rule is based entirely on samples taken at the consumer's tap. As is often the case, the means by which municipalities comply with these regulations creates opportunities for certain segments of the water industry.

Corrosion Control. Corrosion of the internal pipe surfaces is responsible for much of the deterioration of chemical quality in distribution systems. Of continuing concern is the threat posed to the quality of distributed water by corrosion by-products, particularly lead. As the

Environmental Protection Agency's (EPA's) Lead and Copper Rule is now fully promulgated, interest continues to grow in controlling corrosion and reducing lead and copper in drinking water.

To comply with the Lead and Copper Rule, municipalities are actively searching for cost-effective ways to control corrosion and reduce lead and copper in drinking water. Demand continues to grow for chemicals that stop corrosion in distribution systems and prevent the leaching of lead and copper into tap water. Since corrosion involves a transfer of electrons, control methods are aimed at blocking the flow of electrons between the water and the metal that is susceptible to corrosion.

The market for specialty chemicals for the control of lead and copper leaching, scale, and the discoloration of drinking water caused by the presence of iron and manganese in the source water is growing. These products provide a cost-effective alternative to expensive treatment systems and costly replacement of pipe and equipment. Water-soluble liquids are specifically formulated to control a multitude of problems in surface water applications. These formulations are beneficial in controlling lead leaching and form a monomolecular film on pipe surfaces that acts as a corrosion inhibitor in multimetal systems. The blended phosphate compounds are engineered to resist reversion, ensuring that the products remain active through the distribution system.

Other opportunities created by the growing role of distribution systems in the maintenance of water quality at the tap include the demand for upgraded materials used in the pipe network, as well as coatings and liners. The basic types of pipe include steel, concrete, ductile iron, and polyvinyl chloride (PVC), all with different corrosion characteristics. As always, there are trade-offs; for example, ductile iron has greater tensile and impact strength, but PVC is corrosion free.

It is clear that the integrity of a distribution system is a complex matter that must undergo a great deal of additional research. Adding to the uncertainty is that the compliance regulations that impact the distribution system may provide contradictory requirements. For example, the SWTR specifies the use of a disinfectant to minimize risk from microbiological contamination. However, chlorine or other disinfectants interact with natural organic matter in treated water to form DBPs. Raising the pH of treated water can assist in controlling corrosion but may increase the formation of THMs. Despite the need for continuing study, municipalities have compliance deadlines that will not wait. These regulations have created a new role for distribution systems as the interface between the plant and the tap.

As long as water delivery relies heavily on a centralized delivery system, the distribution network will be a critical component in ensuring water quality. It is becoming recognized that the most advanced water treatment technology is pointless if the distribution system degrades the finished product. As this recognition advances, resources will be allocated to the development of superior infrastructure materials, better monitoring and control systems, and enhanced biochemical additives. The need for permanent solutions to the issue of water quality in the distribution system should create significant demand for water companies that aid in that effort.

Stormwater Infrastructure

Stormwater Regulation

Nonpoint sources of water contamination are becoming an increasingly large share of surface water quality impairments. Stormwater runoff is seen as the major contributor. With the governance of point sources of pollution firmly entrenched in the regulatory scheme, the EPA is stepping up its activity to address urban stormwater runoff. The point-source-related National Pollutant Discharge Elimination System (NPDES) has been extended in phases to permits for stormwater discharges from certain industrial and construction sites. New watershed regulations under development, the Phase II rule of the NPDES program that includes ever-smaller construction activity, and the critically important Total Maximum Daily Load (TMDL) program are all designed to address the role of stormwater in surface water contamination. Driven by these regulations, stormwater systems, comprising both the management and treatment of stormwater runoff, is an emerging water industry infrastructure theme.

Stormwater poses an increasing problem as runoff transports pollutants, such as sediment, fertilizers, pesticides, hydrocarbons, and other organic compounds and metals, such as lead, into water bodies. Sediment from development and new construction; oil, grease, and toxic chemicals from automobiles; nutrients and pesticides from turf management; viruses and bacteria from failing septic systems; road salts; and heavy metals are examples of pollutants generated in urban areas. It is estimated that as a result of the gains made in controlling point sources, nonpoint sources now compose over half of the waste load borne by the nation's waters. Runoff from urban areas is the leading source of impairment to estuaries (the ecosystem life zone with the highest net primary productivity) and the third-largest source of water quality impairments to lakes. Urbanization increases the variety and amount of pollutants transported to receiving waters. Population and development trends indicate that by 2010 more than half of the United States will live in coastal towns and cities. Runoff from these rapidly growing urban areas will continue to degrade coastal waters.

In retrospect, the enormous environmental impact of nonpoint sources now appears to have clearly justified a more balanced regulatory policy. Historically, in contrast to the control of point sources, the EPA was given no specific authority to regulate nonpoint sources. Congress saw nonpoint water pollution as a state responsibility; regulation at the federal level wasn't acknowledged until the EPA promulgated Phases I and II of the stormwater program under the Clean Water Act. Phase I relies on NPDES permit coverage to address stormwater runoff from medium and large municipal separate storm sewer systems (known as MS4s). The Phase II rule extends the NPDES stormwater permit requirements to small MS4s and construction activities disturbing more than one acre.

The Phase II rule automatically covers operators who are located within an "urbanized area" that has a total population of 50,000 or more and a density of 1,000 persons per square mile. The EPA estimates that between 3,000 and 4,000 urbanized municipalities (over and above the 900 larger systems) are required to develop comprehensive stormwater management plans.[1] The best management practices (BMPs) can include both structural and nonstructural components such as prohibitions on nonstorm discharges into separate storm sewers, infiltration with pretreatment, detention methods, and treatment controls.

The implications of ensuring the quality of stormwater runoff led to a number of legal challenges both by larger municipalities and smaller urban areas. The issue, of course, is money. According to the EPA, which establishes infrastructure priorities, the United States needs nearly $140 billion over the next 20 years to meet wastewater treatment requirements. The three greatest components over the period were not surprising. They include nearly $45 billion for controlling combined sewer overflows, $44 billion for wastewater treatment in general, and $22 billion for new sewer construction. In addition, the EPA estimates $10 billion for upgrading existing wastewater collection systems, $9 billion for nonpoint source control, and $7 billion for controlling municipal stormwater.[2]

The stormwater rules adopted by the Los Angeles Water Board, and the response by the cities affected, is a good example of the regulatory controversy. Stormwater runoff is a key cause of pollution in Santa Monica Bay and other coastal waters. The Los Angeles region operates under a stormwater consent decree, the result of litigation between the National Resources Defense Council and the EPA. The consent decree mandates the development of over 92 stormwater rules, covering such pollutants as bacteria and heavy metals. In response, the board adopted a 12-year plan to greatly reduce the level of pollutants in the Los Angeles River by requiring new steps for cities to remove them. The cities maintain that they should have been notified of the consent decree and invited to the negotiations, since the cost of the new cleanup programs will fall to local cities.

A report commissioned by a group of Los Angeles cities known as the Coalition for Practical Regulation was issued citing the economic impacts of the Board's stormwater rules.[3] A multidisciplinary team of experts from the University of Southern California released the study and concluded the regulations would cost regional taxpayers from $23 billion to $170 billion over a 20-year period, while causing 20,000 to 400,000 lost jobs annually; capital costs alone were expected to be in the range of $22.6 billion to $169.9 billion. The impacts are based on the cost of building advanced systems for treating stormwater runoff, which would be borne by local taxpayers through some combination of higher taxes or cuts in other services. The Phase II rules have drawn similar controversy from small systems concerned that compliance would necessitate the installation of expensive wastewater equipment. Although the BMPs contemplate a variety of less costly, low-tech solutions, the need for stormwater treatment is a real concern. It is clear that stormwater impacts, regulation, and compliance will emerge as yet another major unfunded infrastructure gap.

Political Runoff

To illustrate how complicated the regulation of nonpoint sources is likely to become, one need look no farther than our own energy policies. U.S. energy legislation established a lofty target for the production of renewable fuels by 2022, of which about 40 percent is allowed to come from cornstarch.[4] The demand for ethanol and rising corn prices prompted U.S. farmers to plant more than 90 million acres of corn, 80 percent of which is grown in the Mississippi and Atchafalaya river basins. Corn responds very well to fertilizer. The resulting nitrogen load coursing through the veins of the largest watershed in the United States is creating hypoxic (low oxygen) water in the Gulf of Mexico—a "dead zone" already larger than the size of Delaware and Connecticut combined.

The runoff of nutrient-rich fertilizer causes extensive algal growth, limiting the penetration of sunlight and decreasing the dissolved oxygen in the water as it is consumed by the decomposing plant material. Clearly, corn-based ethanol production is not the only culprit at work here. Wastewater plants are a factor, but they must comply with the nitrogen limits contained in their NPDES discharge permits (you can now see the logic in applying these permits on a watershed-wide basis). Research, however, has shown that the "Corn Belt" accounts for the bulk of the nitrogen amplifying the hypoxic zone and accelerating the cultural eutrophication of the Gulf. The politically driven corn-based ethanol phase of the biofuels era will only exacerbate the monumental challenge of regulating nonpoint water pollution sources.

Combined Sewer Overflows (CSOs)

In addition, gravity collection systems often overflow and backflow during storms. As a result, flow is only partially treated at the wastewater plant or is bypassed to the nearest stream or river. Increased volumes of runoff also negatively affect groundwater elevations and lessen the volume of water percolating through the soil, thereby lessening the dilution of contaminants entering groundwater. Overflows carry untreated pollutants into watercourses, and backflows can affect the homes of customers within the collection system.

Investment Components

From an investment point of view, the infrastructure challenge of controlling and treating stormwater runoff can be broken down into several components. There are the basic products used in stormwater and sewer systems like concrete and steel pipe and tunnels. Also in this category are the appurtenances, such as valves, backflow devices, and pumping equipment, that are required in nonpoint control systems. Another segment that will certainly grow in importance is technology—that is, the companies that provide technological advances in nonpoint source pollution control. The application of sophisticated technologies in addressing stormwater pollution creates a substantial opportunity for filtration, microfiltration, and separation companies. Treatment is now an optional BMP for complying with the regulations, but the requirements are likely to become stricter over time. Many believe that cities will eventually be required to divert storm runoff to plants for treatment. At the same time, it is not inconceivable that a "separate" stormwater utility, with its own rate structure designed to reflect those distinct costs, could join the group of water and wastewater utilities.

Also of interest are the new technologies that are emerging in response to specific nonpoint problems such as stormwater and agricultural runoff—for instance, a pelletized compost medium that traps particulates, adsorbs organic chemicals, and can remove heavy metals. The filter medium is put into radial flow filter cartridges that are inserted into precast vaults or custom-designed structures and placed, for example, underneath parking lots and next to highways. The technology is promising as a passive stormwater treatment method that goes beyond sedimentation and filtration and requires less land than conventional stormwater treatment methods.

Another segment, which has applications to the stormwater runoff theme, is based on the need to monitor and measure the effectiveness and cost efficiency of any practice or system to meet the regulations.

Metering and real-time data collection and monitoring programs will more effectively control nonpoint contamination in the future. Sewers can then be designed and operated with an optimal peak capacity rather than overdesigning as an approach to controlling peak flows.

For various institutional, economic, and regulatory reasons, nonpoint sources have not received the proper allocation of resources that is deserved given the impact of this category on water quality. It is clear that stormwater runoff is a leading source of surface water impairments. The EPA is committed to dealing with this area, starting initially with stormwater runoff, but the costs will be high. While many of the specific compliance options are still being investigated, the nature of BMPs will certainly encompass structural modifications and technological advances in dealing with the problem. As an investment theme, the treatment, control, and monitoring of stormwater runoff is a growing segment to be watched.

Pipeline Rehabilitation

The world's deteriorating water and wastewater infrastructure will ultimately influence the institutional structures established to alleviate the financing shortfalls. The magnitude of the problem is daunting, both in terms of dollars and political effort. The water infrastructure differs in a critical way from other basic infrastructure systems—such as highways, airports, and transit systems—which have received substantial federal funding. Water systems generally have geopolitical boundaries that inhibit the formation of a national consensus and complicate the relationship between funding and beneficiaries. Figuring all this out simply delays the solution and many municipalities cannot afford to wait. It is for this reason that restoration and rehabilitation, as opposed to the outright replacement, of infrastructure components is a more timely and compelling investment theme.

According to the eleventh Annual *Underground Construction* Municipal Sewer & Water Survey,[5] spending on sewer, stormwater, and water networks remains stable at an average annual level of about $12.5 billion over the past couple of years. Prior periods experienced more dramatic growth, particularly water construction and rehabilitation spending.

Municipal budgets for underground piping infrastructure are very sensitive to economic conditions, both national and regional. The point remains, however, that accelerated spending on piping networks is inevitable over the next decade and that the rehabilitation component will likely continue to outpace new construction spending both in absolute dollars and in the rate of growth. It is estimated that rehabilitation expenditures as a percentage of the total will rise from the current 60 percent to closer to 70 percent since declining Federal Revolving Fund outlays disproportionately impact new construction and strained municipal budgets will seek less costly renovation methods.

Trenchless Rehabilitation Technology

The rehabilitation business is comprised of technologies utilized to upgrade, maintain and restore the vast network of pipes that make-up the backbone of the water and wastewater infrastructure. Trenchless technology is by far the most important aspect of the rehabilitation market and includes a variety of methods such as cured-in-place pipe, directional drilling, microtunneling, pipe bursting, and slip lining. According to the *Underground Construction* survey, 70 percent of the sewer and stormwater rehabilitation market utilizes trenchless technology compared to 30 percent utilization in the water pipe rehabilitation market. In new construction, 16 percent of the sewer and stormwater market and 22 percent of the water market is trenchless. The relatively higher share of trenchless activity in wastewater is a result of EPA mandates relative to combined sewer overflows and other regulations. The positive results of rehabilitation methods in wastewater, horizontal directional drilling in particular, are now spilling over to the water market. The use of trenchless construction methods on the water side is projected to increase, albeit from a lower level, as the more stringent requirements for potable water pipe rehabilitation are addressed by the industry. Municipalities see trenchless rehabilitation as a cost-effective interim solution to many structural and regulatory issues.

Horizontal directional drilling (HDD) has widespread application even though the technology is still in its infancy for the water and wastewater industry. The benefits to drilling under, rather than through, the existing landscapes are clear. The water and sewer markets represents about a quarter of the HDD markets, second only to the once boom- ing telecommunications market. Pipe bursting is another rehabilitation technique used to retrofit aging pipes. During pneumatic pipe bursting, the pipe-bursting tool is guided through a fracturable host pipe. As the tool travels through the pipe its percussive action breaks apart the old pipe, displaces the fragments into the surrounding soil and simultane- ously pulls in the new pipe (usually HDPE).

The ability of water utilities to afford necessary water supply infra- structure improvements has been the subject of numerous studies. Urban areas commonly face problems of deterioration of aging distri- bution systems that have outlived their useful service lives. Because of the large need for restoration of sewers and water pipelines, this seg- ment has compelling investment interest over the long term. The market for rehabilitation technology services is extremely fragmented and the vast majority of these companies are smaller private firms. Some of the larger companies include TT Technologies, Ditch Witch, HOBAS, Astec Industries, and Vermeer. The largest concentrated play in the public arena is Insituform Technologies.

The underground piping infrastructure business is one with a great deal of investment interest due to the potential size of the market and the emotion associated with our deteriorating water systems. Expanded knowledge, skilled personnel, municipal acceptance, and diversity of higher-tech trenchless techniques are the driving forces for trenchless technology. With the proliferation of rehabilitation methods offering viable, practical, and economical alternatives to traditional water and wastewater piping infrastructure needs, this segment is positioned for rapid growth when technological acceptance and political will improve, but patience will be required.

Flow Control and Pumps

No matter what the response of the water industry to growing regula- tory and economic challenges, there is one inescapable fact within the workings of any treatment, process, or supply system: Water must be moved. Gravity often plays a role in water and wastewater systems, but pumps are without a doubt the prime movers in the business of flow control and fluid handling. As a long-standing mainstay of the water industry, pump design was thought to have reached a developmental plateau. But even such a basic component as a pump is not beyond the forces shaping technological innovation in the water industry. Advances in materials, design, and performance have extended markets and created operational efficiencies leading to renewed growth in the pump business.

The function of a pump is basic. It is a mechanical device that adds energy to water or other liquids. In most water distribution systems, pumps are needed to raise the elevation of the water and move it through the network of water mains under pressure. One way of classifying pumps is by their application in the system. For example, there are pumps that lift the water from a river or lake and move it to a nearby treatment plant and there are pumps that discharge the treated drinking water into the transmission and distribution system. And booster pumps are used when it is necessary to increase the pressure within the distribution system or raise the water into an elevated storage tank.

Another way of classifying pumps is according to the mechanical principles on which they operate. The two basic types are positive displacement pumps and centrifugal pumps. A positive displacement pump will deliver a fixed quantity of water with each revolution of the pump rotor. Positive displacement pumps are divided into two broad categories: rotary and reciprocating. The water is physically displaced from the pump casing. These pumps are generally used in high-head, low-volume pumping situations such as with biosolids. Centrifugal pumps are the most common type used in water supply, stormwater, and wastewater systems because they are generally less expensive and require less maintenance. A centrifugal pump adds energy to the water by accelerating it through the action of a rapidly rotating impeller to create internal pressure. The water is thrown outward by the vanes of the impeller and passes through a spiral-shaped casing, where its velocity is gradually slowed down. As the velocity drops in the expanding spiral volute, the kinetic energy is converted to pressure head and the water is discharged.

Other kinds of water and wastewater pumps used are axial pumps, vertical turbine, and mixed-flow pumps. Axial-flow and mixed-flow pumps create flow and head with a propeller and are generally used in low head and high volume applications.

Beyond the definitional aspects of pumps, it is the applications that create an opportunity for growth. Both the physical and economic environments within which pumps are used have changed. Wastewater and process streams can have radically different abrasion characteristics. New materials have increased performance and service life when operating under harsh environments. Further, the judicious positioning and selection of pumps is critical in the economy and operation of the overall system design. Proper planning and design can reduce capital and maintenance costs.

The proliferation of pumps has mirrored other trends in the water industry such as the regulation of biosolids and landfills, the emergence of residential filtration systems, infrastructure rehabilitation, increased population demands, and greater attention to industrial process fluids. These factors have led to an increased focus on customer needs and product development. Stringent landfill regulations require the installation of a leachate collection system for all new landfill construction. Leachate is the often highly contaminated liquid produced by landfill processes that must be prevented from migrating into groundwater. In older landfills that were constructed without leachate systems, and in newer landfills in which the collection piping has clogged, it is often necessary to install leachate collection wells with dedicated pumps. Condensate pumping is usually a vital component in landfill gas recovery procedures. Historically, electric submersible pumps were the only type of pump available for landfill leachate and condensate pumping applications. But the newest and best-adapted pump for larger flow requirements is the self-actuating, controllerless pneumatic pump.

The Part 503 regulations for the reuse of biosolids (see Chapter 13) represent another regulatory requirement that has opened new markets and encourages innovation in pumps. The intent of the regulation is to accelerate interest in sound methods and processes used to handle, condition, and dispose of biosolids. Since a reduction in the volume of sludge being generated results in cost savings, pumps are increasingly used in dewatering activities.

Landfill and biosolids requirements are just two of the specific applications for pumps resulting from regulations that increase the incentive for technological innovations. Advances in materials have also created new markets for pumps because of the enhanced levels of performance, reliability, and longevity. One of the most significant new developments is the introduction of a whole new generation of wastewater pumps with all stainless steel construction that cover a much wider range of waste-handling applications.

Traditional heavy and costly cast-iron pumps have mechanical restrictions that prevent a reduction in wall thickness. Weight, combined with the inability to dissipate heat, places a limitation on cast-iron pump technology. Submersible pumps constructed of stainless steel and synthetic materials can incorporate new technological developments without costing more because of improvements in the manufacturing process. These new pumps have greater mechanical strength, are lighter weight, require less maintenance because of better heat dissipation, and do not use toxic oil to lubricate and cool the mechanical seals.

Materials technology has even advanced to the development of nonmetallic pumps. Thermoplastic pumps are used in handling corrosive and abrasive wastewater, water, and wastewater treatment chemicals as well as corrosive fumes. Other technological developments include pumps with special hydraulic systems suitable for applications with high volumes of solids, built-in failure detection systems, and new vortex impeller systems with greater hydraulic efficiency.

Finally, new markets have emerged for pump manufactures. The growing acceptance of point-of-use water filtration products used in residential and commercial settings has created the need for certain types of pumps in specific situations. Particularly in the international markets for reverse osmosis systems, a booster pump is often required to compensate for low water pressure to achieve the proper performance of the membrane.

Traditionally, the pump business has been highly fragmented. It has undergone considerable consolidation in recent years as a result of the need to lower costs through reduction of excess capacity and customers' preference to align with global full-service suppliers. In addition, the expanding role of pumps in the water industry and industrial processes has led to acquisitions designed to penetrate additional markets and extend product lines.

ITT Industries is a good example of a consolidator in the segment. The acquisition of Goulds Pumps made it the world's largest pump manufacturer, placing it ahead of Japan's Ebara Corporation. ITT also acquired Uniservice Wellpoint, an Italian manufacturer of vacuum primed centrifugal pumps, as part of the ongoing strategy of transitioning its Flygt group from a pump provider to a solutions provider. Demand for pumps is especially strong in developing countries, which need them for new water and wastewater systems.

Table 9.1   Water Transmission and Distribution Companies

Name	Symbol or SEDOL	Country	Water Activity
Ameron International	AMN	US	Water transmission piping
Northwest Pipe Co.	NWPX	US	Welded steel pipe (water transmission) and carbon steel pipe (irrigation)
Astec Industries	ASTE	US	Astec Underground: horizontal directional drilling equipment
Insituform Technology 'A'	INSU	US	In situ pipeline rehab
Wavin NV	B1FY8X2	Netherlands	Plastic pipe systems; plumbing, sewer rainwater management
Geberit AG	B1WGG93	Switzerland	European leader in plumbing, sanitary technology and piping systems
Watts Water Technologies	WTS	US	Water control valves and water quality products; backflow, pressure regulators, flow control, filtration systems, conditioning, POU
KSB Group	4498043	Germany	Pumps and valves; irrigation, process, rainwater utilization. Integrated hydraulic systems; water and wastewater plants

(Continued)

Table 9.1 (*Continued*)

Name	Symbol or SEDOL	Country	Water Activity
Georg Fischer	4341783	Switzerland	GF Piping Systems; drinking water transport, wastewater, irrigation, water treatment, desalination
Kurimoto Ltd	6497941	Japan	Ductile iron pipe for water and sewer, water gates and pipe bridges; Fiberglas reinforced plastic pipe
Nippon Chutetsukan	6643272	Japan	Ductile iron products and plastic pipes for water; water-related civil engineering
Uponor Oyj	5232671	Finland	Plumbing systems focused on conservation and sustainable building; ProPex plastic tubing
Franklin Electric	FELE	US	Submersible motors and pumps
Layne Christensen	LAYN	US	Water drilling, transmission line installation and maintenance, wastewater rehabilitation (Inliner Technologies)
Mueller Water Products	MWA	US	Hydrants and water distribution flow control products (Mueller) and ductile iron pressure pipe (U.S. Pipe)
Roper Industries	ROP	US	Water meter and AMR products and systems (Neptune); pumps and flow measurement (Abel, Roper, Cornell)
IDEX	IEX	US	Positive displacement pumps for water/wastewater industry, cooling towers and industrial markets (Viking; Pulsafeeder; Warren Rupp)
Flowserve	FLS	US	Pumps and systems for transmission, treatment, distribution, wastewater, irrigation and flood control

Despite ongoing consolidation, the pump industry remains highly fragmented with numerous smaller private companies. The water and wastewater industry is expanding rapidly worldwide, with specifiers constantly demanding solutions that will provide increasingly higher performance at lower costs in waste handling, fluid management, and treatment. As a result, the pump business has witnessed both the rapid enhancement of existing pump technologies and the introduction of new products and systems. It is believed that this underrecognized segment of the water industry is poised for above-average growth as a result of demanding operational requirements, expanding specialty markets, such as desalination, and demand from developing countries. See Tables 9.1 and 9.2.

Table 9.2   Pumps, Valves and Flow Control Companies

Name	Symbol or SEDOL	Country	Water Activity
Crane Co	CR	US	Municipal, industrial and commercial pumps; Cochrane water treatment systems
Ebara Corp	6302700	Japan	Full product line of submersible cast iron and stainless steel centrifugal pumps for water, wastewater, sewage, sump, effluent, dewatering and flood control applications
Flowserve	FLS	US	Pumps and systems for transmission, treatment, distribution, wastewater, irrigation and flood control
Franklin Electric	FELE	US	Submersible motors and pumps
Gorman-Rupp Company	GRC	US	Pumps and related equipment (pumps and motor controls) in water, wastewater, irrigation, fire protection (Patterson, Gorman-Rupp)
IDEX	IEX	US	Positive displacement pumps for water/wastewater industry, cooling towers and industrial markets (Viking; Pulsafeeder; Warren Rupp)

(Continued)

Table 9.2 (*Continued*)

Name	Symbol or SEDOL	Country	Water Activity
ITT Industries	ITT	US	Broad range of water pumps (Goulds, Marlow, Lowara), wastewater pumps (Flygt, Grindex, A-C Pump) and treatment systems (Sanitaire, WEDECO, Aquious)
KSB Group	4498043	Germany	Pumps and valves; irrigation, process, rainwater utilization. Integrated hydraulic systems; water and wastewater plants
Met-Pro	MPR	US	Fluid Handling segment manufactures high quality centrifugal pumps for industrial, desalination, water reuse, RO, public aquariums, aquaculture and wastewater applications
Pentair	PNR	US	Broad range of diaphragm and turbine pumps, valves, flow control products (Fairbanks Morse, Jung, etc.) for residential, pool/spa, municipal and industrial applications
Roper Industries	ROP	US	Water meter and AMR products and systems (Neptune); pumps and flow measurement (Abel, Roper, Cornell)
SPX Corporation	SPW	US	Pumps and valves

Chapter 10

Water Analytics

The global water analytical, monitoring, and test market is estimated at over $21 billion.[1] The group includes companies that provide services, manufacture instrumentation or develop techniques for the analysis, testing or monitoring of water and/or wastewater quality. These analytics are applied to achieve, either directly or indirectly, a mandated compliance requirement, a management objective in optimizing operations relative to a specific use, whether municipal or industrial, and now, the objectives of homeland security.

Analytical instrumentation is defined as any equipment or device that is used to test water parameters or analyze water in a process-oriented application in order to determine the identity and concentration of a specific sample component. The equipment is utilized in a number of mission-critical applications in the water industry and is a strategic component in the protection of the water infrastructure.

There are numerous other Environmental Protection Agency (EPA) actions, both existing and pending, that require analytical testing and measurement either as a means of collecting data for future rule making or to gauge compliance with existing regulations. As regulatory mandates increase the need to monitor and measure a variety of water quality parameters, analysis is becoming more than a support function to the municipal water and wastewater industry. Regulatory compliance, cost control, and process monitoring generally require greater amounts of information on increasingly complex processes. All of this portends a growing significance for the nation's environmental analytical equipment manufacturers and service providers.

Metering

What would seem basic to the proper allocation of a resource as critical as water is the simple notion that users pay for their consumption. There are, however, many locations around the world that do not measure water consumption, let alone charge according to a rate design that reflects actual costs and consumption characteristics.

Automatic meter reading (AMR) is a technology that charges according to a rate design that reflects actual costs and consumption characteristics. Once considered the stable, low-technology mainstay of water utility operations, meter reading continues to evolve in tandem with information technologies. AMR is the capture of water consumption data from a meter and transmission to a remote central location using a communication medium. While AMR has been used in the deregulated electric utility industry for some time, the operational advantages and the need for efficient resource management make AMR an attractive theme within the water industry.

There are a number of meter reading variations under the broad umbrella of advanced metering technology from which utility decision makers can choose. Given the advancements in information technologies, however, electronic meter reading is now focused on more sophisticated, two-way, integrated systems to transmit and receive data from an interface unit with imbedded software fixed to the metering point. Such a network requires a communication link to each meter.

Water utilities view electronic meter reading as required technology to be competitive. From an administrative perspective, AMR can reduce meter reading and billing costs, improve cash flow, and largely eliminate estimated bills. From an operational point of view, water consumption data can provide real-time information about leakage, usage patterns, usage distribution, and times of use. The ability to acquire accurate and timely water consumption information has major implications for system design, demand management initiatives, and integrated resource planning. More frequent water usage data can assist in gaining insight into peak demands and thereby the efficient (competitive) pricing of water.

AMR is recognized not only for efficient and reliable meter reading but also as a means to offer value-added products and services to customers. These features include real-time pricing, time-of-use metering, demand billing, outage notification, tamper/theft reduction, leak detection, remote connect/disconnect, multiple meter reading, and home automation. This strategy is already being successfully applied in the deregulated telecommunications environment where the Regional Bell Operating Companies are offering "affinity" products such as voice messaging and caller ID to attract new business and retain the loyalty of existing customers.

Despite the seemingly overwhelming benefits of AMR, there are uncertainties. The ongoing communication costs are not directly under the control of the utility, the technology requires a shift in utility mind-set, careful implementation is critical to controlling costs, and the lack of standardization creates a confusing technology/vendor market. A practical drawback to many existing systems is the power source needed to operate the network, which, given longer distances and the utilization of two-way communications, substantially decreases the battery life to around six years.

A number of technological hurdles also remain. One of several relates to the different pulses emitted by meters of different sizes and makes. A miscoding in the pulse read setting could dramatically alter the usage reading and negate the benefit of precision metering. Manufacturers have yet to completely ensure that this flexibility can be built in and properly managed. Another technological challenge remaining is how to tie the network for different meter devices together.

Although water utility interest in and testing of remote register devices dates back to the 1960s, advanced information technologies, as well as the growing sophistication of vendors, has facilitated large-scale installations of AMR systems. A large and growing number of utilities are actively conducting trials or performing installations. For example, Denver Water converted 220,000 meters to AMR modules that use miniature radio transmitters attached to the water meter. With this process, one driver in a vehicle can read more meters in one day than 33 meter readers. The rapid expansion of participants in AMR is a reflection of the tremendous opportunity potential. From virtually none 10 years ago, there are now over 50 vendors of AMR equipment and related services. These participants range from meter equipment manufacturers to network providers, to the rapidly growing field of systems integrators.

Many smaller firms are becoming very active in the service and installation side of the business, creating a rapidly growing segment known as systems integrators. While AMR equipment and technology vendors continue to wrestle with issues of compatibility and standardization and carriers posture for the right to license the wide area networks, the systems integrators are filling a practical void in the service chain that has been traditionally lacking.

AMR platforms are widely divergent. The basic design allows utilities to read meters using a broadcast technology that does not require a Federal Communications Commission (FCC) license. A growing number of firms that set up the electronic data interchange networks needed in AMR have emerged. The network segment, once thought to be the exclusive turf of large telecom carriers and electric companies, has developed into an expanding market for specialized information technology (IT) providers. Companies such as Itron provide open-architecture data collection systems, including AMR, that are compatible with water meters from all leading manufacturers. Teaming arrangements remain common in the business.

Competitive pressures, escalating operating costs, stringent water quality standards, and conservation needs are changing the rules for water companies. These forces dictate that water utilities must manage their operations in a way that optimizes the delivery and use of water. And while connectivity, licensing difficulties, and battery costs are real concerns, AMR is likely to become standard operating procedure for many water utilities. As such, the fundamentals support an aggressive investment approach to the theme of water consumption measurement. See Table 10.1 for water metering companies.

Table 10.1   Water Metering Companies

Name	Symbol	Segments	Water Activity
Badger Meter	BMI	Flow measurement	Orion®, Galaxy, Itron®, TRACE® manual and automatic meter reading, residential and industrial meters
Itron Inc.	ITRI	Meter Collection Data; Software Solutions	Water usage information technology
Techem AG	Acquired by Macquarie	AMR	Metering and water billing
Roper Industries	ROP	Industrial Technology; RF Technology	Water meter and AMR products and systems (Neptune); pumps and flow measurement (Abel, Roper, Cornell)

Monitoring, Measuring, and Testing

While much is said about the implementation of extensive data collection efforts by the water supply community, there remains the all-too-typical conflict between the economic limitations of promulgating new regulations and the compliance requirements intended to protect the public health. Wedged in the middle is the analytical business—the laboratories, testing, and monitoring companies that are called upon to provide the instrumentation and services necessary to quantify water conditions and determine compliance with regulations. Despite this unenviable position, there is a potential investment opportunity unfolding as governing institutions worldwide struggle with the science behind the law.

The health risk with the highest priority in the regulation of drinking water today is the trade-off between the control of microbiological contamination (bacteria, viruses, and protozoa) on the one hand and disinfection by-products on the other. This risk trade-off arises because typically the least expensive way for a public water system to increase microbial control is to increase disinfection (which generally increases by-product formation), and the easiest way to reduce by-products is to decrease disinfection (which generally increases microbial risk). Microbiological contamination often causes flulike symptoms but can also cause serious diseases such as hepatitis, giardiasis, cryptosporidiosis, and Legionnaire's disease. Disinfection by-products pose the risk of cancer and developmental effects. It is apparent that the health risks are real and that information is critically and quickly needed to address the issues.

The Information Collection Rule (ICR)[2] became the negotiated response by the water industry in the United States to address these concerns. Negotiators reached consensus on a three-part regulatory approach. One prong of this approach is an intensive data collection and research effort to learn more about the occurrence of microbial contamination and disinfection by-products, the health risks posed, appropriate analytical methods, and effective forms of treatment. The ICR was established to meet this component of the regulatory mandate by requiring large public water systems (PWSs) to collect information on the presence and levels of microbial contamination.

The ICR establishes monitoring and data reporting requirements for PWSs. The rule is intended to provide the EPA with information on the occurrence in drinking water of:

- Chemical by-products that form when disinfectants used for microbial control react with chemicals already present in source water (disinfection by-products or DBPs).
- Disease-causing microorganisms (pathogens), including *Cryptosporidium*. The EPA will also collect engineering data on how PWSs currently control such contaminants.

The EPA will use information generated by this rule, along with concurrent research, to determine whether revisions need to be made to the EPA's current drinking water filtration and disinfecting rule and to determine the need for new regulations for disinfectants and DBPs. Analytical instruments that measure specific parameters are utilized for this purpose.

The analytical industry transcends municipal laboratory analysis and reaches well into the business of testing equipment, outsourced laboratory services, and technologically driven monitoring approaches. As regulatory mandates increase the need to monitor and measure a variety of water quality parameters, analysis is becoming more than a support function to the municipal water and wastewater industry. Regulatory compliance, cost control, and process monitoring generally require greater amounts of information on increasingly complex functions. All of this portends a growing significance for the nation's environmental laboratories, suppliers, and analytical equipment manufacturers. Monthly sampling results are entered by the utility into the ICR database as they are received from laboratories, also potential beneficiaries of the information collection effort. But the situation has not always been so promising.

Instrumentation

Analytical equipment is essential to the measurement and monitoring of water quality. As such, the market for analytical instrumentation for the water industry has been relatively untouched by the global economic slowdown. In fact, increased awareness of the need for infrastructure protection due to security concerns has added a growth element to a maturing market. Heightened security, regulatory compliance, the need for quality control, and the emphasis on cost containment all point to a positive environment for analytical equipment manufacturers.

The global water and water-related instrumentation market is, somewhat surprisingly, estimated at over $20 billion.[3] Bear in mind, however, that this segment has a large and rapidly growing industrial component. Analytical instrumentation is defined as any equipment or device that is used to test water parameters or analyze water in a process-oriented application in order to determine the identity and concentration of a specific sample component. The equipment is utilized in a number of mission-critical applications in the water industry and is a strategic component in the protection of the water infrastructure.

Water security is a new reality, and water quality monitoring systems are critical to the timely detection of possible contaminants. The value of real-time environmental monitoring and prediction has increased dramatically with the heightened state of security. This includes sensor and analytical technologies that can provide the equipment needed to continuously monitor water quality variables (chemical and biological); transmit monitoring data in real time; validate, display, and interpret the data; and predict the future state of these variables. Data from sensors create cost control advantages that come from treating algal blooms early, or avoiding drawing water during a turbidity event, but are invaluable as an early warning tool for homeland security protection programs.

In a treatment system, water analysis alone is not sufficient to maintain quality and reduce costs but must be combined with a review of the processes involved. Cost containment is a growing application for analytical instrumentation. Cost and quality control programs that utilize analytical equipment include a comprehensive evaluation of the particular water quality issues. Many times, the only way to effectively control operational and maintenance costs is to optimize the characteristics of the water being treating. This can be achieved by analyzing and then modifying the water before or during the treatment process. For example, pH has a significant impact on the removal of organic matter, a factor in the formation of trihalomethanes, by alum in the coagulation process. Monitoring pH can, therefore, alleviate the need for more expensive treatment options in complying with the disinfection by-product rules. There are many examples of the operational efficacy of maintaining water quality parameters at specified levels—parameters that are measured by analytical instruments.

These parameters can be general or physical, chemical, microbiological, or radionuclide, and the analysis can be part of a monitoring program or cost control plan. Parameters that are commonly measured to describe the physical quality of water include turbidity, temperature, pH, solids, color, taste, odor, and conductivity. While color, taste, and odor may seem to be subjective parameters, each is a proxy for other influences that can be measured, such as the presence of metals, algae, or organic chemicals. Chemical parameters include dissolved oxygen (DO), biochemical oxygen demand, chemical oxygen demand, inorganic chemical, and organic compounds. Solids (e.g., total dissolved solids) can also be classified under chemical examination. Similarly, turbidity is also a parameter used in bacteriological evaluation, one of the more pressing regulatory mandates.

There are many other EPA regulations that require analytical testing and measurement, either as a means of collecting data for future rule making or to gauge compliance with existing regulations. As regulatory mandates increase the need to monitor and measure a variety of water quality parameters, analysis is becoming more than a support function to the municipal water and wastewater industry. Regulatory compliance, cost control, and process monitoring generally require greater amounts of information on increasingly complex functions. All of this portends a growing significance for the nation's environmental analytical equipment manufacturers. And the stormwater regulations contain a list of standard pollutants characterizing urban runoff that must be measured.

The demand for water instrumentation equipment is driven by increasing emphasis on operational efficiency, homeland security issues, and regulatory mandates. However, the intrinsic connection between product price, quality, and features compels manufacturers to provide superior customer and after-sales service to achieve a high degree of differentiation and retain market share. The provision of value-added features is therefore critical to the mix. Instrumentation companies that can design innovative analytical systems to solve a variety of industry issues will reap the benefits.

The market for analytical instrumentation is poised to benefit from the growing global need for sophisticated testing techniques and stringent monitoring requirements. While this segment of the water industry is unlikely to achieve spectacular growth overall in the very short term (approximately 8 percent per year over the next several years),[4] it could very likely be at the center of an IT boom in all-inclusive notion of water resource management—for example, immunoassay field-test kits that are timely, cost-effective, and accurate systems for the detection of contaminants. The tests correlate well with laboratory methods but are used on-site. Other companies are pioneering advanced analysis instruments such as supercritical fluid extraction (SFE) equipment. SFE is a sample preparation method used in laboratories to separate various components from a wide variety of materials prior to their analysis and is cost effective because of reduced time and the replacement of toxic solvents with nontoxic carbon dioxide. Specialty test companies fill the need for on-site accuracy and the simplification of chemical analysis.

These companies manufacture prepackaged test reagents and kits; monitoring instruments such as turbidimeters, spectrophotometers, and colorimeters; process instruments; microbiology products; and electrochemical products. Analytical methods that take longer cannot help a utility monitor its existing water quality and respond quickly and responsibly to safety concerns. What is needed is a number of compatible probe techniques to meet the practical needs of simplicity, speed, and high recovery.

Now that we are able to detect and measure contaminants down to parts per trillion, the policy question is whether trace amounts of proven carcinogens, mutagens, or teratogens represent chronic toxicity to humans. As Paracelsus said in 1540 AD, "The dose makes the poison." The toxicity/dose relationship will become a major issue in the advanced regulatory stages that developed countries are now entering. This will be discussed in greater depth relative to emerging contaminants, for example, the role of disinfection by-products in causing cancer or the impact of pharmaceuticals and personal care products (PPCPs) on the endocrine system. With respect to PPCPs, it is a very good thing that analytical instrumentation can detect trace contaminants down to parts per trillion; if an endocrine disruptor can mimic a hormone, it can do so with an extremely small dose. New laboratory methods have enabled the detection of endocrine-disrupting compounds.

The following are expressions of concentration that serve to provide a basis for comparison:

Parts per million (ppm); one minute in two years
Part per billion (ppb); one second in 32 years
Part per trillion (ppt); one second in 320 centuries

It does not take much study to appreciate the order of magnitude differences; the exponential increase in concentration from parts per million to parts per trillion is mind-boggling. In an example with water, 1 ppt is equivalent to 1 drop of substance in 20 Olympic-size swimming pools filled with 6 feet of water each.

Laboratories

It would seem, given the paramount importance of protecting public health, that the quantitative input provided by a myriad of analyses would equate to a vibrant market for water laboratories. Yet due to a puzzling disconnect between rigorous scientific method and market-driven needs, a cost-efficient network of value-added water laboratories has failed to emerge. There is a huge void between the large, clinical-like labs housed deeply within self-interested engineering firms and institutions and the multitude of fragmented, cookie-cutter localized labs. Granted, many utilities provide their own laboratory services, but indications are that they are more than willing to outsource this function in a cost-saving context to focus on their core operational expertise. And, in fairness, there are several large, privately owned water testing labs, but the approach has been more typical of a consolidative, roll-up model than a full-scale rationalization of an inefficiently fragmented structure. The water laboratory business is a prime example of a segment within the water industry that is an ideal candidate for rationalization.

The segment has suffered for many years from declining hazard-ous waste remediation–related demand and the resulting excess capacity. In addition, an aversion to the perceived low-margin water quality monitoring business blinded laboratories from seeing the potential opportunity in restructuring the industry. As has been mentioned, contract laboratory services were not overlooked by water utilities seeking diversification into nonregulated business. But that trend quickly dissipated as water utilities realized that additional capital expenditures and a diversion of resources made it difficult to turn laboratory services into a revenue center.

Rather than a lengthy diatribe on the circuitous historic evolution and resulting structural failings of the water lab business, an analogy in health care clearly illustrates the idea and the investment potential. Quest Diagnostics revolutionized the medical diagnostic testing business by rationalizing an inefficient and fragmented medical laboratory structure. Importantly, the company continued to develop and integrate innovative health care information technology into its national network of regional laboratories. Now it is the leading provider of routine and specialty analytical and testing services in the health care industry, adding value through secure, Web-enabled, real-time access to patient information facilitating informed decisions. Does that not sound like a model suitable for the mission-critical testing, analysis, monitoring, and compliance functions of the water industry?

There is clear demand from water utilities, let alone industrial clients, for laboratory services that meet their operational and compliance requirements. Testing of tap water under the Safe Drinking Water Act, wastewater discharges under the National Pollutant Discharge Elimination System of the Clean Water Act, and many other existing regulations, require water-quality monitoring. In addition to the basic need for routine and specialty laboratory analytics, there is an enormous pent-up demand for cost-effective and comprehensive integration of these potentially outsourced services within the broader context of water resource management. But it will not happen overnight. And while there is no pure public play in the water laboratory business, investors should be cognizant of the potential as the inevitability of this theme will attract market attention. Instrumentation and testing equipment providers are companies that provide a logical proxy in the interim.

Asset Management

Water and wastewater utilities have a strong incentive going forward to find the most cost-effective means of meeting their critical service requirements. According to the U.S. General Accounting Office,[5] 29 percent of drinking water utilities and 41 percent of wastewater utilities were not currently recovering their full cost of service through user rates. In actuality, when deferred maintenance, marginal supply costs, and distribution system rehabilitation are considered, the true gap generated by artificially low rates is substantially higher.

The previously discussed abysmal shortfall in infrastructure spending, and the government's clear concern for picking up a big piece of the tab, is the impetus behind the accelerating trend of comprehensive management of water and wastewater assets. *Asset management* is the broad term used by the industry to describe the approach to managing capital infrastructure in a way that minimizes the total cost of acquiring, operating, maintaining, replacing, and disposing of capital assets over their disparate life cycles. Recall that cost containment is going to be an enabling force against a variety of institutional and political obstacles;

that is, water and wastewater rates must be adequate to ensure funding for program implementation. A critical feature of the cost minimization component of asset management, therefore, is that it is undertaken in a way that achieves the level of service desired by customers and required by governing bodies. Key assets include treatment plants, collection systems, pipelines, water mains, and other major facilities.

Asset management is all about the analysis of information in order to make informed decisions about capital investments. And information can span the spectrum from the basic collection of key data to an automated plantwide integrated information system with advanced distributed process control. Regulators are likely to focus on the effectiveness of a water utility's asset management efforts in determining rate increases and granting higher rates of return. The application of information technologies to the water industry is destined to become a high-growth investment opportunity in much the same way that automation fed the optimization of energy assets.

Supervisory Control and Data Acquisition (SCADA)

Sophisticated SCADA systems are at the core of the asset management trend. SCADA systems are used to control plant equipment such as pumps and valves according to specific instructions or predictive intelligence. These enterprise solutions ensure continuous monitoring and control of wastewater collection systems, pump stations, distribution systems, remote equipment, and stormwater overflow protection. Enabling information technologies and plant automation can go a long way in creating operational efficiencies and reducing maintenance and energy costs that will mitigate inevitable rate increases, bridge funding gaps, and optimize plant performance and reliability.

Geographic Information Systems (GISs)

GISs are another emerging analytical tool in the water industry. The key to the software is the spatially based approach for mapping and analyzing data. Geographic information can be used in water resource management through watershed and hydrologic modeling, mapping wetlands, and environmental assessments. The spatial attributes of GISs (data referenced to location) are central to advancing utility asset management. The data is used to organize information for managing the physical components of the utility, such as collection systems, pipes, appurtenances, and pumping and treatment equipment. Attribute data, such as customer information, permit requirements, and contaminant transport characteristics can be coupled with spatial attribute data to provide critical problem-solving and decision-making tools.

GIS data sharing with SCADA systems further develops the broader notion of utility asset and resource management by aiding maintenance activities and capital planning.

Homeland Security

Many things changed in the wake of 9/11. The relationship between homeland security and the water infrastructure became the subject of considerable attention. Sadly, very little constructive policy has been advanced and even fewer precautions have been actually implemented. The 2007 Water Sector-Specific Plan (SSP) is the official government response. This plan provides the "overarching" framework for integrating the protection of critical water infrastructure into a program "coordinated" by the Department of Homeland Security (DHS). Key to the water security plan is the need for a strong public/private partnership. That sounds bureaucratically familiar to a host of other water issues languishing in the rhetoric of the phrase; unfunded regulatory mandates, infrastructure spending gaps, alternative supply financing initiatives, outsourced water services, privatization, and the like. So what are the implications for water investors?

The 134-page document was issued by the DHS and the EPA with the title "Water: Critical Infrastructure and Key Resources Sector-Specific Plan as input to the National Infrastructure Protection Plan." The water sector (which includes drinking water and wastewater) is vulnerable to a variety of attacks, including contamination with toxic agents and physical and cyber attacks. The result could be significant numbers of illnesses or casualties or an interruption in water service that would further affect public health and economic activity. The report identifies critical services that would suffer negative impacts such as firefighting and health care, and other dependent and interdependent sectors such as energy, transportation, and food and agriculture.

The SSP discusses the ongoing efforts to identify, prioritize, and coordinate key sector resources and assets that could, if compromised, result in economic or public health impacts. Water and wastewater utilities have undertaken significant activities to assess vulnerabilities and improve plans to respond to security issues. These enhancements include improving control of access to utility assets; expanding physical barriers; increasing control over access, delivery, and storage of chemicals; and the implementation of cyber initiatives. But, while the report exhaustively explores the framework for addressing security threats, it is woefully short of practical recommendations and even less instructive as to how water systems are to pay for any prevention efforts. In fact, the greatest contribution to plant operators, and therefore the most value to investors, is in the identification of additional security-related needs that were apparently outside the scope of the report.

To that end, the DHS has funded another project, entitled the "Domestic Municipal End-to-End Architecture Study," to note any areas where technologies meeting water-security requirements seem to be lacking. This is where the process should have been many years ago. Regardless, with input from the American Water Works Association (AWWA), Water Environment Federation (WEF), and others, it is anticipated that this process will yield actual priorities. The areas identified illustrate the trends that investors should focus on relative to homeland security spending.

Water security is a new reality, and water quality monitoring systems are critical to the timely detection of possible contaminants. Real-time environmental monitoring and prediction has increased dramatically with the heightened state of security. This includes sensor and analytical technologies that can provide the equipment needed to continuously monitor water quality variables (chemical and biological); transmit monitoring data in real time; validate, display, and interpret the data; and predict the future state of these variables. Strategically placed, accurate, and affordable sensors integrated within a utility's asset management network is the vision of the future.

Despite the large number of firms engaged in water monitoring, the sector has not significantly penetrated the opportunities associated with water security. Investors looking at the security aspects should focus on systems integrators providing identifiable solutions. For example, Hach (Danaher) has received Safety Act Designation and Certification from the DHS for an early warning monitoring system designed to help cities protect their drinking water networks from terrorist contamination attacks. The system uses a patented early warning technology to detect, alert, and classify contaminants from cyanide and pesticides to ricin and VX (nerve agent). Emerson Electric is active in creating robust and secure infrastructure architecture and system designs that integrate with advanced SCADA control systems.

It would not be prudent to outline specific actions that could pose a significant threat to our water resources. But the very dismissal by many that it would take a monumental amount of "contaminants" to present a health threat to highly diluted or treated water supplies is just enough denial to make it a perversely attractive option for terrorists. There are more obvious and well-known threats, however. In Baghdad, a pickup truck carrying chlorine gas cylinders killed 5 people and sent more than 55 to the hospital. A more extensive chlorine gas cloud could have extreme consequences. Pentagon officials said the tactic has been used at least three times and has become a new weapon for insurgents. This adds to the need for not only disinfection alternatives to chlorine gas, but also on-site generation of chlorine where it remains in use.

Much must be done to ensure a level of protection that is commensurate with the vital importance of securing such a critical public service as the provision of water. Many of the benefits associated with achieving this goal go well beyond the singular aspect of homeland security. As such, the expenditures designed to ensure the integrity of the water infrastructure represent a unique opportunity for investors going forward. We are only beginning to scratch the surface relative to enabling analytical technologies, but security institutions must be established that aggressively promote and facilitate the use of these technologies.

Drinking water professionals have been aware for a long time of security issues surrounding the provision of drinking water to the public, from securing reservoirs and wells to protecting treatment facilities, to guarding materials on those facilities to the distribution system. Working vigilantly to safeguard our most valuable natural resource, water systems around the nation have had emergency preparedness and response plans in place for many years. They work closely with local, state, and federal officials to identify emergency scenarios and develop strategies for cooperative responses. Many have enlisted the support and resources of professional organizations and agencies, such as the AWWA and the EPA to assist them. Since 9/11, water systems across North America have revisited their emergency response plans and begun taking additional steps to protect treatment plants and pipes.

In the United States, $2 billion has been spent among water suppliers nationwide to address basic physical security needs,[6] but much more is required to reach sophisticated levels of protection. A number of analytics companies are positioning to address the need for improved water quality monitoring devices and sensors to bolster security throughout the water infrastructure. The identification and epidemiological classification of pathogens is central to a vast number of regulatory mandates and policy issues. Advanced analytical methods such as genotyping are becoming increasingly important, particularly in identifying pathogens in drinking water. While not yet a universal tool, gene probe technologies for finished water analyses have significant potential to monitor plant performance.

Chemical security is becoming a big issue for water and wastewater utilities in the next several years. Currently, they are not subject to the Chemical Facility Anti-Terrorism Standard, such exemption being characterized by policymakers as a "significant gap in the regulation." In addition to a congressional removal of the exemption, the possibility of a legislative requirement for "inherently safer" technologies could shift the demand among treatment chemicals, in particular gaseous chlorine used in disinfection. Alternative disinfection methods were previously discussed as one of the compelling investment themes due to the generation of harmful disinfection by-products, and the security issue just adds to that case.

There are a number of public firms that manufacture the instrumentation equipment used to measure the parameters of water quality. Few, however, are pure plays in water instrumentation, but a number have other water and water-related activities, which adds to the possible investment attraction. See Table 10.2.

Table 10.2   Water Analytics

Name	Symbol or SEDOL	Water Segments or Brands	Water Activity
Danaher	DHR	Sigma; Hach	Samplers; extensive line of analytical systems
Teledyne	TDY	Isco	Water samplers
General Electric	GE	Ionics	TOC, carbon, oxygen demand analyzers
Emerson Electric	EMR	Rosemount/ Emerson Process-Water	Analyzers/sensors for range of water quality parameters; PlantWeb digital automation architecture; Ovation SCADA server
O.I. Corporation	OICO	Chemistry analyzers	TOC/VOC analyzers
Strategic Diagnostics	SDIX	On-site tests	Tests/analyzers for range of water quality parameters (e.g.,toxicity, microbial, metals)
Halma Plc	0405207	Palintest	
IDEXX Laboratories	IDXX	Water quality products (7%)	Microbial contamination test kits (Colilert)
Horiba, Ltd.	6437947	Analytical instruments and systems	Water Division: water analysis instruments; online and portable water quality measuring systems
Dionex Corp	DNEX	Instrumentation	Ion/liquid chromatography for wide range of water contaminants; regulated and emerging
Waters Corporation	WAT	Instrumentation	Liquid chromatography/mass spectrometry
Agilent	A	Instrumentation	GC, GC/MS and LC equipment

Chapter 11

Water Resource Management

W hile water resource management is intended to encompass ecological precepts, most, if not all, philosophical ecologists would cringe at the notion of combining water resources with the term *management*. At best, water resource management would be chastised as "shallow ecology"; at worst, indignation would arise from the anthropocentric arrogance implied by the "management" of nature. So-called deep ecology allows only biocentric values, and, ideally, preservation. To the chagrin of investors, the objective of profiting from water becomes oxymoronic. All of a sudden, water resource management doesn't sound so bad and becomes very useful as the "string theory" between ecology and economics. And, in all candor, this is the best that can be expected at this juncture.

While *water resource management* is a term of art in the environmental sciences, it has virtually no parallel recognition in the business world as anything close to an industry classification. Needless to say, there is little associated investment analysis of water resource management companies and none that thoroughly encompass the attributes of the sector envisioned herein. There is a great deal of overlap in the existing framework of water stocks analysis between infrastructure, resource management, treatment, and environmental consulting companies. In this respect, new ground is being broken. More will be said in concluding chapters about investing in the Age of Ecology, but for now the objective is to identify a water industry sector of companies that are positioned to assist in bridging the "knowledge" gap between the severe water problems of the present and the ecocentric solutions of the future.

Water Resource Management Defined

Water resource management is, therefore, the term used to describe an interdisciplinary approach to reconciling human needs and activities (human ecology) with the planet's hydrologic cycle. It represents a systems-oriented approach to the integration of the principles of resource sustainability with complex water challenges. Restated, the rationale behind the resource management sector represents the embodiment of a comprehensive, forward-looking, integrated approach to solving water resource issues and ensuring sustainable use for the benefit of future generations. As forewarned, it is far from a perfect designation and, accordingly, the companies within the category are less than perfectly aligned with the concept. But this topic is far too important for us to avoid the interim state of flux.

The sectors that are tangential to water resource management are delineated by limiting treatment to equipment and systems suppliers, infrastructure as centered on distribution (once the water leaves the plant) and resource management as including the environmental engineering and consulting services (E/C) firms that are theoretically technology and product neutral but are engaged in system design and construction. This makes more intuitive sense because treatment companies are not responsible for plant build-out, infrastructure should be more focused on the delivery network, and E/C companies design and specify the plant systems in concert with environmental considerations. It is important, therefore, to understand not only what the dimensions of water resource management are, but the types of companies, existing and future, that are likely to benefit from capturing the shift to sustainability.

The Principle of Sustainability

There are as many definitions of resource sustainability as there are ideas about how to achieve it. To complicate matters, the notion of sustainability is so overapplied that the value of its intended message has become blurred. It is not that the anthropogenic bias in many definitions is necessarily problematic from an environmental perspective but that sustainability is suggested as an economic activity, the outcome of which is presumed to be satisfactory, rather than focusing on the limitations imposed by the carrying capacity of the environment and then working backwards to avoid that limitation indefinitely. There is no "sustainability" inherent in nature. Only change itself is sustainable; in other words, nature is "kept" sustainable by changing. But before this commendable movement is vilified, recall that sustainability is one of the goals of water resource management.

Economics and Sustainability

Sustainable resource usage cannot be divorced from economic development. Even Aldo Leopold, who laid much of the foundation for modern ecological thought, recognized the inevitability of economic development. In his pivotal essay on the land ethic,[1] Leopold stated that, "a land ethic of course cannot prevent the alteration, management, and use of [these] 'resources,' but it does affirm their right to continued existence, and, at least in spots, their continued existence in a natural state." This speaks to the reality that absolute resource preservation would have a chilling effect on economic development, but falls short of the instantaneous gratification encompassed in the exploitive implications of the "wise-use" principle espoused by early conservationists (discussed subsequently).

A line in the sand must be drawn in order to effectively address the planet's current water crisis. And while the tide of ecology can erase the demarcation, to be subsequently redrawn, it is logical to expect that much more progress must be made in elevating the level of healthy drinking water available and basic sanitation before preservationist thought will creep into the mainstream. Witness the problems with the Kyoto Protocol that drew a line in front of the economic expansion of developing countries that is proving to be so difficult to gain international consensus, especially from emerging economies.

Sustainability must obviously be defined before there is any chance of achieving it. In this respect, economic theory can serve as a starting point. Granted, the conceptual framework used in economic models to address environmental issues necessarily views the environment as an asset, which may be repulsive to some. But the sustainable use of nature's capital implies that the asset must not be diminished; if you tap into your capital, you move from a sustainable to an unsustainable condition. You may not have to file for bankruptcy, but your heirs will. This fits nicely with the sustainability criterion that emerges from Rawls's hypothetical "veil of ignorance" example in deriving a general theory of justice. At a minimum, sustainability requires that future generations are left no worse off than current generations. Despite the subjectivity in defining "no worse off," this criterion allows a society to judge the fairness rather than the efficiency of water resource usage; if the use or abuse of our water assets in one period impairs the usage by future generations, then that violates this sustainability criterion. Therein lies the importance of the "veil"; all members of present and future generations decide on the rules for allocating resources among generations without knowing which generation they will be a member of. Hypothetically, then, they will not be overly preservationist nor overly greedy.

The intriguing attribute of this definition of sustainability lies in what it does not preclude. Namely, it is not unjust for current generations to avail themselves of resource availability at the expense of future generations as long as they do not make them worse off. This exclusion is particularly timely given the debate over energy policy and the frenzy over dependence on foreign oil; its application to water is not far behind. Accordingly, despite the fact that the present exploitation of a depletable resource precludes its future availability, it is not valid to conclude from the criterion that this violates the sustainability principle. Remember, it would run afoul of sustainability only if the consumption caused future generations to be worse off. To deplete oil reserves while transitioning to renewable sources of energy is a sustainable policy. If, however, the depletion of oil and the burning of fossil fuels alters the atmosphere to the detriment of future generations, then that is not acceptable under the criterion.

The implications for water resource management now become apparent. If the consumption of water interjects scarcity (e.g., the depletion of groundwater or the lack of conservation) or degrades water supplies (industrial contamination) or alters the environment (ecosystem impairment), sustainable management practices must take the marginal cost into account. The oil analogy becomes useful yet again. If we continue to deplete oil reserves through the use of fossil fuels in energy generation, the cost of alleviating global warming must be included in determining the efficient resource allocation. Why not require oil producers to acquire carbon credits for every barrel sold? Otherwise, the maximum sustainable yield is not synonymous with efficiency. With respect to water resource management, sustainable use must incorporate the marginal cost of alternative supplies, advanced treatment, and conservation initiatives. The challenge then comes back to the methods, whether market-based, institutional, regulatory, or altruistic, by which sustainability is achieved.

Water Policy and Sustainability

The critical question, then, is how is sustainability being incorporated into water policy? An example of this is encompassed in the shift in policy emphasis toward managing water resources at a scientifically practical level; that is, based on watershed units. At first blush, this may seem overly broad. But, by definition, watersheds penetrate everywhere, from a backyard to the Mississippi basin. The scalability of watersheds enables policy making to take place on a variety of levels and facilitates many key water resource management initiatives such as nonpoint source pollution, reuse and recycling, and the determination of water quality impairment through the Total Maximum Daily Load (TMDL) program.

Watershed Initiatives. Water quality improvements have traditionally focused on specific point sources of pollution, such as wastewater discharges, or specific water resources, such as a river segment or wetlands. While this approach may be successful in addressing readily identifiable contaminants, it often fails to address the more complex and chronic problems that contribute to water quality. For example, pollution from a wastewater treatment plant may be significantly reduced by advanced treatment technologies, yet a receiving body of water may still be contaminated if other factors in the watershed, such as runoff, go unaddressed. Watershed protection is emerging as a central tenet of water resource management and promises to be a significant area of growth for companies engaged in the business.

Watersheds are the basic land unit of the hydrologic cycle; all land on Earth is in a watershed. Watersheds are defined as the topographically delineated geographic area of land that drains water, sediment, dissolved materials, heat, biota, and the like, to a common outlet. The drainage system (and the watershed) includes the geographic area surrounding the stream system that captures precipitation, filters and stores water, and determines water release into stream systems. Since watersheds are defined by natural hydrology, they represent the most logical basis for managing water resources.

Many water quality issues are better solved at the watershed level than by addressing individual problems within a watershed. Watershed management attempts to comprehensively address natural resource issues in a manner that includes multiple jurisdictions and cuts across political boundaries, integrates concerns about surface water and groundwater quality and quantity, and coordinates insights from the natural and social sciences. A holistic watershed management approach provides a framework for addressing all stressors within a hydrologically defined drainage basin instead of viewing individual sources in isolation. Unique to the concept of watershed management is recognition of the relationship between land use, soil erosion, and productivity; water quantity and quality; wildlife populations and habitat; and social and economic factors. It is a systems approach rather than a single-pollutant approach to solving water quality problems.

The federal budget backs up the economics of this approach with a number of watershed initiatives. The Watershed Protection Approach

(WPA) describes efforts within the Environmental Protection Agency (EPA) and other federal, state, and local agencies to use a watershed-oriented approach to meeting water quality goals. The WPA is a comprehensive methodology that takes into account all threats to human health and ecological integrity within specific watersheds. To some extent, this approach requires a departure from the EPA's traditional focus on regulating specific pollutants and pollutant sources and instead encourages integration of traditional regulatory and nonregulatory programs to support natural resource management. The budget also funds the EPA's Targeted Watershed Grant program (formerly called the Watershed Initiative) that encourages the implementation of water quality trading programs on a watershed basis.

In addition to these programs, the EPA strongly supports the development and issuance of National Pollutant Discharge Elimination System (NPDES) permits on a watershed basis. The EPA believes that watershed-based permitting can:

- Lead to more environmentally effective results
- Provide greater opportunities for trading and other market-based approaches
- Reduce the cost of improving water quality
- Foster more effective implementation of TMDLs
- Facilitate regulatory integration of key water programs

In fact, there is a great deal of interplay between watershed management initiatives and existing requirements under the Clean Water Act of 1977. For example, water quality standards are the driving force behind state water quality programs, and one goal of any watershed management plan is the ultimate attainment of water quality standards.

Watershed-based permitting is defined as an approach that produces NPDES permits that are issued to point sources on a geographic or watershed basis to meet watershed goals. There are numerous permitting mechanisms that may be used to develop and issue permits within a watershed approach. The most common approach is to reissue NPDES permits according to a rotating basin schedule wherein each source receives an individual permit, and the permits are issued based on basin or watershed management areas. Another approach includes a general permit but to categories of common point sources within a watershed, such as all publicly owned treatment works (POTWs) or all confined animal feeding operations or all municipal stormwater discharges. A variation on this is a general permit that collectively addresses all point sources within the watershed. The most significant difference between a traditional general permit and the watershed general permit for common or collective sources is that permit requirements reflect watershed-specific water quality standards. Several other approaches include a watershed-based individual permit that covers multiple permittees and integrated municipal NPDES permits.

Effectively managing a watershed requires knowledge attainable only through thorough research, monitoring, and evaluation. Since watershed protection is largely an information-based concept associated with planning and management rather than the isolated application of treatment methodologies, it is an activity suited for engineering and consulting companies. These companies include a broad range of specialized water resource management projects: integrated watershed planning, Phase II stormwater permits, hydraulic modeling, surface water management, and professional design and consulting services in support of sustainable water and wastewater infrastructure solutions.

Watershed management focuses on water and its interrelationship with everything else in the watershed. The unique environmental, social, economic, and political scene of a watershed must be combined with traditional natural resource science to successfully manage a watershed. Watershed management is a water quality and quantity tool that is rapidly growing in significance as regulators transition from isolated treatment solutions to total water management. Table 11.1 presents a list of companies engaged in the water resource management sector.

The Engineering and Consulting segment has a number of different monikers, including Engineering and Environmental Services; Engineering and Consulting (E/C); and Engineering, Procurement, and Construction (EPC). The environmental E/C tag is the one used herein, but the point is made. These are service firms that provide the technical knowledge to address the broad range of water resource management issues. Most grew from the early days of command and control, where remediation response was more prevalent than prevention.

Table 11.1   Resource Management: E&C Companies

Name	Symbol or SEDOL	Country	Water Aspects
Aecom Technology	ACM	US	AECOM Water; water, wastewater, water resources, watershed management (Boyle, Earth Tech, Metcalf & Eddy); AECOM Environment; remediation, emerging technologies, water resources Earth Tech, ENSR, STS, Metcalf & Eddy)
ARCADIS NV	5769209	Netherlands	Water and wastewater infrastructure, biosolids, advanced treatment technologies, watershed management, and strategic environmental consultancy (Geraghty & Miller); comprehensive water resource management activities
Jacobs Engineering	JEC	US	DoD/DOE environmental restoration; Water Resources Development Act flood control; water and wastewater projects
Shaw Group	SGR	US	Water and wastewater plant design-build; bioreactors, ion exchange, biofiltration, MTBE/perchlorate remediation
Stantec	SXC	Canada	Water supply, treatment and distribution systems including advanced technologies such as membrane filtration, desalination, UV; wastewater engineering with specialization in advanced conveyance and enhanced nutrient removal (MBR); comprehensive water resource management activities
Tetra Tech	TTEK	US	Water supply, wastewater/stormwater treatment, flood control, watershed protection, groundwater; comprehensive water resource management activities
URS Corp	URS	US	Water resources infrastructure activities; water and wastewater, supply planning, water storage and transmission, and water quality management planning; comprehensive water resource management activities

Remediation

With the growing concern of consumers about drinking their own tap water, it would seem logical to assume that such awareness would spill over into the macro environment as well. Consumers are certainly thinking locally, but have seemingly lost interest in the global nature of environmental issues. This partially explains the relatively favorable investment climate for companies engaged in point-of-use water treatment compared to the lagging performance of the broader water remediation stocks.

Perhaps as a result of perceived satisfaction at the individual level, while frustrated about political and regulatory failings, the remediation market has lost the public's attention over the severity of generalized water quality problems. Following the positive outlook of the late 1980s, when environmental issues were highly visible and investors saw the opportunities in cleanup efforts, economic realities and regulatory stalemates have put a damper on the environmental remediation business. The remediation market continues to decline in light of declining governmental work, the successful resolution of many point sources of contamination, and a shift in regulatory priorities and the political will that drives it. In short, remediation activity is a declining portion of the E/C business mix. For investors, the positive fundamentals of these companies rests with the transition toward sustainability and the role of the E/C firms in linking ecological imperatives with economics.

The environmental remediation industry is comprised of E/C companies that apply a broad range of consulting, engineering, and construction services to environmental projects, as well as the equipment and technology firms that service remediation activity with specific equipment and technology. While the lines are becoming blurred, environmental E/C firms are distinguished from other environmental service companies in their role in project management and product specification and by their contractual relationship with the ultimate customer.

The publicly traded environmental E/C firms are generally national firms that are highly diversified and provide varying levels of engineering, construction, and consulting services. Growth in the 1980s and early 1990s was derived primarily from private sector spending to characterize wastes on Superfund sites, to remediate underground storage tank sites, and to facilitate real estate transfers. But the problem with many Superfund projects is that a significant amount of the federal money set aside for site cleanups is spent deciding who is at fault, rather than on the actual cleanup. Because of this, the market for environmental remediation activity has shifted dramatically from private-sector spending on relatively small-scale site assessment and remediation projects toward large-company and public-sector spending on complex site remediation and cleanup.

Public-sector spending was greatly expanded by the Federal Facilities Compliance Act of 1992, which put federal facilities under the same regulatory and oversight framework faced by the private sector. This prompted a significant amount of government action and has been one of the few bright spots in the otherwise beleaguered environmental remediation sector. The EPA has estimated that the cost to restore federal sites and manage the waste could amount to as much as $400 billion over the next 30 years.

Even now, the Department of Defense (DOD) market remains strong as it attempts to resolve the environmental problems in its installation, restoration and base closure programs. Significant military base closures and the desire to transfer the properties to the private sector have provided the impetus for growth in this remediation activity. The DOD and Department of Energy (DOE) estimate that spending over the next five years could reach $65 to $100 billion. Still, new government contracts are difficult to secure and competition is fierce. Contract opportunities have declined, while the number of E/C firms remains high despite attrition and consolidation.

The list of listed E/C firms has declined dramatically in the last decade. Familiar names that fed the growth of the existing E/C behemoths include Air & Water Technologies, Harding Lawson, ICF Kaiser, Dames & Moore, Stone & Webster, Geraghty & Miller, and Fluor Daniel. The dynamics of the industry have led to a significant amount of consolidation activity and a few full-scale meltdowns (e.g., Morrison Knudsen). The need for growth and diversification is fueling acquisitions by dominant players seeking to expand geographically and into capabilities that complement core businesses or open niche opportunities necessary to replace dwindling revenues. Examples include the

Fluor Daniels/Groundwater Technology combination, the purchase of Rust International by U.S. Filter via Wheelabrator Technologies, and the acquisition of Geraghty & Miller by Heidemij N.V.

Firms must aggressively pursue business in new and established selected market sectors focusing on higher-margin, value-added solutions for customers, while controlling costs. International markets, such as the Asia-Pacific region, also hold significant future potential. From an investment point of view, selectivity remains the key to investing in the environmental E/C group. There are many uncertainties associated with the future course of environmental policy as well as the enabling technologies. Many of the small-capitalization stocks, which includes the majority of companies, are experiencing severe earnings deterioration because of technological dependence, niche operations that lack market demand, and the inability to compete with larger firms for full-service procurements. In addition, many of the large-capitalization E/C firms, while of interest because of their exposure to the water industry, also tend to have significant nonenvironmental E/C.

The shift in emphasis from specialized environmental consulting to full-service project management is a result of competitive and cost-containment pressures. This shift will benefit large-capitalization companies because they possess complex project management expertise and the financial strength to deal with liability challenges. Particularly with respect to DOD and DOE contracts, the complexity and size of the cleanup at many of the sites requires E/C firms with extensive project management experience to provide comprehensive assessment, remediation, and closure expertise. This attribute is especially important given the continuing deterioration in private-sector work.

It is anticipated that the remediation business will continue to experience little, if any, earnings growth due to excess industry capacity, a general lack of projects (especially in the private sector), and regulatory uncertainties. In the short run, new growth initiatives seem limited and the group in general lacks earnings visibility with respect to this component of their business. As a side note, the eventual shift toward actual cleanup operations creates significant opportunities for technology and equipment companies that have specific contaminant removal capabilities and innovative new procedures. Bioremediation, for instance, is increasingly being called upon to clean a broad variety of sites and contaminants. Biochemicals firms should benefit, as would equipment suppliers that market cost and efficiency advantages over traditional treatment techniques. While perhaps the riskiest area for investors, new and innovative remediation procedures offer substantial promise as more technologies are proven and approach commercialization.

Due to the duration of the slump in core remediation businesses, there are fewer E/C firms that focus solely on the cleanup of contaminated water. On the positive side, the adjustment to such a stagnant environment is creating possibilities for leading firms in this segment. Diversification into government outsourcing at federal facilities, leveraging core competencies into high-growth remediation activities and shifting from areas that are dependent on regulatory enforcement, are trends that are sure to transform the traditional E/C remediation business. Although the best investment vehicles remain unclear, the magnitude of the market insures that it will remain a key area of the water industry, gaining respect as the segment adjusts to a changing economic and regulatory environment.

Water Supply: Reservoirs and Dams

The construction of dams on the planet's rivers and streams is as old as the human need to augment natural hydrologic sinks with water stores. In modern times, dams have become synonymous with development, inextricably linked to the landscape of economic growth. Unfortunately, they are also tethered to the natural landscape, diverting flows and altering ecosystems. The benefits of dams are undeniable but, to many, the costs are simply unacceptable in an age of heightened environmental and social awareness. And, importantly, negative impacts can often be avoided. The critical need for irrigation, drinking water supplies, and hydropower are likely to overwhelm growing objections to the construction of dams. In addition, the effects of global warming serve to exacerbate the spatial and temporal water problems that dams are constructed to ameliorate. This would be a good place for socially responsible investors to turn the page, for despite the seeming contradiction between sustainability and capturing limited freshwater supplies, the damming of easily accessible surface water is often juxtaposed with sustainable water resource management.

It is not the intent to screen any potential investment associated with the water industry, despite any professional position. The construction of dams is big business, and there is a high probability that many parts of the world will see a dramatic increase in activity. Nelson Mandela captured the state of mind in the developing world at the time of the Report of the World Commission on Dams (WCD) in 2000.[2] In his words, "The problem is not dams. It is the hunger. It is the thirst. It is the darkness of the township." Food plus water plus energy equals economic development. If that was the mentality at that time, you can imagine it is magnified ten-fold in this time of even greater climate change awareness, agricultural demands, and energy volatility.

There has not been a comprehensive study of the number of large dams worldwide since the WCD report. That document put the number of large dams worldwide at a minimum of 45,000. The database of some 80,000 dams of all sizes in the United States was pulled from the web by the Army Corps of Engineers shortly after 9/11. But precision is not required in order to understand the dynamics of the dam and reservoir construction business worldwide. Dams have long been the subject of considerable controversy.

Easily accessible surface freshwater is overappropriated. A majority of the world's large river systems are encumbered by dams. Half of the world's dams were built exclusively or primarily for irrigation. Logically, the number of single-purpose dams built for irrigation is highest in the Middle East, at 86 percent, and Africa, at 66 percent.

The Hetch Hetchy Valley

At no time were the central tenets of sustainability more fiercely debated than in the controversy over the use public lands in the United States in the early twentieth century. The conservationist school, led by Theodore Roosevelt and Gifford Pinchot, advanced the proposition that sustainability meant the "wise use" of wilderness areas. However, the preservationist movement, led by Sierra Club founder John Muir, viewed the absence of human exploitation as the path to sustaining wilderness areas. In other words, to the conservationists, future generations would be best served by wise and scientifically based management of public lands by the current generation. For the preservationists, the legacy was ensured only if left completely untouched.

In 1901, Pinchot and the mayor of San Francisco proposed to dam the Tuolumne River flowing through the Hetch Hetchy Valley (in what is now Yosemite National Park) to supply drinking water for the rapidly urbanizing city of San Francisco. As a geologist and naturalist, John Muir spent many years studying and exploring the wilderness of California's Yosemite Valley and was adamantly opposed to the dam. The stage was set for the iconic controversy of the early American environmental movement. It is constructive at this point to quote Pinchot's description of the wise-use principle:

> The first great fact about conservation is that it stands for development. There has been a fundamental misconception that conservation means nothing but the husbanding of resources for future generations. There could be no more serious mistake. Conservation does mean provision for the future, but it means also and first of all the recognition of the right of the present generation to the fullest necessary use of all the resources with which this country is so abundantly blessed. . . .
>
> The first principle of conservation is development, the use of the natural resources now existing on this continent for the benefit of the people who live here now. There may be just as much waste in neglecting the development and use of certain natural resources as there is in their destruction.[3]

Congress passed the Raker Act in 1913, allowing the city of San Francisco to build the dam and flood the Hetch Hetchy Valley. The divisive battle lasted 12 years, and the war continues today. Having been in remission for over 40 years, the construction of massive dams in the western United States is gaining momentum again, fueled by the need for irrigated crops, inexpensive hydropower, and concerns over climate change. Ironically, the consideration of new dams is rising just as older dams are being decommissioned as a result of environmental concerns. Globally, the advent of large dams continued unabated with potentially devastating environmental consequences and few lessons learned.

The Hetch Hetchy Valley Revisited: The Three Gorges Dam

The Three Gorges Dam is the largest hydroelectric power plant in the world with a width of a mile and a half, rising 600 feet, and flooding 630 square miles along the Yangtze River in China. Officials estimate that the dam will save 50 million tons of coal per year, reduce CO_2 emissions by 100 million tons, prevent massive flooding, generate a substantial amount of the country's electricity requirements, and create a reservoir of 1.4 trillion cubic feet. The dam displaced 1.4 million people to the densely populated hillsides, where landslides and erosion are growing problems. Sedimentation, silting, and nutrient retention not only threaten the dam's efficiency, but also have potentially catastrophic ecological impacts. See Table 11.2.

Rooftop Reservoirs: Rainwater Storage

To end the dam discussion on a positive note, innovation in sustainable water resource management is being planned in Queensland in Australia, where homes are harvesting rainwater. The roofs of the homes provide collection for reuse in nonpotable applications and diversion to advanced treatment systems before being fed into the central drinking water system. The rooftops of houses could be the water reservoirs of the future—the so-called urban dam. The bottom line is that the severity of water problems must be lessened before a foothold can be gained for alternatives to the manipulation of the hydrologic cycle through the construction of dams.

Table 11.2 Reservoirs and Dams

Name	Symbol or SEDOL	Country	Activity
Alstom	B0DJ8Q5	France	Leader in hydro-electric power generation
Harbin Power Equipment	6422761	Hong Kong	Dam construction
Kurimoto Ltd	6497941	Japan	Dam construction
Fomento de Construcciones	5787115	Spain	Dams, canals, transfers, outlets

Irrigation

Agriculture is by far the largest user of groundwater and surface water throughout the world. The agricultural complex could not come close to meeting the demands of our growing planetary population without the irrigation of crops. While almost 70 percent of the world's freshwater withdrawals go toward irrigation, the allocation differs widely across regions depending on a variety of factors such as the role of agriculture within the economy. Within the European Union, irrigation of agricultural land represents about 30 percent of the total consumptive water withdrawals, and most of that is in the southern countries of France, Italy, Greece, Portugal, and Spain. In the United States, irrigation withdrawals are about 40 percent of total freshwater withdrawals. Excluding thermoelectric power, the allocation of freshwater withdrawals rises to 65 percent nationwide.[4] Surface water accounts for about 58 percent of the total irrigation withdrawals, leaving groundwater accountable for 42 percent. In many western states, however, the allocation to agriculture rises to over 90 percent.

In developing countries, irrigation takes on additional complexities. There are many water allocation, conservation, and management issues facing irrigated agriculture in emerging economies. Irrigation plays a major role in food production and food security. In many developing countries, irrigation represents up to 95 percent of all consumptive water use. Future development not only depends on the basic fabric of agricultural activity as an underpinning of economic sustenance, but also places demands on water resources from uses other than irrigation. Many developing countries are dependent upon flows from outside of their borders, thereby increasing regional tensions and the potential for water conflicts. For example, 97 percent of Egypt's total water flow originates from outside of its political boundaries.[5] Population growth, climate change, and shifting diets combine to create demand for efficiently irrigated land; harvests can increase only if additional land is cultivated or if higher yields are achieved.

Technological Flow: Low to High

The demand for mechanized irrigation comes from the following sources: conversion from dryland farming, conversion from flood irrigation, and replacement of existing mechanized irrigation machines. The associated metrics of market potential bears this out. First, world-wide, only 17 percent of agricultural land is irrigated. Second, some 85 percent of global agricultural irrigation is accomplished by the flood irrigation method. Mechanized irrigation can improve water application efficiency by 40 to 90 percent compared with traditional irrigation methods. And third, innovation and improvements in irrigation technology have reduced the life cycle of low-tech mechanized equipment, making the replacement market a significant component of demand. According to the Worldwatch Institute,[6] at least a doubling of water productivity in U.S. agriculture is necessary to meet food demand in a sustainable manner.

Quality Considerations. The quality of water used in irrigation is important for the quantity and yield of crops, maintenance of productive soil characteristics, and ecological impacts. Reduced water runoff from advanced mechanization improves water quality in riparian water bodies such as rivers and streams and in underlying aquifers.

Innovation in Irrigation. The demands on groundwater supplies for irrigation are driving innovation, such as the trend away from flood irrigation (principally used in international markets) to center-pivot systems or localized drip irrigation. The impact of center-pivot systems is best visualized as those lush circles that can be seen as we traverse the country at 30,000 feet. These are true "crop signs," an indication that irrigation is pivotal in squeezing greater yields from crops. While corn-based ethanol is part of the recent irrigation equation, global food demand fueled by rising real incomes in the developing countries is the more permanent fixture. Demand for irrigation is growing rapidly in Brazil, Argentina, and eastern Europe, as well as Australia.

Water and, in some instances, chemicals are applied through sprinklers attached to a pipeline that is supported by a series of towers, each of which is propelled via a drive train and tires. A standard mechanized irrigation machine ("center pivot") rotates in a circle, although extensions ("corner" machines) are available that can irrigate corners of square and rectangular fields as well as conform to irregular field boundaries (referred to as a "corner" machine). One of the key components of the irrigation machine is the control system. This is the information technology that allows the machine to be operated in the manner preferred by the grower, offering control of such factors as on/off timing, individual field sector control, and rate and depth of water and chemical application. Control system innovation allows growers the option of controlling multiple irrigation machines through centralized computer control or mobile remote control It is these features that allow improvements in productivity and address sustainability issues.

Since the purchase of an irrigation machine is a capital expenditure, the decision is based on the expected return on investment. The benefits a grower may realize through investment in mechanical irrigation include improved yields through better irrigation, cost savings through reduced labor, and lower water and energy usage.

Investment Landscape. While there are no significant barriers to entry, competition has largely been consolidated over the years, making irrigation one of the few subsectors that has reached a market-driven structural state. Valmont Industries and Lindsay Manufacturing are the

Table 11.3 Irrigation Companies

Name	Symbol or SEDOL	Country	Activity
Jain Irrigation	6312345	India	Irrigation systems
Eurodrip Irrigation Systems	4151227	Greece	Irrigation systems
Xinjiang Tiayne Water Saving Irrigation	HKG0840	Hong Kong	Irrigation systems
Lindsay Corporation	LNN	US	Irrigation products and management systems; Zimmatic
Valmont Industries	VMI	US	Irrigation products and systems; wastewater reuse in agricultural irrigation; Valley brand

Table 11.4   Resource Management: Other Companies

Name	Symbol or SEDOL	Country	Applicable Segments
Andritz Group AG	B1WV68	Austria	Biosolids; sludge thickening, centrifuges, dewatering, belt drying systems, turn-key plants
Cadiz, Inc.	CDZI	US	Water rights
Bayer AG	2085652	Germany	Efficient water use in agriculture
Flexible Solutions Intl.	FSI	Canada	Watersavr brand evaporation loss control
Halma Plc	0405207	UK	Leak detection/flow analysis (Palmer, Fluid Conservation Systems, Radcom)
Hyflux Water Trust	B29HL02	China	Invests in water infrastructure assets
Itron Inc.	ITRI	US	Water usage information technology
Layne Christensen	LAYN	US	Hydrogeological investigation/modeling
Monsanto	MON	US	Efficient water use in agriculture
PICO Holdings Inc.	OICO	US	Water rights
Pure Cycle Corp	PCYO	US	Integrated water and wastewater service provider

Table 11.5   Resource Management: Multi-Business Companies

Name	Symbol or SEDOL	Country	Applicable Segments
Fomento de Construcciones	5787115	Spain	Full service water management, sewer system maintenance, hydraulic works
Veolia Environnement	VE	France	Total water cycle management
Suez Environnment	B3B8D04	France	Total water cycle management

leaders in the irrigation segment, combining to conservatively account for more than 75 percent of the global irrigation business (see Table 11.3). Because of the obvious seasonality of the irrigation business, both have diversified outside irrigation, but this is one instance in the water industry where it should not be viewed as a negative; the irrigation component is the major earnings driver and will represent an increasing percentage of the overall mix for the foreseeable future.

Tables 11.4 and 11.5 further delineate company groupings engaged in the broad category of resource management.

Chapter 12

Desalination

With nearly three fourths of the earth's surface covered by water that contains too much salt to sustain human life, the prospect of producing potable water from seawater has long held a certain intrigue in helping to solve the planet's water scarcity issues. Desalination refers to the water treatment process that removes salts (dissolved minerals and other solids) from water. Desalting the vast oceans for drinking water is akin to perpetual motion, cold fusion, and, less theoretically impressive, fuel cells. But energy costs have been the perennial roadblock. And rightly so, thanks to those anomalous properties of water. Whether changing phase using thermal desalination or distillation or overcoming osmotic pressure using reverse osmosis membrane desalination, a great deal of energy, and therefore expense, is required to separate salts from water. But that is rapidly changing.

The Promise of Desalination

While large-scale desalting is well established worldwide in areas that have limited or no freshwater supplies, there are also a growing number of applications that utilize desalination technologies as a treatment process. It is the development of variations of existing desalting technologies that enhances the potential for desalination as an economically viable water supply option.

According to the February/March 2008 issue of *International Desalination & Water Reuse Quarterly*, there are approximately 14,000 larger-scale desalting plants worldwide.[1] The total installed capacity is about 10.5 billion gallons per day. The desalination market is expanding significantly, with some estimates approaching 15% per year. The contracted capacity of seawater desalination plants is growing even faster. Desalting equipment is now used in about 120 countries, with almost half of the capacity used to desalt seawater in the Middle East and North Africa. Saudi Arabia ranks first in total capacity, with most of it being made up of seawater desalting units that use the distillation process. At present, Spain is the second-largest market for desalting plants. The estimates of the global number of units and of installed and contracted capacity are not nearly as informative as the percentage of the world's population that is currently served by desalination. Worldwide, that number is only 1 percent, and in the United States, it is less than half of 1 percent.

The Process of Desalination

Desalination is essentially a separation technology wherein saline water is separated into two streams: one with a low content of dissolved salts, the other a concentrate of contaminants. Separation is achieved with traditional technologies such as thermal and membrane processes as well as developing methods such as freezing, membrane distillation, and solar humidification.

The thermal process of distillation includes multistage flash (MSF) distillation, multieffect distillation, and vapor compression distillation. The MSF distillation process uses steam, often from a power plant, to heat seawater to a point at which it is "flashed" or vaporized in a flash chamber. The vapor generated goes through mist eliminators where it is condensed and collected. MSF is a well-established technology developed primarily by foreign companies, including Polymetrics (subsidiary of U.S. Filter/Siemens), MHI/Sasakura and Hitachi Zosen of Japan, Doosan Heavy Industries, and Fisia Italimpianti of Italy.

Multi-effect distillation is another approach that uses distillation fundamentals. This technology is based, not on the principle of flashing, but on evaporation and condensation. Steam is condensed inside horizontal tubes while boiling occurs on the outside. The boiled water, or steam, flows to the next effect, condenses, and then gives up the heat to boil more water. The process is repeated in each effect. The more effects the more water is obtained per unit of steam. Although this technology is supplied by several international firms, the leading company is privately owned IDE Technologies, Ltd. in Israel (although it should be noted that IDE is on track to become a public company). Another version of distillation for desalting seawater is a vapor compression process where a compressor boosts the pressure of the steam and allows it to condense. IDE Technologies, Sidem in France, and Sashkura Company in Japan all provide advanced vapor compression units.

The United States ranks roughly second in overall capacity but with an important distinction. In the United States, most desalination plants utilize reverse osmosis (RO) to treat brackish groundwater (rather than seawater), and the numbers include a significant industrial component. RO is one of two membrane processes used in desalting. In an RO system, impure water is forced under pressure against a semipermeable membrane designed to block passage of impurities and salts. Pressure forces water through the membrane, purifying it in the process. There are a number of RO desalination plant and membrane suppliers. The largest include DuPont, Hydranautics (a subsidiary of Nitto Denko of Japan), Dow Filmtec, Ionics (GE), Koch Fluid Systems, and Toray. Other companies that supply membrane elements specifically for brackish water include Osmonics (GE), PWC/Crane Environmental (Crane), and Toyobo of Japan.

Electrodialysis (ED), another membrane desalination process, allows the passage of ions through ion selective membranes. By applying direct current electric power, the ionized impurities in the feedwater are driven through the membrane cells, desalinating the water. Because of the unidirectional nature of the process, the concentrate side of the membrane is subject to various operational problems. This has led to the introduction of electrodialysis reversal (EDR). In EDR, the polarity is reversed two to four times per hour, providing an automatic self-cleaning system that enables improved efficiency in operation and less downtime for periodic cleaning. Ionics was an early developer of these processes and is by far the market leader in this technology.

In terms of the actual number of desalination units installed, the United States holds the lead. Desalination units have been constructed in every state in the United States. Again, this is due in part to the fact that in the United States desalination technologies are used for a wider application of brackish waters. Here, desalination technologies are utilized in a variety of other applications and are subject to specific economics that create an opportunity for dramatic growth. In most of the United States, the cost of available freshwater supplies has yet to challenge the relatively high cost of seawater desalination. In addition, many inland rivers, such as the Brazos, Colorado, and Rio Grande, contain high levels of salinity. An important aspect of desalting technologies in drinking water applications is that they allow plants to be built in stages to meet demand, unlike traditional water development, with its high initial capital outlay.

The technologies used in seawater and brackish water desalination are also becoming recognized for their potential in pretreating and demineralizing industrial process water and in water reuse. To meet more stringent federal drinking water regulations, water suppliers and businesses are turning to desalting techniques to remove contaminants (dissolved minerals, heavy metals, dissolved organics and pathogens) from groundwater and surface water supplies as well as industrial waste streams. Desalting is also used to treat wastewater for direct or indirect use. For example, vapor compression is ideal for reclaimed water applications.

At the same time that a growing global population is increasing the demand for safe and affordable drinking water, conventional freshwater supplies are disappearing. As a result, many municipalities are faced with transporting water from a distance at great cost, or finding a way to use the presently unusable water that may be within close proximity. In the oceans and under much of the surface of North America and throughout the world, vast quantities of brackish or highly mineralized water can be found, as well as in many lakes and rivers. Desalination technologies can unlock these reserves.

Innovative applications and emerging variations are creating opportunities. These processes are increasingly being used in home water treatment systems, to clean up agricultural drainage and industrial and municipal wastewater, to produce high-quality water for industrial purposes and to improve the quality of drinking water from sources high in dissolved minerals. There are many definitions of salinity with respect to quantifying the "salt" concentration associated with freshwater, brackish water, and seawater. While water with total dissolved solids (TDS) concentrations under 1,000 mg/L are generally deemed acceptable by the World Health Organization in terms of human health, aesthetic factors such as taste and color often dictate treatment options for drinking water sources between 900 and 1,200 mg/L. The Environmental Protection Agency (EPA) suggests that TDS concentrations as low as 500 mg/L are distasteful. The key point, however, is that desalination technologies are increasingly being applied to a wider range of water quantity and quality issues.

Brackish Water Supplies

Under much of the surface of North America and throughout the world, vast quantities of brackish or highly mineralized water can be found, as well as in many lakes and rivers. Desalination technologies can unlock these reserves to augment the existing supply and meet increasing demands. In addition, a growing number of coastal areas are experiencing saltwater intrusion in groundwater wells. Membrane technology, RO in particular, can cost-effectively treat these brackish water sources and is expected to capture a greater portion of the desalination market. As such, this is another positive fundamental for companies engaged in RO systems and membrane manufacturing.

While the large-scale desalting of seawater is well established in coastal areas worldwide, there are also numerous sources of brackish water that can be desalted to obtain potable water. Brackish water is a plentiful, relatively drought-proof water resource for inland populations and reduces dependency on imported water. The sheer number of planned brackish water treatment plants is an indication of its potential as an economically viable water supply option. Especially in the United States, the desalting of brackish water is a rapidly growing market for membrane technology.

Yet water suppliers in the United States have historically not been very responsive to desalination, viewing it as an inefficient, expensive treatment option. But severe droughts, dwindling supplies, growing populations, and cheaper methods of desalting brackish water have created a growing interest among American suppliers. Brackish water, defined by most sources as water that has a TDS content (salinity) ranging from 1,000 mg/L to 25,000 mg/L (i.e., more salts than freshwater but less than seawater), exists in a variety of inland conditions. In the United States, groundwater is the main source of brackish water, but surface waters can meet the definition as well.

The attractive water delivery price for desalinated brackish water provides evidence of how rapidly the cost of desalination has been declining. This has made desalination of brackish water a very viable supply option for many communities around the world. Desalting brackish water costs between three and five times less than desalting seawater. According to the International Desalination Association (IDA), total production costs for U.S. plants treating brackish water range from $0.25/m^3 ($0.95 per 1,000 gallons) to $0.60/m^3 ($2.27 per 1,000 gallons) for systems with capacities of 4,000 m^3/d to 40,000 m^3/d. A representative example of the potential of brackish water reverse osmosis (BWRO) is the world's largest inland desalination plant in El Paso, Texas.

El Paso's water sources include the Hueco Bolson (aquifer) and surface water from the Rio Grande. As a city in the desert Southwest, El Paso desperately needed to embrace a forward-looking strategy to diversify its water sources to meet expected demand. The Department of Defense also recognized an opportunity to supply the strategically important military base at Fort Bliss with a reliable source of water. In a unique cooperative effort, El Paso Water Utilities (EPWU) and Fort Bliss officials collaborated on a brackish water desalination project that increased freshwater production by 25 percent.

The Hueco Bolson provides about 40 percent of El Paso's municipal water supply. But the groundwater is being extracted from the aquifer 25 times faster than it can be replenished, a rate that would easily deplete the Texas portion of freshwater within 30 years. Furthermore, the amount of brackish water in the Bolson exceeds the amount of freshwater by approximately 600 percent. As such, tapping into this previously unusable brackish groundwater represents a major addition to the region's sustainable drinking water supply.

Table 12.1 Desalination Plant and Equipment Suppliers

Name	Symbol or SEDOL	Country	Desalination Activity
IDE Technologies Ltd.	IPO Anticipated	Israel	Broad-based water solutions/desalination
General Electric	GE	US	Ionics/Osmonics
Nitto Denko	6641801	Japan	Hydranautics; membrane supplier
Dow Chemical	DOW	US	Membrane supplier
DuPont	DP	US	Membrane supplier
Energy Recovery, Inc.	ERII	US	Energy recovery devices for SWRO desalination
Gruppo Acciona SA	5579107	Spain	Acciona Agua; water and wastewater plants; RO desalination
Veolia Environment	VE	France	Sidem/Weir
Impregilo S.p.A	B09MRX8	Italy	Fisia Italimpianti; thermal and mechanical desalination
Doosan Heavy Ind.	6294670	South Korea	40% share of multi-stage flash market
Suez Environment	B3B8D04	France	Ondeo/Degremont
Siemens AG	SI	Germany	US Filter
Sasakura Engineering	6786683	Japan	Diverse desalination applications
Mitsubishi Heavy Ind.	6597067	Japan	Seawater and brackish water
Hitachi Zosen	6429308	Japan	Conglomerate; desalination in Power Systems business
Consolidated Water	CWCO	Cayman Islands	Desalination-focused water utility and contractor
Hyflux Ltd.	6320058	HK/ Singapore	Broad-based water treatment with desalination exposure

The brackish water RO plant provides 27.5 million gallons of freshwater daily (mgd); enough to meet the future needs of the city and the base. EPWU has determined that the plant's water production costs are as low as $1.65/1,000 gallons, which is right at the midpoint between the IDA's range of brackish water desalination costs. Approximately 83 percent of the water is recovered, while the remainder is output as a concentrate. Deep-well injection was selected as the ecologically preferred solution to the problem of concentrate disposal. With respect to the financial structure of the plant, $29 million of the $87 million total plant cost was provided with federal money, making it the largest public-public project of its kind in the United States (and hence the name, the Kay Bailey Hutchison Desalination Plant).

Since each desalination application possesses different source water characteristics, it is difficult to generalize much about the comparative effectiveness of the technologies. But there is an identifiable trend toward membrane desal plants. Further, with respect to the participants in desalination, the periodic nature of large desalination plant construction renders a ranking of the global providers somewhat transient. Nonetheless, Table 12.1 summarizes the top desalination plant suppliers.

Given the enormous potential associated with this reliable and virtually unlimited supply of water for the increasing number of water-stressed regions, the fact that there are no exclusively dedicated desalination plant suppliers should not deter investors. The segment is currently dominated by multinational companies that either construct desalination plants as an adjunct to other water and wastewater plant activity (mostly private companies) or as part of a diversified portfolio of businesses that apply their construction expertise to other markets as well. In either case, the actual desalination plant suppliers are generally subsidiaries within larger global companies. Accordingly, investors should first consider companies that are primarily water infrastructure companies, and then select the multibusiness firms where the unrelated activity also meets an investment objective (e.g., hydropower, petrochemical, or nuclear power plants or environmental services).

Despite the somewhat convoluted structure of the current desalination segment, it should be considered an essential core theme for water investors. The rapidly growing desalination market is large enough to offer opportunities for existing participants as well as new entrants to the business. With several hundred private companies competing in the desalination plant market, there is the likelihood of more specialized, particularly membrane, desalination companies going public.

Part Three

WATER BEYOND THE TWENTY-FIRST CENTURY

Chapter 13

Emerging Issues

T he list of issues emerging within the water industry is constantly expanding. Such issues range from regulatory agendas
with respect to individual or classes of contaminants to broader
areas of regulatory concern that are the subject of more comprehensive
programs and research. Regulatory oversight is a complex interaction of
governing institutions and stakeholders with no one model prevailing.
Accordingly, the outcome of many of these challenges is far from clear.
At the same time, the governance of water resources with respect to
human health and ecological considerations represents an enormous
opportunity for investors as these concerns create a pipeline of business
for companies engaged in all aspects of the water industry.

The focus on the U.S. Environmental Protection Agency (EPA),
with respect to the regulation of emerging contaminants, provides a
comprehensive list that is either paralleled in the other developed countries or will provide future guidance for developing countries as they
advance beyond more basic water quality priorities. For example, microbial contaminants are a universal challenge due to the omnipresence

of human pathogens, while perchlorate, an oxidant used in solid rocket propellant, is not likely to be present in the groundwater of sub-Saharan Africa. Given the extensive amount of research undertaken by the EPA, and the very vigorous advocacy climate that monitors this process in the United States, it is reasonable to adopt their water agendas as representative of the future. Emerging topics in the water industry include not only pure regulatory drivers but also economic drivers associated with compliance of existing regulations.

Unregulated Contaminants

It is instructive to peer into the future to determine which contaminants are of regulatory concern. Regulations drive business in not only the treatment sector as the best available technologies are adapted as a solution, or the analytical sector where measurement for occurrence and testing for compliance create additional applications, or the resource management sector where firms are paid to design systems that prevent or processes that remediate, but also, significantly, the water utility sector that must fund the capital expenditure to implement to regulation in the first place.

Contaminant Candidate List (CCL)

In the United States, the EPA is required to maintain a list of contaminants that are not currently subject to any proposed or promulgated national primary drinking water regulations, but that are known or anticipated to occur in public water systems, and which may require future regulation under the SDWA. They are divided into three categories: priorities for more research, priorities for more occurrence data, and priorities for regulation. The EPA is currently on their third version of the list (Contaminant Candidate List 3 or CCL 3), which includes 93 chemicals or chemical groups and 11 microbiological contaminants.

The key is to remember that inclusion on the CCL is still a potential and points to the regulatory risk inherent in the industry. For example, as will be seen, perchlorate has been the subject of exhaustive regulatory debate and, after several states adopted their own perchlorate standards, it was assumed that the EPA would as well. Now the EPA has said that a national standard for perchlorate may never be promulgated. It has been some time since regulatory risk has been a factor for water stocks.

A table of the microbial contaminant candidates and a table of the CCL 3 candidates can be found in Appendix A: Water Contaminants.

Case Study 1: Perchlorate

Perchlorate, a strong oxidant used as an ingredient in solid rocket fuel and in the manufacture of munitions, automotive air bags, and batteries, is showing up in a growing number of the nation's drinking water supplies. Although little research has been conducted on the effect of long-term, low-level exposure to perchlorate, the EPA has included it on the CCL and considers it to be a probable human carcinogen. While the treatment of wastewater containing perchlorate is more established compared to drinking water, there is a rapidly growing need to address the treatment methods for removing perchlorate from drinking water. The perchlorate saga is a case study in the market-driving capability of regulations, this time to the downside. It seemed so probable that a national drinking water standard would emerge that it became the primary attraction for the Basin Water, Inc. initial public offering.

The Science Behind the Regulation. Perchlorate (ClO_4^-) is the most highly oxidized form of chlorine and originates from the dissolution of ammonium, potassium, magnesium, or sodium salts. Perchlorate is an oxidizing anion, but in dilute aqueous solution is very stable and inert and can persist for many decades under typical groundwater and surface water conditions. An important characteristic of perchlorate is its high aqueous solubility, which makes it exceedingly mobile in water. Perchlorate can migrate in subsurface systems substantial distances from the original site of contamination. This contributes to the difficulty in removing low quantities with conventional treatment processes.

Perchlorate is both a naturally occurring and man-made chemical. A major source of perchlorate contamination in the United States is associated with the manufacture of ammonium perchlorate for use as the oxidizer component and primary ingredient in solid propellant for rockets, missiles, and fireworks. Because of its limited shelf life, it must be periodically washed out of missiles and rockets and replaced with a fresh supply. Thus, large volumes of the compound have been disposed of over time.

Perchlorate salts are also used in the manufacture of munitions, automotive air bags, matches, and batteries. Other uses of perchlorate salts include their use in nuclear reactors and electronic tubes, as additives in lubricating oils, in tanning and finishing leather, as a mordant for fabrics and dyes, in electroplating, in aluminum refining, and in the production of paints and enamels. Chemical fertilizer also has been reported to be a potential source of perchlorate contamination. It is because of the diversity in the industrial use of perchlorate that there is serious concern that the occurrence of the chemical will grow now that detection technology has substantially improved.

Wastes from the manufacture and improper disposal of perchlorate-containing chemicals are increasingly being discovered in soil and water. Perchlorate has been detected in water supplies in at least 20 states. Those states most affected by perchlorate occurrence are western states such as California, Nevada, and Utah, where facilities that have manufactured or tested rocket fuels are located. In the western United States, perchlorate is estimated to affect the drinking water of more than 23 million people. In California alone, perchlorate has been detected in 284 drinking water sources. All told, there are 44 states that have confirmed perchlorate manufacturers or users based on EPA information request responses. The possibility of widespread occurrence of perchlorate contamination raises obvious concerns over the effects on human health.

Perchlorate interferes with iodide uptake into the thyroid gland. Because iodide is an essential component of thyroid hormones, perchlorate disrupts how the thyroid functions (i.e., is considered an endocrine disruptor). In adults, the thyroid helps to regulate metabolism. In children, the thyroid plays a major role in proper development in addition to metabolism. Impairment of thyroid function in expectant mothers may impact the fetus and newborn and result in effects including changes in behavior, delayed development, and decreased learning capability.

Changes in thyroid hormone levels may also result in thyroid gland tumors. The EPA's draft analysis of perchlorate toxicity states that perchlorate's disruption of iodide uptake is the key event leading to changes in development or tumor formation. The EPA concluded that the potential human health risks of perchlorate exposures include effects on the developing nervous system and thyroid tumors.

The EPA has not issued a health advisory for perchlorate or categorized it as a priority chemical for regulation. However, because of extensive occurrence data, California has moved to regulate the contaminant. In September 2002, California established the country's first drinking water standard for perchlorate. California currently has an action level for perchlorate at 6 parts per billion (ppb) and has mandated that utilities monitor for its presence. Below 6 ppb, perchlorate is not thought to pose a health risk to humans. Massachusetts has set the standard at a more restrictive 2 ppb.

The EPA's draft assessment includes a reference dose (RfD) that is intended to be protective for human health risks. The RfD is defined as an estimate, with uncertainty spanning perhaps an order of magnitude, of a daily exposure to the human population that is likely to be without appreciable risk of adverse effects over a lifetime. As with any EPA draft assessment document containing a quantitative risk value, that risk value is also draft and does not represent policy. Thus, the draft RfD for perchlorate of 1 μg/L is still undergoing science review and deliberations both by the external scientific community and within the EPA.

Treatment methods for removing low levels of perchlorate from drinking water are also under considerable investigation. Perchlorate is known to resist most conventional treatment processes. Abiotic methods, such as biological treatment and ion (anion) exchange systems, are among the technologies that are being used, with additional treatment technologies under development. Because of the ongoing research efforts on the part of the EPA, there is as yet no best available technology (BAT) designated. Most of the research efforts employ biological treatment methods or ion (anion) exchange technology, although reverse osmosis (RO), nanofiltration (NF), and chemical reduction are being investigated. All ion-exchange processes produce a concentrated perchlorate solution, which must be disposed of or further treated.

Biologically catalyzed perchlorate reduction is also a promising treatment alternative for the removal of perchlorate. Although biologically based treatment of perchlorate-contaminated wastewater has been practiced since the 1970s, biological perchlorate removal technologies have only recently been applied to drinking water. Biologically active carbon (BAC) filtration, which destroys the perchlorate molecule and converts it to chloride, is one approach.

Biotreatment holds a great deal of potential due to the chemical properties of perchlorate. Because the chlorine atom within the perchlorate molecule is in its highest oxidation state, the reduction of perchlorate is highly thermodynamically favorable. Since perchlorate is a strong oxidant (i.e., accepts electrons readily), it provides a large amount of energy to microorganisms as an electron acceptor. Thus, in biologically active carbon, greater reduction of perchlorate is achieved. Because perchlorate is displaced by other ions in water that are more strongly attached to straight granular activated carbon (GAC), GAC filtration has not been shown to be an effective means of remediating perchlorate-contaminated water.

Savvy investors will see that treatment technologies for the removal of perchlorate from drinking water supplies is likely to be a niche growth opportunity within the water industry. But with the EPA's decision not to establish a federal drinking water safety standard for the contaminant, investors also see a good example of the regulatory risk that can, albeit not too frequently, limit a market application. Specifically, a company like Basin Water was very dependent on the promulgation of a federal standard for perchlorate levels in drinking water. It now remains to be seen just how many states will act on their own. This is the purpose behind the several case studies: to impart an appreciation for the impact that regulation, or the lack thereof, has on investments in water.

Case Study 2: Methyl Tertiary Butyl Ether

Like perchlorate, methyl tertiary butyl ether (MTBE) is not a regulated contaminant under the Safe Drinking Water Act. However, since the EPA considers it to be a possible human carcinogen, MTBE is included on the CCL for further evaluation to determine whether or not regulation with a National Primary Drinking Water Regulation is necessary. All large community water systems are required to monitor for MTBE, and the EPA has issued an MTBE health advisory (based on tastes and odors) for drinking water at 20 μg/L (20 ppb or 0.02 ppm).

Made from methanol and a by-product of the oil-refining process, MTBE is added to gasoline to promote complete burning and to reduce emissions of carbon monoxide and organic combustion products, and it is showing up in ground and surface water all over the United States. MTBE is a synthetic compound that was first used in the late 1970s as a replacement for lead to boost octane. In 1990, in response to concerns over air pollution, Congress amended the Clean Air Act (CAA) to require the use of fuels that add oxygen to gasoline. In 1992, the Oxygenated Fuel program was initiated by the EPA to meet these requirements. The program required 2.7 percent oxygen by weight in gasoline in certain metropolitan areas during the winter months. The Reformulated Gasoline (RFG) program, initiated in 1995 also in response to CAA requirements, requires 2 percent oxygen by weight year-round in areas of the United States where air quality standards are exceeded.

MTBE was favored over other potential oxygenates because of its low cost, ease of production, and favorable blending characteristics with conventional gasoline. What was originally thought to be good for air quality has become a curse for water quality. Evidence of the detrimental effects of MTBE on drinking water supplies is mounting rapidly.

As a result, state regulatory agencies are increasingly mandating that MTBE contamination be addressed. California has enacted four bills relating to MTBE and has now adopted the primary contaminant level of 35 μg/L. Dallas imposed its toughest water use restrictions in nearly 50 years after a pipeline rupture spilled 600,000 gallons of gasoline reformulated with MTBE at a site that drains into a key drinking water reservoir. Numerous other states have set regulatory guidelines or standards for MTBE. New Jersey also has a drinking water maximum contamination level standard of 70 μg/L. The concerns are justified.

MTBE is especially problematic because it has a low taste and odor threshold, tends to migrate in subsurface systems much faster than other constituents of gasoline, and is difficult to remove from water at low concentrations via conventional treatment processes. MTBE, like other ethers, is hydrophilic, meaning it has a chemical attraction to water molecules. In fact, it is 30 times more soluble in water than other compounds of gasoline. Once MTBE is in groundwater systems, its high aqueous solubility makes it a fairly mobile contaminant. In addition, MTBE partitions weakly to soil and resists natural degradation. As a result of these factors, MTBE contamination spreads farther and faster in groundwater than other gasoline components.

The main sources of MTBE in groundwater supplies are leaking underground storage tanks and pipelines, spills, contaminated sites, and MTBE manufacturing and storage facilities. The primary sources of MTBE in urban surface water supplies are releases from gasoline-powered recreational watercraft and atmospheric deposition through precipitation of industrial or auto emissions. Stormwater contaminated with MTBE from gasoline leaks and spills also contributes to groundwater and surface water pollution.

Water industry officials generally support the EPA's position but emphasize that existing contamination must also be addressed. According to the American Water Works Association (AWWA), communities around the nation face $1 billion in potential MTBE cleanup costs, yet no federal funds have been allocated to pay for it, nor has a best available technology been identified to deal with the problem. To this end, the EPA has assembled a work group to conduct field evaluations of technologies and processes to treat drinking water and groundwater contaminated with MTBE. Compared with other components of gasoline, MTBE is more difficult to remove from contaminated water. There are several treatment technologies that have been advanced for the removal of MTBE.

The more commonly considered strategies include air stripping, advanced oxidation processes (e.g., UV photooxidation or chemical oxidation such as ozone hydrogen peroxide), biological filtration, and adsorption with activated carbon or other sorbents. Because of MTBE's relative inability to partition to the vapor phase, air stripping is less effective for MTBE removal than for other volatile organic chemicals usually encountered in contaminated groundwater. Advanced oxidation processes can be effective for destroying MTBE, although the concurrent formation of bromate from ozone or ozone hydrogen peroxide treatment may be a concern for some water supplies. Application of biological filtration following oxidation can reduce the concentrations of oxidation by-products. Removal via activated carbon adsorption is typically not cost effective for MBTE, but other sorbents are being examined for their efficacy and cost effectiveness. These findings support the consensus view within the water industry that typical water treatment processes designed for removal of other organic chemicals are not adequate for MTBE removal.

Other approaches that are being examined include application of traditional processes in series, optimization of existing treatment systems, and use of novel sorbents. Calgon Carbon, for example, has introduced Filtrasorb, an activated carbon product that is used in combination with the company's adsorption systems and is specifically designed to remove MTBE from water. Groundwater remediation has been achieved by air stripping within specially designed density-driven convection wells. And pilot-scale compost-based biofilters have been developed with the ability to degrade MTBE. The bottom line is that there is not yet a clear consensus on a cost-effective solution for the removal of MTBE.

The United States produces, distributes, and consumes extensive quantities of gasoline, much of which contains MTBE. It is the third most produced organic chemical in the country. The concern is that we have only seen the tip of the iceberg with respect to MTBE contamination. A substantial amount of research is therefore being conducted on issues related to MTBE health risks, effects on air quality, environmental occurrence, fate and transport, site remediation, and water treatment technologies. As the research mounts, it is evident that the cleanup of MTBE will be an emerging niche within the water treatment business.

Case Study 3: Arsenic

After a lawful limit of 50 ppb for nearly half a century, and considerable debate, the EPA lowered the level for arsenic to 10 ppb in 2006. In a classic example of the trade-off between the protection of public health and the cost of compliance, the science behind the debate prevailed, identifying the potential risks to human health. The prevalence of arsenic in the environment, and the potentially significant impact on numerous drinking water systems, ensures that arsenic removal will be a niche growth market for treatment technologies.

Arsenic is an extremely poisonous semimetallic element. It is both a naturally occurring substance and an industrial by-product. Arsenic ranks about 52nd in natural abundance among the elements in crustal rocks and can combine with other elements to form inorganic and organic arsenicals. It is primarily the inorganic forms that are present in water and are of greatest concern. Most arsenic enters water supplies from erosion of natural deposits in the Earth's crust or from industrial and agricultural pollution. The weathering of rocks, burning of fossil fuels, volcanic activity, forest fires, and mining and smelting of ores also contribute to releases in the environment and can lead to contamination of groundwater.

Commercial arsenic has been used in the manufacture of glass and military poison gases, for the hardening of lead, and as a pesticide. The most common compound, chromated copper arsenate, makes up 90 percent of the industrial arsenic in the United States and is used to pressure-treat wood. Arsenical compounds are among the most widely distributed elements in the earth's crust and in the biosphere. The presence of arsenic in drinking water is of global concern. In Bangladesh, for example, it is estimated that 25 million people are exposed to arsenic levels far above 10 ppb from millions of shallow wells tapping groundwater supplies.[1] In the United States, arsenic is found at high concentrations in western mining states.

The International Agency for Research on Cancer has classified inorganic arsenic compounds as demonstrating sufficient evidence of being skin and lung carcinogens in humans. Long-term exposure to even low concentrations of arsenic can lead to skin, bladder, lung, and prostrate cancer and may lead to kidney and liver cancer. Noncancerous effects include cardiovascular disease, diabetes, and anemia, as well as reproductive, developmental, immunological, and neurological effects. Studies indicate that arsenic disrupts the glucocorticoid system; that is, it is an endocrine disruptor. Furthermore, arsenic promotes the growth of tumors triggered by other carcinogens.

The Safe Drinking Water Act amendments require the EPA to set the maximum contaminant level for contaminants such as arsenic based on peer-reviewed health effects research, studies of treatment, analytical

methods, occurrence, and cost-benefits. After delays in setting a standard, a number of groups grew concerned that the EPA was unnecessar-
ily prolonging the process. Lawsuits by the Natural Resources Defense
Council prompted the Clinton administration to propose a standard of
5 ppb in drinking water. After industry protests, it was set at 10 ppb, and
three days before Clinton left office the 10 ppb standard was adopted.

The Bush administration, however, suspended that action, citing
costs to local communities and questioning the scientific basis behind
the new standard. According to an AWWA Research Foundation study,
a 10-ppb standard would cost drinking water suppliers nationwide
$600 million a year, with capital costs of $5 billion. While the compliance costs are admittedly going to be high, the report by the National
Academy of Sciences stated that the EPA had greatly underestimated
the risks to public health.

Christie Whitman, the EPA administrator from 2001 to 2003, asked
the academy to study the health effects of establishing a standard of 3,
5, 10, or 20 ppb. At each level, the study found that the cancer risks
were much higher than the EPA had estimated. The academy report
stated that, even at 3 ppb, the risk of bladder and lung cancer from
arsenic exposure is between 4 and 10 deaths per 10,000 people. The
EPA's maximum acceptable level of risk for the past two decades for all
drinking water contaminants has been 1 death in 10,000. As a result of
seemingly compelling scientific evidence, the Bush administration had
no choice but to accept the tougher arsenic standard. On October 31,
the EPA formally announced the new arsenic standard of 10 ppb in
drinking water. Despite the delays (the initial rule was promulgated
in January 2001), the compliance date for the new standard was January
23, 2006.

According to the AWWA, nearly 97 percent of the water systems affected by the rule are small systems that serve less than 10,000
people each. The EPA will provide technical assistance and training to
the operators of these small systems in an effort to reduce their compliance costs. The agency will work with small communities to maximize grants and loans under current State Revolving Fund and Rural
Utilities Service programs of the Department of Agriculture. The effectiveness of a given treatment process depends on the type of arsenic
compound being removed and the oxidation state. Many technologies

perform most effectively when treating arsenic in the form of arsenic(V). Arsenic(III) can be converted to arsenic(V) through preoxidation. Oxidants such as ferric chloride, potassium permanganate, ozone, and hydrogen peroxide are effective for this purpose. Several conventional processes are effective for the removal of arsenic, including coagulation with ferric sulfate or alum, lime softening, activated alumina/adsorption, and ion exchange. Other technologies that can potentially meet the lower arsenic standard include RO, NF, and electrodialysis reversal (EDR).

Coagulation and lime softening are not appropriate for most small systems because of the high cost and the need for trained operators. In addition, these methods alone may have difficulty in consistently meeting the lowered arsenic maximum contaminant level (MCL). Activated alumina can also be inefficient to the extent that adsorptive capacity is lost with each regeneration cycle. For systems with existing conventional treatment, implementation of enhanced coagulation may be a feasible option. Ion exchange can effectively remove arsenic and is recommended as a BAT for most small groundwater systems with low sulfate and total dissolved solids levels. Each of these methods suffers from the problems associated with concentrated waste streams and sludge disposal.

RO can provide removal efficiencies of greater than 95 percent when operating pressure is ideal. If RO is used by small systems in the western United States, 60 percent water recovery will necessitate an increased need for raw water. Water rejection in the RO process is an issue in water-scarce regions, and recovery leads to increased costs for arsenic removal. Although NF has slightly lower removal capability than RO, water recovery levels can be lower, thereby allowing for greater efficiency. When compared to RO and NF, EDR is not considered to be competitive with respect to costs and process efficiency.

Since it is anticipated that the new arsenic standard will disproportionately impact small systems, point-of-use (POU) technologies are considered a viable option for arsenic removal. For POU methods, the key is to clearly define the size of the community where cost alone would make it a preferable alternative. For systems without existing treatment or small systems, membrane technologies offer a versatile approach. There are a wide variety of companies that engage in arsenic removal technologies. Clearly, there is a substantial amount of research and development that must yet take place to demonstrate the relative cost effectiveness of new and existing arsenic removal methods. Until the results of numerous studies have been analyzed, it is difficult to predict a single best technology. Investors must be patient as the EPA continues its research efforts.

There is probably more information to support the arsenic rule than most regulations that have been adopted in the last 30 years. At the same time, some believe that the arsenic standard could be the most expensive drinking water regulation ever. It is this combination that creates a positive outlook for technologies that cost-effectively remove arsenic from drinking water. Given that arsenic contamination is a global problem, companies that provide solutions in this arena should experience increased demand for their products and services.

Biosolids Management: There's Money in Sludge

The management of wastewater treatment by-products is a business that continues to undergo transition subject to a regulatory landscape that is fraught with peaks and valleys. The potential growth in biosolids management is fueled by the need for treatment and disposal of growing quantities of product and the fact that residuals can be a beneficial resource. At the same time, the commercial use of biosolids is hampered by a negative perception associated with sewage sludge that politicians and consumers are having a hard time getting around. On balance, while the growth rate may be modest by current market standards, the residuals management segment remains a viable growth component of the water industry.

Dispersion of biosolids at sea is no longer permitted, and there is pressure on dischargers to use land-based options other than landfills. The Water Environment Federation estimates that 36 percent of biosolids are recycled, 38 percent landfilled, 16 percent incinerated, and 10 percent disposed of in other surface methods. Concerns with leachate control is likely to continue to divert organics like biosolids away from surface landfill disposal, and changes in air emission standards limit the use of biosolids incineration. In short, the demand for higher-quality biosolids will greatly influence processing choices. The EPA estimates that 7.1 million tons of biosolids were generated in 2000 and that by 2010 the amount will have increased to 8.2 million tons.

The labels given to wastewater by-products are often confusing and sometimes misleading. The shift in nomenclature from "sewage sludge" to "biosolids" underlies the intention to encourage the beneficial use of certain classes of waste materials. The term *biosolids* appears in the preamble of the Part 503 regulations that govern residuals. Coined by the Water Environment Federation, this term refers to those solids produced by domestic wastewater treatment and septage that can be beneficially reused. *Webster's Collegiate Dictionary*, Tenth Edition, defines biosolids as "solid organic matter recovered from a sewage treatment process and used, especially as fertilizer." But the EPA, to be consistent with language used in the Clean Water Act (CWA), often uses the term *sewage sludge* for the same type of material. The key concept is that biosolids are derived through the treatment of sewage sludge to quality criteria levels.

The requirements of the Part 503 biosolids regulations are very extensive and complex, including sections on land application, surface disposal options, strategies to reduce pathogens and vector organisms, and incineration. Overall, the regulations seek to encourage the reuse of sewage sludge while protecting public health and the environment; that is, it is a risk-based rule. The rule sets national standards for pathogens and limits for 12 pollutants with potential for adverse effects on humans and the environment.

Spurred both by regulation and technological advances, the cost-effective treatment, disposition, and management of sewage sludge is a controversial yet growing business. It is clear that the mandate on sludge reuse and management is a priority in the EPA's regulatory scheme. Because of a lack of outlets for the beneficial use of biosolids, the current investment opportunity is primarily one of equipment manufacturers and service providers. As advanced treatment technologies are utilized to generate high-quality biosolids, the industry will be able to tap into markets with greater commercial appeal. This eventuality favors the residual management companies that provide solutions to the entire spectrum of municipal needs.

Biotechnology

In addition to bioremediation, there are a number of possible uses of biotechnology in the water industry. While conventional water and wastewater treatment methods utilize a variety of biological processes, the potential lies in commercializing new and innovative technologies that develop as products or services. Biochemical products for the consumer market, bioindicators, on-site testing and cleanup applications, and waste minimization through biological technologies are examples of first-generation biotechnology applications in the environmental industry.

One of the more intriguing areas of bioenvironmental research is biosensors, which combines biotechnology with materials and electronics to produce sophisticated monitoring devices for detecting pollutants in water. The first generation of biosensors utilizes immunoassay technology. This new technique relies on an antibody that is developed to have a high degree of sensitivity to the target compound. In the environmental industry, immunoassay methods provide timely, cost effective, and accurate information on contamination levels of key pollutants. Strategic Diagnostics Inc. is a leader in the development of immunoassay-based test kits for environmental contaminants.

Regulation

The regulatory environment is critical to investors because it helps drive the allocation of resources within the water industry. A review of the regulatory trends, legal mandates, and the EPA's docket reveal the direction of policy issues and identifies the industry segments that may benefit as the regulations are implemented. Drinking water regulations are intended to reduce the risk of adverse health effects from exposure to contaminants that may be present in tap water. Specifically, the EPA has the authority and obligation under the Safe Drinking Water Act (SDWA) to set a National Primary Drinking Water Regulation (NPDWR) for contaminants. The 1996 amendments to the SDWA mandated the establishment of a series of new drinking water regulations. Since then, the EPA has been actively developing, proposing, and finalizing a number of regulatory actions. These regulations largely determine the landscape of the water industry and the framework for the provision of drinking water.

Several NPDWR revisions are currently in progress under EPA rule-making procedures. The agency is proceeding with revision of the

Total Coliform Rule (TCR), which is intended to address unintentional fecal contamination and monitoring. Related to the TCR is a consideration of regulations targeted at distribution systems. The TCR, however, does not address the possibility of deliberate biological contamination of source waters and distribution systems. A consideration of deliberate microbiological contamination will require rethinking of not only how indicator organisms are used to reveal microbiological contamination, but also reconsidering which organisms should be monitored and what analytical techniques should be used. This is one factor that supports growth in the use of diagnostic tools and analytical devices.

Another regulatory front, and an area of considerable debate, is the proposed rule-making regarding Total Maximum Daily Loads (TMDLs). Much of the current TMDL debate focuses on the CWA efforts to control point sources of pollutants. Municipalities are concerned that implementation of the TMDL program will translate into increased controls on point source pollution, leading to significant increases in resources needed to meet the federal mandate. Despite the fact that the Water Pollution Program Enhancement Act of 2000 authorizes financial resources for programs related to implementation of TMDLs, the AWWA believes that it is critically important to include nonpoint source controls in the regulatory scheme. The EPA, however, has indicated that this will not be addressed in the final TMDL rule. Much more debate on the TMDL program can be expected, given the high-stakes nature of the outcome.

The EPA has also released the proposed Ground Water Rule (GWR), which specifies the appropriate use of disinfection in groundwater and establishes multiple barriers to protect against bacteria and viruses in drinking water systems that use groundwater. The proposed rule is the first to extend protections to underground sources of drinking water and will apply to all 157,000 U.S. public water systems that use groundwater. The GWR was issued as a final regulation in late 2001. The GWR must be promulgated no later than the promulgation date for the Stage 2 Disinfectants/Disinfection By-products (D/DBP) rule.

Currently, only surface water systems and systems using groundwater under the direct influence of surface water are required to disinfect their water supplies. A monthly source-monitoring requirement is included for systems that are "sensitive" to microbial contamination or have contamination in their distribution systems. In addition, a compliance-monitoring requirement applies to all groundwater systems that notify states they disinfect in order to avoid source water monitoring, and to systems that disinfect as a corrective action. The proposed strategy of the GWR addresses risks through a multiple-barrier approach and will clearly benefit the disinfection and monitoring segments of the water industry.

As expected, the EPA proposed slashing the current arsenic standard from 50 μg/L ppb to 5 μg/L parts per million (ppm) to reduce public health risks. The significance of the current proposal is that this is the first time that a maximum contaminant level (MCL) has been set higher than a feasible level based on cost-benefit factors. The AWWA has recommended that the standard be set no lower than 10 μg/L. The proposed arsenic rule will impact many community water systems and provide additional protection to at least 22.5 million Americans. It is estimated that the lower arsenic standard will cost $1.5 billion annually. Water systems in western states and parts of the Midwest and New England that depend on underground sources of drinking water will be most affected by the proposal. The BAT for meeting the proposed standard includes ion exchange, activated alumina, RO, modified coagulation-filtration, modified lime softening, and EDR.

Another significant debate is swirling around the regulations for the balance of radionuclides (primarily alpha and beta emitters, radium, and uranium). The balance of radionuclides is an extremely complex regulation, due to the very nature of radiochemistry, and due to the different isotopes involved in the rule-making. Because of this complexity, and the difficulty in implementing the monitoring requirements, the costs associated with the regulation are expected to be significant. Other areas of regulatory activity include the implementation of aluminum standards, revisions to the lead and copper rule, and the chloroform maximum contaminant level goal (MCLG) (which is driven by the disinfection by-products rule). Each of these regulations requires advanced filtration technologies and/or alternatives to existing treatment methods.

Water utilities are giving particular attention to planning for compliance with the anticipated Stage 2 D/DBP rule and the associated Long-Term Enhanced Surface Water Treatment Rule (LTESWTR). Although the EPA is still developing a proposed rule, the Stage 2

Federal Advisory Committee Agreement contains enough detail for water systems to begin planning for their compliance with these rules. This would entail an evaluation of disinfection by-products data, identifying actions that could be taken to reduce DBPs, and evaluating alternative microbial treatment technologies.

While regulations are an important factor in generating demand for a particular process, technology, or capital investment, the reality is that compliance costs money. And given the usually substantial cost of these mandates, funding is often a concern. The Drinking Water State Revolving Funds (DWSRF) legislation is, therefore, of great interest to municipalities and firms supplying the water industry. Through DWSRF, public water systems can get assistance with financing the costs of infrastructure needed to achieve or maintain compliance with regulations. These funds can be used to develop and implement programs for capacity development and source water protection.

To date, Congress has provided $3.6 billion in funding for the DWSRF program. By the end of the 2002 fiscal year, the EPA expected that 2,100 loans will have been made and more than 450 DWSRF-funded projects will have begun operating. To further address drinking water infrastructure needs, $825 million has been requested by the EPA for the DWSRF in the 2002 fiscal year budget. Despite the fact that appropriations are nowhere near what the water supply community would like to see, the DWSRF legislation continues to be a crucial mechanism by which technology is transferred to the marketplace. The bottom line is that this funding helps fuel demand in several segments of the water industry, namely, privatization initiatives, new treatment technologies, and infrastructure development.

Filtration and disinfection methods that deal effectively with microbial concerns are likely to receive increased attention. Monitoring (diagnostic and analytical) is also seen as a high-growth segment due to importance of cost-benefit analysis, information gathering, and compliance.

The draft proposal of the Stage 2 D/DBP rule contains an MCLG for chloroform, a by-product of chlorine disinfection, of 0.070 mg/L. This would be the first nonzero MCLG ever set for a carcinogenic contaminant. The draft requires a comprehensive program of identifying peak DBP levels over the entire distribution system and sets a time frame to comply with the current total trihalomethanes (TTHM) standards. The draft of the Long-Term 2 Enhanced Surface Water Treatment Rule (LT2ESWTR) seeks to enhance the existing level of protection against pathogens afforded by the interim rule. The preproposal draft requires most filtered and unfiltered surface water systems to monitor for *Cryptosporidium* for the first time and sets the stage for the use of ultraviolet (UV) disinfection.

While regulations are an important factor in generating demand for a particular process, technology, or capital investment, the reality is that compliance costs money. And given the usually substantial cost of these mandates, funding is often a concern. The DWSRF legislation is, therefore, of great interest to municipalities and firms supplying the water industry. Through DWSRF, public water systems can get assistance with financing the costs of infrastructure needed to achieve or maintain compliance with regulations. These funds can be used to develop and implement programs for capacity development and source water protection. Despite the fact that appropriations are nowhere near what the water supply community would like to see, the DWSRF legislation continues to be a crucial mechanism by which technology is transferred to the marketplace. The bottom line is that this funding helps fuel demand in several segments of the water industry, namely, privatization initiatives, security, new treatment technologies, and infrastructure development.

The BATs for complying with these regulations are a good way of anticipating treatment trends and the relative demand for competing technologies, equipment, and services. Filtration and alternative disinfection methods that deal effectively with microbial concerns are likely to receive increased attention. Monitoring (diagnostic and analytical instrumentation) is also seen as a high-growth segment due to the importance of cost-benefit analysis, information gathering, and compliance.

Regulating Nonpoint Sources of Water Contamination

In broad terms, the sources of water pollution can be categorized in two ways. One is contamination that originates from an identifiable point, for example, the end of a pipe or a channel. The other is nonpoint sources, which affect water quality in a more indirect and diffuse way, such as agricultural activity or urban runoff. With point sources of pollution firmly entrenched in the regulatory scheme, the EPA is stepping up its activity to address nonpoint sources—a challenge with significant water quality implications. Given this developing interest, the management of nonpoint sources of contamination is an emerging investment theme moving forward into the next decade of water quality protection.

It is estimated that as a result of the gains made in controlling point sources, nonpoint sources now compose over half of the waste load borne by the nation's waters. In retrospect, the enormous environmental impact of nonpoint sources now appears to have clearly justified a more balanced regulatory policy. Historically, in contrast to the control of point sources, the EPA was given no specific authority to regulate nonpoint sources. This type of pollution was seen by Congress as a state responsibility and is a large part of the paucity of regulation regarding nonpoint pollution.

Nonpoint sources of contamination do not exhibit the same economic characteristics as point sources. That is, a particular source cannot always be isolated with some specific activity held accountable. Because of this, economics cannot govern as efficiently. While some market solutions have emerged, such as point/nonpoint trading formats, as a means of creating additional point source discharges, the regulation of nonpoint sources must be intensified. And this is the case as the EPA has promulgated an extensive array of regulatory mandates aimed at dealing with nonpoint sources of water pollution.

The EPA is developing a strategy for strengthening nonpoint source management and intends to dramatically pick up the pace in nonpoint source control and watershed management. The initial focus is on runoff. The EPA has adopted the approach of best management practices for the control of urban nonpoint stormwater runoff. Under the final rule, municipalities must ensure that new construction projects have proper stormwater management systems in place. Stormwater runoff is seen as the major contributor to nonpoint water contamination.

Stormwater is posing an increasing problem as runoff transports pollutants, such as sediment, fertilizers, pesticides, hydrocarbons, and other organic compounds and metals, such as lead, into water bodies. This has major ramifications for the degradation of coastal life zones and the eutrophication of freshwater bodies. In addition, gravity collection systems often overflow and backflow during storms. As a result, flow is only partially treated at the wastewater plant or is bypassed to the nearest stream or river. Increased volumes of runoff also negatively affect groundwater elevations and lessen the volume of water percolating through the soil, thereby lessening the dilution of contaminants entering groundwater. Overflows carry untreated pollutants into watercourses, and backflows can affect the homes of collection system customers.

The overflow and backflow occurrence is commonly ascribed to infiltration and inflow (I/I) and is a continuing problem despite newer construction techniques and system components (joint design, pipe material and installation, and manhole fabrication). An early response to the problem was to overdesign for peak storm I/I. As much as eight times normal dry-weather peak flow capacity was provided in the 1950s. Yet, after just a few years, sewers all too typically ran full during storm events. Because manhole lids were bolted down, pressurized sewers delivered much more flow to the plant than could be fully treated.

Still today, problems associated with stormwater runoff, sanitary sewer overflow, and combined sewer overflows are attacked in a rather haphazard fashion by operators and engineers. Collection mains and overflow outlets are often localized solutions that only treat the symptoms of the problem. The EPA is working with the wastewater industry to standardize sanitary sewer overflow control policy. The operators of wastewater treatment plants and collection systems are concerned about the way that discharge permits are applied to sanitary sewer overflows and that the requirements of the CWA are consistent with engineering realities and health and environmental risks. Their concerns are justified.

According to EPA reports,[2] which are used to establish infrastructure priorities, the United States needs nearly $140 billion over the next 20 years to meet wastewater treatment requirements alone. The three greatest components over the next 20 years were not surprising. They include nearly $45 billion for controlling combined sewer overflows, $44 billion for wastewater treatment in general, and $22 billion for new sewer construction. In addition, the EPA estimates $10 billion for upgrading existing wastewater collection systems, $9 billion for nonpoint source control, and $7 billion for controlling municipal stormwater.

From an investment point of view, the infrastructure challenge of controlling nonpoint sources of water contamination can be broken down into several components. There are the basic products used in wastewater and sewer systems like concrete and steel pipe and tunnels or high-density polyethylene. Also in this category are the appurtenances, such as valves, backflow devices, and pumping equipment, that are required in nonpoint control systems.

Another segment that will certainly grow in importance is technology—that is, the companies that provide technological advances in nonpoint source pollution control. Also of interest are the new technologies that are emerging in response to specific nonpoint problems such as stormwater and agricultural runoff. For instance, a pelletized compost medium that traps particulates, adsorbs organic chemicals, and can remove heavy metals has been patented. The filter medium is put into radial-flow filter cartridges that are inserted into precast vaults or custom-designed structures and placed, for example, underneath parking lots and next to highways. The technology is promising as a passive stormwater treatment method that goes beyond sedimentation and filtration and requires less land than conventional stormwater treatment methods.

Due to the magnitude and complexity of agricultural runoff, microfiltration systems are being designed specifically to remove nutrients, sediments, selenium, and pesticide residues. The application of sophisticated technologies in addressing nonpoint source pollution creates a substantial opportunity for filtration, microfiltration and separation companies.

Another segment that has applications to the nonpoint source theme is based on the need to monitor and measure the effectiveness and cost efficiency of any practice or system to meet the inevitable nonpoint regulations. Metering, real-time data collection, and monitoring programs will more effectively control nonpoint contamination in the future. Sewers can then be designed and operated with an optimal peak capacity rather than overdesigning as an approach to controlling peak flows.

For various institutional, economic, and regulatory reasons, nonpoint sources have not received the proper allocation of resources that is deserved, given the impact of this category on water quality. It is clear that uncontrolled nonpoint sources of water contamination must be addressed with the same vigor that point sources have been regulated to date. The EPA is committed to dealing with this area, starting initially with stormwater runoff, but the costs will be high. While the specifics of any regulation of nonpoint sources are a long way from being known, the nature of best management practices will certainly encompass structural modifications and technological advances in dealing with the problem.

Water Reuse

Despite an understandable lack of public acceptance toward drinking treated wastewater, the fact is that all water is eventually reused—the hydrologic cycle is a closed system. The notion of water reuse can take on a variety of applications, from groundwater recharge to industrial recycling to direct potable reuse. The common thread is economics; different uses and reuses can be addressed with differing water quality levels. It makes little sense to use water treated by RO, for instance, to flush toilets. It is the necessity of differentiating water supply needs that will inevitably govern the growth of water reuse.

While on a macro scale water has traditionally been thought of as a replenishable but depletable resource, the accumulated degradation of supplies and burgeoning demand has modified its economic status on a micro level. Because of the imbalance of supply and demand, and the lack of a workable structure to achieve local equilibrium, water reuse presents a mechanism to efficiently allocate water, that is, replenishing a depletable resource through "recycling."

Water reuse generally refers to the use of wastewater following some level of treatment and is often analyzed in terms of an emergency water supply, a long-term solution to a local water shortage, or a fringe benefit to water pollution abatement. Water reuse can be inadvertent, indirect, or direct. Inadvertent reuse of water results when water is withdrawn, used, treated, and returned to the environment without specific plans for further withdrawals and use, which nevertheless occur. Such use patterns occur along many rivers and, in fact, are accepted as a common and necessary procedure for obtaining a water supply. That is, dilution is the solution to pollution.

Indirect water reuse is a planned endeavor, one example of which is using reclaimed wastewater to recharge groundwater supplies. Artificial recharge of depleted aquifers using treated municipal wastewater is increasingly common. Direct water reuse refers to treated water that is piped directly to the next user. For now, the "consumer" is industry or agricultural activity in most cases. But indirect and even direct potable reuse remain viable options.

As competition for groundwater increases, particularly in the western United States, so does the need for innovative ways to manage water efficiently. The National Research Council's Committee on Groundwater Recharge recommends strategies for using artificial recharge in areas where supplies have been depleted. It has not been shown that water recovered from recharged aquifers poses any greater health risks than currently acceptable potable water supplies. However, it is stressed that due to uncertainties and possible health risks, these sources should be considered for potable purposes only when better-quality water is unavailable.

One growth area within the reuse category, therefore, is pretreatment. Wastewater must receive a sufficiently high degree of pretreatment prior to recharge to minimize degradation of groundwater quality and the need for posttreatment at the point of recovery. As the regulations that govern effluent discharged to receiving waters become increasingly stringent, industry—as well as municipalities—has an economic incentive to reuse or recycle process water and wastewater.

Nonpotable reuse is well established in some areas of the United States and is drawing attention in other areas. Since there is not a general regulatory framework for reclaimed water at the federal level, states are responsible for setting the criteria for nonpotable uses such as irrigation and recreation. The question under debate is whether these criteria are adequate to protect public health from chemical constituents and microbial pathogens, including viruses and parasites such as *Giardia* and *Cryptosporidium*.

As an indication of the current interest in this topic, the American Water Works Association and the Water Environment Federation recently sponsored Water Reuse 2001. The conference agenda addressed the latest developments in water reuse technology and applications. While irrigation and industrial, urban, and indirect nonpotable reuse are developing applications for reclaimed water, the challenge is public acceptance and protection in the application of reclaimed water to potable uses. Critical to this evolution, and a major opportunity, are disinfection and membrane technologies that will drive the expansion of water reclamation.

Relative to drinking water regulations, standards were developed piecemeal to address problems in traditional water sources. They do not fully address the problems of converting reclaimed water into drinking water in the areas of virus control and organic matter. As such, significant progress must be made in legislating additional criteria for controlling contaminants in the water reuse process. While surface water augmentation with reclaimed water is being practiced under strict state guidelines, an interim step in the evolution of water reuse is the dual distribution system.

California has taken a leading position on the regulation of water reuse and requires filtered, disinfected water for such areas of concern as swimming and irrigating vegetables. In the Irvine area, reclaimed water has been used for 20 years to irrigate crops and lawns. Now, officials want to expand the use of reclaimed water. Dual water systems, which distribute both potable and reclaimed grades of water to the same service area, are becoming prevalent, particularly in California and Florida. The main disadvantage of building and operating a dual system is economic. In San Diego it was found that unit cost tends to be high for a fairly limited distribution system. As the dual system is expanded, the optimum unit cost is reached. Beyond this optimum range, the unit cost rises and the project's cost effectiveness may be lost.

An advantage of dual systems is that the suppliers that operate the drinking water distribution system can handle the reclaimed water using the same technology. As more systems explore alternative disinfection and advanced filtration methodologies, the opportunity for institutionalizing water reclamation becomes more compelling. In addition, nonmonetary factors such as reliability and environmental effects will increasingly influence the decision.

Two of the largest reclamation systems are in Irvine, California, and St. Petersburg, Florida. The fact that these systems were built without subsidy indicates that they are economical. In new developments, both lines are installed at once, and buildings are plumbed for both grades of water. The costs are low compared with the costs of retrofitting older areas. Thus, as time goes on, dual systems will increase in potential.

It is clear that water reuse is an economic proposition that is inevitable in the future of the provision of water. As a general category, it has yet to fully emerge as an industry segment of the water industry capable of defined investing. Nonetheless, it has broad implications for existing segments such as privatization, distribution systems, infrastructure components, disinfection technologies, and membrane utilization. And as the public accepts reclaimed water as part of the recycling ethic, reuse will secure a permanent position in the scheme of efficiently providing water for all consumptive uses.

Water Conservation

One of the major platforms of the water supply industry in recent times is the notion of water conservation. Having been denounced for the expansion and development of environmentally sensitive and costly water supplies, the only other option in the equilibrium equation available to water purveyors is to reduce demand. The concept has caught on among water providers and the crescendo increases with every annual convention that pays homage to its political might. With such a forceful movement under way in the water industry, the opportunist must ask the logical economic question, namely, who will benefit from the conservation of water?

The conservation issue with respect to water resources is an interesting combination of the characteristics peculiar to the water industry. Why conserve at all? Although only 0.3 percent of the earth's total water supply is fresh water available for human consumption, the absolute amount, some 1 million cubic miles, is very large indeed. Therefore, the argument for water conservation is generally not based on a limited global supply, as it has been with other natural resources. The major reason for water conservation is not its scarcity but rather the environmental costs of supplying it.

An important distinction under the notion of conservation is the difference between involuntary and voluntary conservation. The former is more accurately called rationing and is dictated by municipal authorities, much like the gasoline rationing of the late 1970s. The notion of voluntary conservation is to be distinguished on the basis of behavioral change as a response to institutional or structural occurrences, that is, conservation motivated by economic forces. This is the type of conservation significant to the water industry, both because of the implications of reduced demand and the impetus for new participants to enter the market.

One way to view the investment opportunities in water conservation is by analyzing the various conservation measures. For instance, there is significant investment potential in metering. Water metering is a structural measure that is critical to reducing water demands because users pay according to the actual amount of water they use. Water meters are thought to be commonplace, but some major cities in the United States remain partially unmetered, and as a percentage of taps, unmetered accounts are still large. As imagined, the international potential is huge. Water meter manufacturers such as Badger Meter, Inc. and meter service providers such as Itron, Inc. are direct ways to play the conservation theme. Other companies such as Health Consultants Inc. provide water accountability services such as meter testing and leak detection.

Other conservation measures involve water-saving devices. About 63 percent of residential water use occurs indoors. The bathroom alone accounts for approximately 75 percent of indoor use, so it is an ideal target for municipal water conservation measures. Low-flush and ultra-low-flush toilets use 19 to 28 percent less water than conventional toilets (defined as = 3.5 gallons/flush). The ability to save water by reducing the amount of water consumed in toilets is validated by the myriad of low-flush devices. There is Mini-Flush, Frugal Flush, and FlushSaver, to name a few. But the best way to invest in water-saving devices is through the large, national plumbing fixture manufacturers such as Eljer, Inc. Improved irrigation technology, particularly in agriculture, is another good way to invest in water conservation. Valmont Industries and Lindsay Manufacturing hold over two thirds of the U.S. irrigation equipment market for center pivot and lateral move systems, which address efficiency issues in agricultural water usage.

The basis for residential water conservation is not only the physical amount of water involved but the large—and growing—environmental costs related to its procurement, transmission, treatment, and distribution. While agricultural and industrial water consumption obviously entails environmental costs, there are relevant differences that are addressed within other components of the water industry. Agriculture, which accounts for 85 percent of consumed water, is affected by the dynamics of groundwater usage with little distribution required, and industrial consumption is subject to internal costs that are increasingly captured in the production process. This is not to minimize conservation in other than the residential context but to emphasize that the main reason for developing new water sources is demand from municipal systems, the largest component of which is residential. Conservation would not be a viable concern unless reduced demand had a leveraged impact on costs, both economic and environmental.

The evolution of water conservation from primarily an emergency measure to mitigate short-term water shortages to its new status as a long-term policy concern has challenged the traditional engineering approach to water supply problems. To be institutionalized, water conservation must impact the economic decisions of consumers using water. As such, pricing can be a powerful measure in influencing the amount and timing of water usage. Judging by the political furor that often accompanies water utility pricing policy, it is often not clear just how economic principles are to be applied to water resource problems. Economic principles of resource allocation dictate that when costs are incurred in the acquisition and transport of water supplies to customers, the principle of equimarginal value in use is combined with the principle of marginal cost pricing.

Marginal cost pricing is widely touted in the water supply industry, but few water utilities actually incorporate it into their rate schedules. Concerns over revenue stability and equity often prevail over the logic of charging for the true cost of service. It is precisely because of practical considerations, such as location, use patterns, type of service, and so on, that the marginal costs of serving all customers will not be the same. The consumption characteristics of residential customers indicate that the real price of providing water must increase to reflect the true costs associated with the particular patterns of demand imposed on the system. It is this concept that provides much of the impetus for change in water pricing as a conservation measure.

While the regulatory setting indicates that the real cost of providing water will rise, the conservation trend virtually guarantees it. The use of pricing in particular has a dramatic effect because it links the supply and demand for water. As this occurs, the alternatives to the way we traditionally obtain water—from the tap—become attractive. So, in addition to nonprice considerations (quality concerns) that are currently driving the market for tap-water substitutes, price will reinforce the shift in demand. The answer, then, to the original question as to who will benefit from the conservation of water is that POU treatment technology will gain. The reason for the reluctance of the water supply industry to implement exactly what they espouse then becomes clear.

Nanotechnology

Nanotechnology, at least relative to scale, is nothing new to the water industry. NF is one in a range of filtration methods. In fact, NF is an order of magnitude above where more advanced separation levels occur. By definition, reverse osmosis (also referred to as hyperfiltration) takes place at the nanolevel, dealing with separation in the ionic range, which is much smaller than the molecular range of NF. The interest of nanotechnology to the water industry, however, is more premised on the various applications of nanomaterials than it is the basic filtration of contaminants at the nanolevel. But as important as nanotechnology is to emerging markets in water, the potential market for removing nanoparticles from water represents an enormous, yet still unknown, aspect of treatment. The nanowastewater market is likely to be a huge growth subsector of wastewater treatment, rising in parallel with the widespread commercialization of nanotechnologies.

Algal Toxins

Stormwater runoff, nonpoint source pollution, and wastewater discharge are each distinct water quality challenges. Yet all share a common impact on receiving waters that is becoming a water quality issue in its own right; namely, the increasing occurrence of algae. Combined with a substantial increase in the use of surface water, eutrophication of water supplies presents a growing problem for municipalities. Increased nutrient loading from urban runoff, farming, and improperly treated wastewater has raised the incidence of algal blooms. Toxins produced by algae can have adverse health effects on wildlife, aquatic biota, and humans and is becoming an increasing concern for regulators and treatment plant operators.

The frequency and duration of harmful algal blooms have shown a dramatic increase in recent years. Most occurrences of cyanobacterial (blue-green algae) toxins are caused by nutrient overenrichment or eutrophication. Eutrophication is a process whereby water bodies, such as lakes, estuaries, or slow-moving streams, receive nutrients that stimulate excessive plant growth such as algae. Nutrients can come from many sources, such as fertilizers applied to agricultural lands, golf courses, and lawns, the erosion of soil-containing nutrients, and wastewater treatment plant discharges. The loading is often magnified by decreased water flow caused by improper watershed management or drought. And growing populations suggest that more algae-prone surface waters will be used to meet future demands.

The EPA's CCL includes freshwater algae and their toxins as one of the microbial contaminants selected for regulatory consideration, but it does not specify which toxins should be targeted. In May 2001 a panel of scientists was convened to assist in identifying a target list of algal toxins that are likely to pose a health risk in drinking water. The EPA is reviewing the list and will select the final toxins to be monitored under the Unregulated Contaminant Monitoring Rule (UCMR) when analytical standards are validated. A third of freshwater cyanobacteria are capable of producing harmful toxins. Microcystin, cylindrospermopsin, and anatoxin-a are the toxins identified by the panel as having the highest priority relative to drinking water health effects.

Cylindrospermopsis is an expanding subtropical toxin that has been observed in the waters of many mid-Atlantic states as well as Kansas, Oklahoma, and Florida. An AWWA Research Foundation report found that of the samples collected in utility waters in the United States and Canada, 80 percent were positive for microcystins. It is now being found in finished (treated) water as well. Florida has detected as much as 90 µg/L of cylindrospermopsin in finished water, and several counties served from a plant on the Peace River had water that tested at five times safe levels for microcystin. In drinking water treatment, the coagulation/sedimentation/filtration process is reported to be between 90 and 99.9 percent successful at removing algae, but it is not effective at removing dissolved toxins. Physical removal of cells may be effective for toxins that tend to be retained in healthy cells such as microcystin, but is less effective for toxins that are released by healthy cells such as cylindrospermopsin.

The mechanisms of algal biotoxin's toxicity are very diverse, ranging from hepatotoxic, neurotoxic, and dermatotoxic to general inhibition of protein synthesis. Studies on the occurrence, distribution, and frequency of algal toxins have suggested that hepatotoxins are the most prevalent. Animal and epidemiological studies suggest that low-level chronic exposure to microcystins increase human health risk of cancer and tumor growth promotion in the liver. Cylindrospermopsin's primary target is also the liver, although recent studies have also found it to be carcinogenic and genotoxic (affects fetal development). In animal studies, the effects of this toxin have been widespread and progressive tissue injury, with cell necrosis in the liver, kidneys, adrenals, lung, heart, spleen, and thymus. Although the lack of markers for toxins has hindered the understanding of algal toxin health effects, it is clear that the presence of algae, and the production of secondary metabolites or toxins, is an emerging regulatory issue.

Since the World Health Organization (WHO) has developed a guideline value for the concentration of microcystin in finished drinking water (1 μg/L), the EPA has been reviewing the science behind the study and has accelerated its efforts to make regulatory decisions related to algae. Because regulatory decisions regarding contaminants on the CCL require information on health effects, susceptibility to treatment, and occurrence, a great deal of information gathering on algal toxins must first be completed. One of the main impediments to rule making is the lack of critical information (i.e., occurrence data) that must be obtained through the development and validation of analytical detection and monitoring methods.

Measuring Chlorophyll-a

While gas chromatography and immunosorbent assay methods can be used in a laboratory setting, there is an enormous demand for detection methods in the field as well. Lab analyses can become expensive and do not provide the continuous in-line monitoring desired by extensive field studies as will be required under the UCMR. One way to monitor for algal blooms is through the measurement of photosynthetic pigments, particularly chlorophyll-a, which estimates phytoplankton productivity. For the purposes of long-term monitoring and management programs, chlorophyll-a is the most widely used indicator of algal biomass.

Given the recent advancements in LED technology, the fluorometric method has become practical for field instrumentation. Chlorophyll, when excited by an external light source, absorbs light in certain regions of the visible spectrum and fluoresces (emits) light at longer wavelengths. By measuring the fluorescent intensity, chlorophyll concentration can be inferred, and early detection of toxin-producing algae can be achieved. In addition to the need to measure algae as part of the measurement and eventual regulation of toxins in drinking water, the EPA recommends that chlorophyll-a be monitored as a response variable under its water quality criteria for nutrients within ecoregions.

Algae and the toxins that they produce is an emerging regulatory issue that the EPA is examining. With the realization that algal toxins can pass through many conventional treatment methods, the water industry and regulators are moving forward to advance the science of algal toxins, gather information on occurrence, and ultimately provide guidelines and recommend treatment methods that potentially remove the health threat. The first beneficiaries within the water industry will be the analytical and/or instrumentation companies that develop standard methods for rapid detection, monitoring, and analysis.

Pharmaceuticals and Personal Care Products

Pharmaceuticals and personal care products, known in the water industry as PPCPs and in the medical community as endocrine disruptors, have been detected in trace amounts in surface water, drinking water, and wastewater effluent sampling conducted in both Europe and the United States. PPCPs are a group of compounds consisting of human and veterinary drugs (prescription or over the counter) and consumer products, such as fragrance, lotions, sunscreens, housecleaning products,

Table 13.1 Potentially Strategic Water Investments

Name	Symbol or SEDOL	Water Segments or Brands	Water Activity
Crane	CR	Fluid Handling (Barnes, Deming); Treatment (Crane Environmental)	Pumps; submersible, sewage. effluent; treatment; Cochrane, Environmental Products
Met-Pro Corp.	MPR	Product Recovery/ Pollution Control; Fluid Handing; Filtration/ Purification	Odor control at wastewater plants and degasification for treating contaminated groundwater (Duall/ Strobic); centrifugal pumps for RO, desalination, reuse (Fybroc); POU and industrial water filters (Keystone) and proprietary chemicals (Pristine Water Solutions)
Ahlstrom	B03L388	Disruptor nanotechnology	Water filtration; nanoalumina fibers
Robbins & Myers	RBN	Fluid Management; Moyno, Tarby	Wastewater; progressing cavity pumps, sludge grinders, dewatered sludge transfer systems
Bayer AG	BAY2085652	Water treatment chemicals; Bayer CropScience (Agriculture)	Sustainable water management; drought-resistant, water efficient crop species; pipe coating innovation
Monsanto	MON	Agriculture	Agricultural water use efficiency; drought-tolerant crops and agronomic practices
Ashland Corp.	ASH	Drew Industrial	Municipal and industrial water and wastewater treatment chemicals
Dow Chemical	DOW	Dow Water Solutions; Rohm & Haas, FilmTec, Dowex, Adsorbsia GTO	Leading RO membrane manufacturer (desalination), ion exchange resins, contaminant removal media (arsenic), water reuse and EDI

and others. Water professionals have the technology today to detect more substances, at lower levels, than ever before. These compounds are being found at levels 1,000 times lower than where drinking water standards are typically set. As analytical methods improve, many compounds such as those listed above are being found at extremely low levels, typically single-digit parts per trillion. Drinking water standards are typically set in the parts-per-billion range, which is 1,000 times higher. PPCPs are the subject of extensive research to determine the human health impact from long-term exposure to trace amounts.

The fact that a substance is detectable in drinking water does not mean the substance is harmful to humans. While these trace substances may be detected at very low levels in source waters, people regularly consume or expose themselves to products containing these substances in much higher concentrations through medicines, food and beverage, and other sources. The level in which they are found in source waters is very small in comparison. PPCPs are fairly common in our society and environment and come from many sources. Research on health effects for humans from PPCPs has focused on two areas:

1. While PPCPs are found in very low levels in drinking water, there is a concern of possible cumulative effects of long-term exposure.

2. PPCPs may react in ways that are different from their intended purpose once they are introduced into the environment.

Water professionals are researching the effectiveness of current treatment techniques on removal of PPCPs and other organic compounds. Because of the wide array of chemical structures and properties associated with PPCPs, no one single treatment can remove them all. Technologies under investigation include membranes and GAC, which physically remove compounds, and ozone or UV, which breaks them down. The EPA's CCL does not currently include any PPCPs. See Table 13.1 for other potentially strategic water investments.

Chapter 14

Water as an Asset Class

With the focus on water as a thematic or sector-based investment, the protocol of the financial community is to categorize water neatly within the existing analytical framework. The exercise has proved difficult and the categorical progression telling: services, alternative investments, natural resources, commodities, infrastructure, and now, just water. As water is becoming an investment classification unto itself, it begs the question as to whether an asset-class distinction is appropriate. Water, if it were a class, does not have enough cohesive history to determine long-run return predictability, especially in relation to assets such as oil, gold, and other commodities. The expected risk and return parameters for water are just beginning to be tested by the markets. If similar beta characteristics determine an asset class, then the verdict on water is still out. Resorting to alpha returns (those that beat the markets) is therefore left to directly investing in water stocks or selecting a fund that is managed to earn better returns than the broader asset classes.

For the present, index funds (e.g., water exchange-traded funds) or derivatives can be utilized by investors to achieve a better total risk-adjusted return through a mix of the two sources of return. The discussion in this chapter is intended to contribute to this ongoing dialogue.

Is Water an Asset Class?

Or, perhaps more appropriately at this juncture, *should* water be an asset class? To arrive at a conclusion, it is critical to explore two preliminary questions. First, what is the definition of an asset class? And second, what is the significance of an asset-class distinction? Giving away the ending, water should be an asset class. The easy question first: Why does it matter? The easy answer: It matters to investors. It has been shown empirically that investment performance is predicated more on the timely identification of the optimal asset-class allocation than on the selection of any specific security. In other words, investment performance is more highly correlated with getting the broad asset-class allocations right than with picking the right individual security time after time. In fact, one study found that about 90 percent of the variation of returns of a typical fund is explained by asset allocation decisions.[1] Asset allocation is an adjunct of diversification—the strategy of reducing portfolio risk and volatility through the selection of securities, or classes of securities, that perform independently under varying market conditions. But all of this very much presumes that we have complete knowledge of what the appropriate asset classes are and that we understand the relative movement among and between categories at any given point in global macroeconomic time; that is, what percentage of a portfolio should be devoted to various asset classes? That begs the next question.

What Is an Asset Class?

There are a daunting number of definitions for *asset class*, spanning the spectrum from overly broad to unrealistically narrow. The broader definition is the more traditional, defining an asset class by inclusion. Under this basic definition, an asset class is a grouping of financial instruments with similar features, such as stocks (equities), bonds (fixed income), or cash equivalents. Almost immediately, it can be seen that this definition is not very helpful in a financial landscape that has changed dramatically with a proliferation of new and innovative investment vehicles. This definition is about as helpful as the definition of *class* in the Linnaean taxonomy of living things; that is, below phylum and above order. According to that logic, an asset class is defined as being above an individual security but below an instrument type. Nevertheless, the central point of any classification system is the sharing of characteristics at a specified level of detail.

Continuing the taxonomic analogy, the broad categorization of financial assets into equities, debt securities, and cash equivalents falls more in the kingdom range than class. At the other end of the definitional spectrum, to say that an exchange-traded fund is, per se, an asset grouping (vis-à-vis an index) creates as many categories as there are species on the planet. Can a "category" become an asset class? A finer level of distinction is required, and this still does not accommodate all of the investment vehicles available in this world of derivation. Institutional investors often have an "alternative investments" category that serves as somewhat of a catchall asset class in justification of a broad spectrum of investment strategies. This category typically includes commodities, private equity, real estate, natural resources, and, increasingly, water.

A survey of the literature suggests that the following factors weigh heavily in the determination of what constitutes an asset class:

1. A distinguishing asset definition
2. Consistently independent and identifiable asset movement (beta)
3. The ability to reduce overall portfolio risk
4. Diversification of returns from low or noncorrelation.

Thus, in the traditional sense, it is problematic to say that water is *currently* an asset class.

One must look at the inherent characteristics of the water "market." As argued previously, water itself is not yet a commodity; there are few organized markets for purchasing raw water and certainly no global market for reconciling supply and demand. By and large (assuming that the acquisition of land for the water rights is prohibitively expensive for most), investors must purchase a specific water company or invest with others in a water fund. But water is such a fundamentally distinct asset that its value and usage characteristics will undoubtedly elevate it to asset-class status over time. So, despite the current arguments for and against water as an asset class, the bottom line is that water should be *considered* an asset class in making allocation decisions; it is simply too compelling a theme to be strategically ignored in any portfolio.

Correlation and relationship are vastly different statistical constructs (something climatologists should keep in mind). The problem lies in a lack of definitional precision. Investors explain the correlation between two securities, or two asset classes, as a measure of the *relationship* between price movements. Don't forget that as an economist, I am just a stone's throw from conceding that a dart thrown at the stock page is just as effective as any modern or postmodern portfolio theory. Economic theory focuses on events "at the margin." Investment theory, in contrast, is critically dependent on normally distributed returns, where extreme events are, *ceteris paribus*, assumed to be just too many standard deviations away. If anything, modern financial crises have exposed the reality that standard deviation may no longer be an appropriate metric for risk.

In statistical data analysis, correlation coefficients are used to quantify the strength (magnitude of the number) and direction (sign of the coefficient) of the *linear* relationship between two variables. In financial data analysis, the correlation between two securities or asset classes is mistakenly considered as a measure of the causal relationship between price movements. Enter noncorrelation and the difference between beta and correlation: beta moves with the market (volatility); correlation moves with another asset. *Asset class* is defined as a category of investments that has similar beta characteristics. By definition, then, alpha is a zero-sum game among asset classes (in the spirit of Lester Thurow); one investor's alpha is another investor's lack of alpha. Given that, what is there to do now but to create an index, set up an exchange-traded fund (ETF), and call it an asset class?

Given the problems of modern portfolio theory, the investment community is in desperate search of a postmodern theory of portfolio management to capture a new and greater return labeled alpha.

Unfortunately, rather than improving theory, the financial community simply created more asset classes on which to tout the ability for generating alpha returns. There will come a day when reversion to the mean comes back in fashion.

Water Funds

In addition to direct investing in the water industry, the choices afforded to investors continue to grow through the expansion of water funds and structured products. While historically there have been a limited number of private equity funds and fewer publicly traded mutual funds, the crescendo over investing in water has been building dramatically ever since the launch of the first water ETF, the PowerShares Water Resources Portfolio, in 2005.

The definition of low risk and high returns has shifted back to more fundamental industries. With the volatility in the broad markets reaching unprecedented proportions, many investors are looking for themes that exhibit more stable growth prospects. The dynamics of the water industry fit the model, creating growing interest from investment funds.

During any interval of time, the growth and value investment styles demonstrate very different levels of volatility and investment returns. Investors in growth stocks expect that the long-term earnings potential of the companies that they are invested in will outpace the market's expectations. Value stocks tend to have slower and more stable earnings growth rates, but carry the expectation that at some point in the future, the value will be recognized. One of the attractions of the water industry at this juncture is that many water stocks represent a unique combination of value and growth characteristics. Value is derived from the essential nature and demand characteristics of increasing water consumption. Growth is a function of accelerating earnings as the global water industry transitions to market-based solutions.

Exchange-Traded Funds

Index investing is a common tool in today's investment landscape. An index is a "basket" of stocks selected according to preestablished rules. Indexes serve as barometers for an asset class, a particular market, or a specific industry against which financial or economic performance can be measured. Suffice it to say, contrary to conventional wisdom, that the simple act of forming an ETF does not an asset class make. The unprecedented proliferation—dare I say unbridled propagation—of ETFs has presented investors with an extensive array of choices. When it comes down to capital markets, however, choice is a good thing. The application of index investing to water provides investors with an attractive vehicle for investing in the compelling fundamentals of the global water industry.

The inherently fragmented and diverse structure of the global water industry, comprised of large international companies as well as specialized smaller-cap companies, dictates that the methodology of the underlying index be designed to optimize exposure to a constantly changing industry. Despite the obvious appeal associated with investing in the fundamentals of the water industry through a diversified, tax-efficient, highly liquid product such as an ETF, investors must fully understand the underlying index design and methodology in order to make informed decisions. The goal of this discussion is to objectively analyze the various water index designs and methodologies and the relative merits of each as a proxy for measuring the true potential of the global water industry.

With the number of choices for water investors now expanding, it is critical that investors understand the style and sub-asset-class considerations (such as currency exposure and market capitalization) of the underlying components in order to determine whether a particular ETF coincides with their investment objectives.

Weighting Methodology. The weighting methodology of the index is critical. There are several basic weighting approaches: market-capitalization, fundamental, equal-dollar, and hybrid. The market-cap approach is generally considered one of the less favorable. A market-cap weighted index methodology is intrinsically inefficient and often leads to underperformance. The shortcomings of a market-cap weighted index are magnified in an index based on the water industry where there are a number of very large global companies engaged in water activities that often have a multibusiness structure. A market-cap-weighted index overweights all stocks that are trading above fair value and underweights those trading below their fair value; that is, it overweights the overvalued stocks and underweights undervalued stocks. The sum of these errors impedes the performance of capitalization-weighted indexes. This conclusion has been empirically studied and supported by analysts such as Robert Arnott, among others. The theory is that since the weighting errors cannot be quantified because fair value cannot be known for any of the index components, an index should be constructed in a way in which the errors are randomized.

According to Arnott, "Equal-weighting an index is one good way to randomize the errors. Half of the stocks will be overweight and half will be underweight. Some that are above true fair value will be underweight; some that are below true fair value will be overweight."[2] That solves about half of the market-cap-weighted challenge. This is where Arnott's Fundamental Indexation methodology comes in—to alleviate the problems introduced by equal weighting. As Arnott goes on to say, "So equal-weighting fixes part of the problem but introduces its own, very serious problems. Equal-weighted indexes are capacity constrained, high-volatility, and result in high turnover in some of the least liquid companies in the market." Fundamental weighting based on objective measures associated with a company is his alternative to market-cap weighting. Several water indexes avoid the market-cap-weighted approach and are defined as modified, equal-dollar-weighted indexes. By this it is meant that the indexes are modified to include sectors within the water industry that are fundamentally weighted and within the sectors the components are equally weighted.

Accordingly, not only is the market-cap-weighting objection overcome, but any shortcomings of equal weighting are mitigated; that is, the weight of each stock within a sector is weighted equally based on the overall fundamental weight afforded that sector. Since the fundamental weighting is applied at the sector level, the metrics that are applied by Arnott relative to firm size are not applicable. Here, the fundamentals relate to industry-specific measures such as the size of the infrastructure funding gap, the relative impact of regulations, the price of water, best available treatment methods, trends in resource sustainability, convergent technologies, and so on. This combination of fundamental and equal weighting further randomizes any error variance from alpha and optimizes the returns available to investors in the water industry.

Frequency of Review

The frequency by which an index is rebalanced and reconstituted is another factor to be considered. Generally, more frequent review by the index providers is an extremely positive attribute of index maintenance. Granted, a more frequent rebalancing can lead to tracking errors (temporary time lags) by the ETF managers. But this must be weighed critically against the benefits. Given the dramatic increase in merger-and-acquisition activity in the water industry, the advent of private equity participation, and the overall dynamics of an industry in transition, it is intuitive that a more frequent adjustment is preferable. As has been mentioned, there is significant restructuring momentum under way within many facets of the water industry, and this expected to increase substantially. The number of acquisitions, spin-offs, and initial public offerings is on the rise, and it is anticipated that this trend will accelerate rapidly over the next decade, creating a window of opportunity to invest in water. A sample of stock listings completed or contemplated include American Water Works, Cascal N.V., Mueller Water Products, GL&V, AECOM Technology, Basin Water, Polypore International, Suez Environment, and IDE Technologies. These are the type of events and companies that create significant investment potential within the industry and contribute to the compelling fundamentals. Water investors want exposure to these opportunities as reflected in an ETF as soon as possible.

The Water Universe

The compilation of the "universe" of water stocks from which the index population is selected is equally important. While the water indexes available generally are equivalent in the size and liquidity requirements by which inclusion is determined, the inclusion approaches can vary significantly. The S&P Global Water Index employs a mechanical approach based on a generic search for "water" in the business description. The International Securities Exchange (ISE) Water Index and the Palisades Water Indexes utilize a more selective approach based partially on a qualitative review of a company's contribution to the water industry.

Table 14.1 Summary of Major ETF-Based Water Indexes

Feature	Palisades Water Indexes[a]	S&P Global Water Index[b]	ISE Water Index[c]
Weighting methodology	Fundamentally modified, equal-dollar weighted	Modified market-capitalization weighted	Modified market-capitalization weighted
Rebalance/ Reconstitution frequency	Quarterly	Annually	Semiannually
Index Subclassifications	Six fundamental water sectors	Two "clusters"	None
Index universe	Palisades' proprietary water database	Mechanical search of S&P Capital IQ database	Subjective
Investable universe	Market-cap, liquidity, and water-related requirements	Market-cap and liquidity requirements	Market-cap and liquidity requirements
Index constituents	Fundamentally determined by sector or component	Market-cap ranking	Market-cap ranking
Index maintenance	Palisades' water industry-specific analysis	S&P Global Thematic Committee	Semiannual review by ISE

SOURCE: WaterTech Capital, LLC, and ETF/Index provider information.

Disclosures: (a) Steve Hoffmann is a co-founder of Palisades Water Indexes LLC, the developer of the Palisades Water Index™ and the Palisades Global Water Index™, which are licensed for use by PowerShares Capital Management LLC in connection with the PowerShares Water Resources Portfolio ETF (symbol PHO) and the PowerShares Global Water Portfolio ETF (symbol PIO), respectively. PowerShares is a trademark of PowerShares Capital Management LLC. The Palisades Water Index™ and the Palisades Global Water Index™ are trademarks of Palisades Water Index Associates, LLC. (b) The S&P Global Water Index™ is a trademark of Standard & Poor's, Inc. (c) The ISE Water Index™ is a trademark of the International Securities Exchange, Inc.

The ISE Water Index, however, does not include any water companies traded on an international exchange. The inclusion of foreign companies in an index is a key consideration in allocating investment funds to the water sector. Both the Palisades Global Water Index and the S&P Global Water Index include foreign exchange–listed companies (see Table 14.1).

Table 14.2   Sampling of Water Funds

Name	Type	Index/Manager/Affiliation
Aqua International Partners, LP	PE	Texas Pacific Group
Aqua Terra Asset Management LLC	PE	Boenning & Scattergood, Inc.
Claymore S&P Global Water	CGW	ETF; tracks the S&P Global Water Index
Clean Water Asia	Hedge	Clean Resources Asia Management Pte Ltd
First Trust ISE Water Index Fund	FIW	ETF; tracks the ISE Water Index
Global Water & Infrastructure Fund	Hedge	Perella Weinberg Partners
KBCAM Eco Water Fund	Hedge	KBC Asset Management
Kinetics Water Infrastructure	KWINX	Mutual Fund
PFW Water Fund	Mutual	Crowell, Weedon & Co.
Pictet Global Water Fund	PGWRX	Pictet Asset Management
PowerShares Global Water Portfolio	PIO	ETF; tracks the Palisades Global Water Index
PowerShares Water Resources Portfolio	PHO	ETF; tracks the Palisades Water Index
SPDR FTSE/Macquarie Global Infrastructure 100	GII	ETF; tracks the Macquarie Global Infrastructure 100 Index
The Water Fund	Hedge	Terrapin Asset Management
TRF Master Fund (Cayman), LP	Equity	Water Asset Management, LLC; public and private water-related companies
SAM Sustainable Water Fund	Hedge	Sustainable Asset Management

The Palisades Water Index (index symbol ZWI) was the first index to be published as a proxy indicator of the stock performance of U.S. exchange-traded companies (including American Depositary Receipts and American Depository Shares) engaged in the water industry. It is firmly established as a benchmark water index and is the tracking vehicle for the PowerShares Water Resources Portfolio ETF (AMEX: PHO). The global companion water index is the Palisades Global Water Index (index symbol: PIIWI) and is the tracking index for the PowerShares Global Water Portfolio (AMEX: PIO). The global index components are selected from the full spectrum of global water companies, thereby providing exposure to foreign water companies not easily available to many investors. The Palisades Water Indexes were designed to be a complementary "family" of interrelated water indexes. This approach optimizes the exposure to the global water industry and gives investors a choice when allocating funds to the sector.

The foregoing discussion aside, there is no one "right" ETF to take advantage of the water theme. The various index-ETF attributes may coincide with very different investment-style objectives, and each should be judged accordingly. In addition to ETFs, there is a diverse field of funds that are designed to invest in the water industry. These are structured as hedge funds, private equity funds, or mutual funds. Accordingly, investors must make an independent determination as to management capabilities, investment approach, and fund characteristics. Many are available only to accredited investors and institutions (see Table 14.2).

There is little doubt that water funds (public and private) will continue to proliferate in response to the growth prospects of the global water industry. Associated with this visibility is the danger that water funds will overpromise on returns that, while unquestionably attractive over the long term, may take some time to materialize.

Chapter 15

Climate Change and the Hydrologic (Re)Cycle

V ariability in weather is a fact that the water industry has always had to deal with. What is different about global warming, and more specifically climate change, is that the short-term fluctuations in weather conditions are unprecedented, and longer-term changes in climate appear to be under way. The spatial and temporal variation caused by climate change will all take place at the margin. This has a number of significant ramifications for water resource management. These include:

- Planning for greater uncertainty
- Impacts on water quality
- Operational and structural considerations in infrastructure design
- The inevitability of supply dislocations
- Institutional adaptations

Planning for Uncertainty

If there is only one thing that can be agreed on with respect to the impact of global warming on the water business, it is that the element of uncertainty associated with variations in weather is increasing. While it is not the intent of this book to debate the causes of global warming, there are a number of statistics that cannot be ignored by water providers: greenhouse gases exist at higher levels than in the past 650,000 years,[1] the last eight 5-year periods ended with 2006 were the warmest pentads in the last 100 years of national records,[2] and the western United States is experiencing less precipitation as snow and more as rain. Changes in seasonal precipitation can be more important than annual averages. Even if precipitation is unchanged, higher temperatures make conditions drier by reducing soil moisture, stream flow, and lake levels through increased evaporation.

Water planners take historical statistics into consideration when developing their forecasting models. To the extent that long-term patterns such as temperature, stream flows, snow pack, and the like are impacted by climate change, the assumption of stationarity no longer holds. This has major implications for plant design, capacity considerations, system reliability, and water quality.

Impacts on Water Quality

Few scientists today doubt that the atmosphere is warming. Most also agree that the rate of climatic change is accelerating and that the consequences of this temperature change could become increasingly disruptive. Climate changes can significantly affect the hydrologic cycle and therefore water resources. And while much of the attention has been directed to localized droughts and floods, falling reservoir levels, and strings of record high temperatures, there are more than just quantity issues at stake. There is mounting concern and evidence that atmospheric warming has a negative impact on water quality and will increase the global incidence of waterborne disease.

Weather becomes more extreme and variable with atmospheric heating in part because the warming accelerates the hydrologic cycle. A warmed atmosphere heats the oceans (leading to faster evaporation), and it holds more moisture than cooler air. When the extra water condenses, it more frequently creates a dramatic storm event. While the oceans are being heated, so too is the land, which can become extremely dry in areas. This dryness enlarges the pressure gradients that cause winds to develop, leading to other powerful storms. The altered pressure and temperature gradients that accompany global warming can also shift the distribution of when and where storms, floods, and droughts occur.

Human-induced climate variability is associated with the addition of greenhouse gases that diminish the ozone layer and change the radiation balance of the planet. The more predictable consequences of an atmosphere heated up by a thinning of the ozone layer include warming oceans, shifting agricultural patterns, melting glaciers, and rising sea levels. Yet less familiar effects could be equally detrimental. Revised weather patterns, by upping the frequency and intensity of floods and droughts, promote the emergence, resurgence, and spread of infectious disease. Some of the worst are waterborne.

Warming itself can contribute to the change, as can a heightened frequency and extent of droughts and floods. It seems perverse that droughts would favor waterborne disease, but they can diminish supplies of safe drinking water and concentrate contaminants. Further, the lack of clean water during a drought interferes with good hygiene and safe rehydration. The increased climate variability accompanying warming will probably be more significant than the rising heat itself in fueling outbreaks of waterborne diseases.

Floods favor waterborne disease in different ways. They wash sewage and other sources of pathogens (such as *Cryptosporidium*) into drinking water supplies. They also flush fertilizer into water supplies. Fertilizer and sewage can each combine with warmed water to trigger expansive blooms of harmful algae. Some of these blooms are directly toxic to humans who inhale their vapors. Others contaminate fish and shellfish that are consumed. As algal blooms grow, they support the proliferation of various pathogens, among them *Vibrio cholerae*, the causative agent of cholera.

Drenching rains brought by a warmed Indian Ocean in the late 1990s set off an epidemic of cholera in the Horn of Africa. In the aftermath of Hurricane Mitch, Honduras reported thousands of cases of cholera; floods created by unprecedented rains and a series of cyclones has spread cholera in countries such as Mozambique and Madagascar. In the United States, cholera is not as much of a threat as other etiological agents. Nonetheless, as many as 900,000 cases and 900 deaths from waterborne disease occur annually in the United States. Dramatic outbreaks affecting a community's water supply have been linked to both droughts and floods. Massive flooding also results in contamination from spilled sewage. The largest outbreak of waterborne disease in recent U.S. history (400,000 illnesses and 100 deaths) was due to contamination by *Cryptosporidium* after spring rains in Wisconsin.

The U.S. National Assessment on the Potential Health Impacts of Climate Variability and Change has specifically identified the effect of climate on waterborne disease outbreaks as a research priority. Rainfall and runoff have been associated with individual outbreaks of waterborne disease caused by fecal-oral pathogens. Fecal-oral microorganisms originating from human or animal wastes include bacteria such as *Escherichia coli (E. coli), Campylobacter, Salmonella,* and *Shigella*; viruses such as Norwalk virus, small round structured viruses, and hepatitis A virus; and protozoa such as *Cryptosporidium* and *Giardia.* The transport of water contaminated with these microorganisms is enhanced during periods of drought and flooding.

The effects of extreme weather on municipal water supplies is a growing problem. Meteorological data for the United States show that downpours averaged less than 8 percent of the total annual precipitation at the beginning of the twentieth century and that they had increased to 10 percent of the total at the end of the century.[3] It is not clear whether this increasing trend will continue. However, if the projected changes in global warming translate to climate variability resulting in changes in the frequency, intensity, and geographic distribution of extreme weather in the United States, there is likely to be a significant effect on both drinking water and wastewater systems.

In a recent analysis[4] of waterborne disease outbreaks in 2,105 U.S. watersheds, between 20 and 50 percent were associated with extreme precipitation. The relationship between waterborne disease and storm events was found to be statistically significant for both surface water and groundwater, although it was more apparent with surface water outbreaks. The health toll taken by global warming will depend to a large extent on the steps taken to prepare for the dangers. Many of the current regulatory themes focus directly or indirectly on these issues.

The Safe Drinking Water Act and the Clean Water Action Initiative have both emphasized the need to focus on watershed management. Stormwater runoff is the subject of a great deal of industry discussion. And the control of pathogens is central to numerous regulatory requirements and technological initiatives. Spending on water and wastewater infrastructure is also likely to be influenced by climate variability. When a system is built or upgraded, billions of dollars can be saved if the potential for extreme weather is taken into account. In short, the ramifications of greater climatic variation and intensity will drive demand across the board for the products and services of the global water industry.

Occurrence of Drought

As investors ponder the potential associated with water, one of the first things that comes to mind is drought. In Texas, the summer of 2006 entered the meteorological record books. The National Weather Service reported that the January-through-June period of that year was the hottest since 1895, the year it started keeping records. The average temperature for the period was 5.7 percent above the norm. Precipitation statewide was the lowest since 1998 and 25 percent lower than the 100-year average for the first six months of the year. In fact, the entire Great Plains as well as Arizona and Alabama experienced intensity levels from moderate drought (D1) to exceptional drought (D4). Fully two thirds of the United States experienced abnormally dry, or worse, drought conditions in that year.

And drought is not limited to the United States. According to the Chinese Ministry of Water Resources, hot weather and severe drought recently left 18 million people in 15 Chinese provinces and regions short of drinking water. Although possessing the fourth-largest freshwater reserves in the world, China, by virtue of its burgeoning population, has the second-lowest per-capita water stocks in the world, averaging about 2,200 m^3 of water per person. A generally recognized measure of water "stress" (defined as water scarcity manifested as increasing conflict over usage, a decline in service levels, crop failure, and food insecurity) is 1,700 m³. By 2025, China, as well as India, will be below that threshold.

From a global perspective, one of the first impacts of drought is on agriculture. The drought in China was reported to have damaged millions of hectares of cropland. As previously written, agriculture (read irrigation) is by far the largest consumer of available freshwater worldwide.

Under the pricing schemes imposed by many water utilities, the more water used by consumers, the greater the revenue generated by the utility. Common sense would dictate that in a drought situation consumers would require more outdoor water and therefore revenue for the utility would follow. In fact, water utility stocks traditionally rose and fell according to the precipitation patterns within their service areas. This was why the large, geographically diverse utilities are often a preferred way to mitigate climatological risk. Before the audacity of imposing restrictions on water, the stock price of water utilities was often correlated to the particular amount of rainfall in their operation regions.

The bottom line is that water utilities can no longer be perceived as beneficiaries of drought conditions. Not only do droughts often lead to usage restrictions, but many utilities have rate structures in place that penalize extreme usage to encourage conservation. "Regulatory lag" associated with rising costs ahead of rate relief will increase only for utilities in drought-plagued regions that are constrained by the price granted by regulators as costs are spread over a dwindling consumption base.

Drought conditions also presuppose that a way to alleviate supply shortages is to drill more wells. Pertinent to the prospects for drillers, such as Layne Christensen, demand for water-well-drilling services is driven by the need to access groundwater, which is affected by many factors, including shifting demographics and regional expansions, new housing developments, deteriorating water quality, and limited availability of surface water. Groundwater is a vital natural resource that is withdrawn from the earth for drinking water, irrigation, and industrial use. In many areas of the United States and other parts of the world, groundwater is the only reliable source of potable water. But it is also the main source of irrigation for agricultural production.

Again, droughts can be a double-edged sword. In the United States, the recent droughts in the Great Plains have focused attention on the limits associated with the production of wheat, beef, corn, and other crops. An initial response is to drill more wells, a situation that has clearly driven interest in the stock of Layne. But water costs and conflicts over the vast but shrinking Ogallala aquifer have prompted restrictions on irrigation. For example, Nebraska has put a moratorium on new wells and taken farmland out of production in the Platte River Valley to limit the draw on the Ogallala Aquifer. As demographics shift to more water challenged areas combined with an increasing amount of regulated contaminants and impurities, the demand for water recycling and conservation services, as well as new treatment media and filtration methods, is expected to remain strong.

Investing in Drought

Ruled by the emotion associated with the "preciousness" of water, and without adequately reflecting on just what that means from an investment perspective, many assume that drought equals scarcity equals opportunity. It is prudent to put droughts into investment perspective. It is a far more complex issue than it seems to be on the surface. The occurrence and frequency of droughts dictate that investors understand the implications for water stocks over and above the simplistic notion that scarcity means increased value. Just as the occurrence of widespread drought varies greatly across the planet so does the impact on companies engaged in the water industry. It is the institutional response to drought or water shortage conditions that is likely to determine the extent of the opportunity.

It is important to put the perceived investment opportunities derived from drought conditions in perspective. As we have learned from other resources (oil comes to mind), "scarcity" does not equate to an unbridled shift in economic rents from one group to another. Even with a resource such as oil, which is governed by sophisticated market mechanisms, a point can be reached wherein the structure of the market itself comes into question. This is why it is said that institutional responses to severe droughts, especially under the auspices of global warming, may in some respects serve to shift the financial "windfall" of droughts from one sector to another: that is, from water drilling to integrated resource management and from the depletion of groundwater sources to reuse/recycling and desalination.

Chapter 16

Forward-Looking Thoughts for Water Investors

I f there is one thing that remains certain, even when the fabric of economic systems is unraveling, it is that the foundation of all civilizations are dependent upon the resources that originate from the natural environment.

The advantage of investing in water—even in a difficult investment environment—is that, no matter how you define it, water has intrinsic (i.e., inherent) value. Generally speaking, anthropocentrism and ecocentrism are the philosophical bookends of the intrinsic value continuum. At one end of the spectrum is the belief that nature exists, and is to be utilized, for the benefit of the human species. The contrasting view is that the ecology of the planet is the focus of existence and humans are simply part of the whole of nature. As has been alluded to throughout the book, these contrasting beliefs often bring economics and ecology into a head-on collision And, as has also been suggested, this need not, and should not, create the competition that it presupposes.

In fact, water is truly unique in that it possesses intrinsic value all along the continuum. It is argued by some ethicists that intrinsic value, when viewed as the inherent worth of something independent of its value to anything else, cannot really exist without an evaluator. Such futility aside, at the utilitarian end of the spectrum (recall the economics) the intrinsic value of water is embedded in its utility to mankind. At the biocentric end, the intrinsic value of water rests in its causality of the right of everything to exist. As such, the philosophical underpinnings of the intrinsic value of water can satisfy a very broad range of investment rationales, from price to priceless.

It is in vogue to capture the value of water through the context of the value of oil and to compare the promise of water companies to the evolution of the oil industry. The discussion is important from several perspectives associated with intrinsic value. One is the extent to which the definition of the intrinsic value of oil can be transferred to water. Another is the extension of the economics of oil to the economics of water. And a final perspective is whether a misguided notion of oil's intrinsic value created problems that can be avoided with respect to water resources. These are critical to fundamental investment analysis; that is, determining the underlying value of a water company separate from its stock price. But all of this presumes the validity of the analogy between oil and water.

Is Water the Next Oil?

Like everyone else when it comes to making a decision, investors want a simple "yes" or "no" to the interrogatives that serve as informational inputs. As much as I would relish the opportunity to definitively put to rest the answer to this question, it is simply not that straightforward. Lest I disappoint readers, I will say that in many key respects water will indeed be analogous to the "next oil." This is said based largely upon the perspective from which the question frequently emanates—namely, that water, like oil, is a critical factor in global economic development and the source of potential competitive advantage and conflict.

The flavor of the answer is often dependent on the particular agenda being served, the present investment objective notwithstanding. From an investment perspective it is also necessary to consider a time horizon within which a correlation between water industry dynamics and company performance can be reasonably projected.

Some baseline observations are as follows:

- Oil is a depletable, nonrecyclable resource.
- Water is a replenishable but depletable resource.
- Oil is a private good and commodity.
- Water is often considered a public good.
- Oil has a transferable and enforceable property right structure.
- Water rights, where they exist, are legally variable.
- The price of oil is determined by expectations of supply and demand.
- The price of water is artificially set.
- Oil is an economic commodity.
- The UN has declared access to water a human right.
- Oil is an energy resource for which there are alternatives.
- There are no substitutes for water.

The discussion of the merits of comparing the water business to the modern development of the oil industry is purposefully placed at the end of the book so that readers have had exposure to the myriad of factors that influence the global water market and, therefore, have a frame of reference with which to judge a response. In that regard, the obvious starting point is scarcity.

The "Myth" of Water Scarcity

Scarcity is often cited as a prominent similarity between oil, the commodity, and water, the resource. But this becomes somewhat problematic when science is consulted; there can be no aggregate scarcity of water, but there can be an aggregate scarcity of oil. Granted, this scientific fact means precious little at the practical level of regional or local water distribution. There can certainly be temporal and spatial scarcity and, ultimately, a limit on the carrying capacity of water resources to support a given species-driven mix of life. Accordingly, with water, scarcity is relative:

> If you are born in the tundra, you demand no wood. If you move to the tundra from the forest, wood is scarce. If you are born in the desert, you demand no more water than is available. If you move to the desert from the rain forest, you better bring water with you.

At first blush, these anecdotes seem to take on an air of belligerence and even outright arrogance. Such perception could not be farther from the intent. While the "myth" of water scarcity is not meant to inflame, it certainly is meant to challenge the traditional wisdom. The problem with the management of water resources is that it is led not by scientists, but by managers and politicians. As such, the rhetoric is largely one of semantics, totally divorced from the reality that humankind need not suffer the heinous situation of a lack of safe drinking water. Indulging in that war of semantics, the title seeks to take a provocative position; water is not scarce on Planet Earth; it suffers from allocational and distributional mismanagement.

The vital resource of water is at the inflection point with respect to the capacity to meet the demands placed upon it. To the detriment of many peoples of the world, water is summarily categorized as a public good for which there are textbook remedies that simply cannot meet the complexity of a uniquely ubiquitous resource. Because water can become scarce, it has economic value. But the way in which markets deal with scarcity is very different for oil than for water.

Supply and Demand. Investors are all too familiar with the "sophistication" of the oil markets. Oil as a commodity is an asset class that has an enormous supporting financial infrastructure. Without getting into the artificiality imposed by an oil cartel, the supply and demand for oil is a very fluid mechanism that translates in real time to a price. Nor is it the intent to discuss in detail the difference between movement along the supply and demand curves and shifts in the curves themselves. This is not, however, to be interpreted as a dismissal of the importance of shifting curves since the factors that give rise to changes in positioning represent many of the fundamental drivers of the supply and demand for water going forward, such as the cost of new supplies, climate change, conservation, technological innovation, and food production. A change in the *quantity* supplied or demanded is very different than a change in supply or demand. And a key distinction between oil and water is that, generally speaking, econometric models indicate that the price level of water has had little impact on demand.[1] But that will change; the "diamond-water paradox," along with the institutional structures that pay homage to its origins, is no longer an enigma in an age of a growing water crisis. With respect to true scarcity, the prospect of diminishing oil reserves is most comparable to groundwater (a depletable resource) and the availability of readily accessible freshwater supplies. But again, water is not scarce in the same universal sense that oil is, and where it is scarce, there is no pricing mechanism to bring supply and demand into balance. Nonetheless, water is rapidly approaching oil as a good with the ability to constrain economic development. And there are no substitutes for water.

Water as an Economic Good. The classification of water as a resource, commodity, or public good is discussed extensively in Chapter 3. The conclusions therein were premised upon the current reality and the future imperatives. But the underpinning is clearly that water has significant and growing economic value that is not even remotely accommodated by the potpourri of existing classifications. When compared to oil, there is clearly no glimmer of a commodity-type market for water or clean (refined) water and barely a market for water rights. As such, the supply and demand for water is left to its own devices without the equilibrating benefit of a price. Nowhere in economics is there an efficiently functioning market for a private good without a price.

From the perspective of whether water shares the same position of a fundamental ingredient in standards of living, geopolitical stability, and economic advancement, there is little question that water and oil are analogous. Any invaluable economic good that is disproportionately distributed across the planet possesses the trigger for geopolitical conflict. This is but one reason why water policy makers must learn from energy policy or the lack thereof; namely, are the solutions to a lack of water the same as the solutions to a lack of oil?

Water and Oil Must Mix

On the molecular level, water being dipolar and oil nonpolar, the two cannot chemically mix. But politically, economically, and environmentally, it is imperative that they do. The fact that water and energy go hand in hand is more a testament to their concordance than resemblance. I do not necessarily view the prospect of water's being the next oil as particularly positive. It would be much more in the interest of the water industry, and investors in water, to wish for the advantages associated with water as a pure economic good while avoiding many of the pitfalls associated with oil: geopolitical conflict, environmental degradation, and price instability.

Much is written about the age of "water wars." Yes, wars are waged over oil, and there will certainly be conflicts over water; humans have never been wanting for reasons to go to war. But it is unlikely that there will ever be a geopolitical risk premium in the price of water.

The way that the interrelationships between water and oil are addressed from an environmental perspective is critical to water investors for a number of reasons. First, the water industry has much that can be gleaned from the years of incentive-based solutions to oil industry–related environmental concerns, both successes and failures. Second, energy is a major factor in water production, and any environmental concerns with respect to oil will ultimately translate to water in the form of a cost. Third, climate change is both a water and a carbon problem. The hydrologic and carbon biogeochemical cycles are far more integrally linked than the global warming discussion indicates.

Oil is part of the carbon cycle, while the hydrologic cycle governs the movement of all water. Average temperature and average precipitation are the main determinants of a region's climate. Warmer temperatures create a positive feedback loop for global warming in that they increase water vapor (through increased evaporation of surface water), which in turn can amplify the warming. When both the carbon and hydrologic cycles are considered, global warming becomes exceedingly complex with an exponentially increasing number of both positive and negative feedback loops, the net effect of which is nowhere near understood.

Certainly, one attribute of oil that has yet to play out with water is price instability. Without a market price for water, commodity deflation is not possible. Water may contribute to commodity risk in other commodities, but there is no commodity risk inherent in water. We cannot eliminate oil price volatility, but with a coherent energy policy, it would be easier to manage demand volatility. Water must not succumb to this roller-coaster approach. As an exercise, take the transcripts of the congressional hearings on oil industry profits and substitute the word *water* for *oil*. If we do not come to grips with the reality of our global water challenges, we are destined to replay a scenario where the price of water plays catch-up to decades of institutional mismanagement, and then markets are forced to allocate a scare resource in the only way they can—recalibrating supply-and-demand equilibrium through price. This could lead to rampant price increases and the political will to redistribute profits, an analogy to a windfall profits tax on oil. But before investors rush off to buy water producers and refiners (utilities) under the theory that their coffers will be flush with cash from runaway water rates, consider that a redistribution of wealth caused by a crisis-induced pricing of water will likely take many other more insidious forms: the price of food, geopolitical conflicts, environmental degradation, and a global economic crisis.

Water and the Global Economic Crisis

To every reader: Recognize that in the granularity of the present, you are forging new neurofinancial pathways that will define a post-neomodern portfolio theory. The purpose of this book is to convey the influence and confluence of factors that portend a historic investment opportunity. The current financial crisis only serves to catapult forward the transitions under way in the global water industry. The ongoing deleveraging process is the mechanism for transferring the financial crisis to an economic crisis. And it is the response to the economic crisis that is likely to usher in a realignment (i.e., convergence) of social and private returns. It is not that the deleveraging cycle will disproportionately impact the water industry, but that already fragile governments are leveraged to the point of lockdown.

There will be a capitalist lesson that emerges from this. The lesson may refine capitalism and selectively scrutinize core values, but the structure will survive—stabilizing natural selection, so to speak. It remains to be seen exactly what traits emerge that enable the adaptation of economic systems to the institutional conditions that will have changed in response or reaction to the historic Economic Crisis of 2008.

Cultural Carrying Capacity

I have talked about the concept of carrying capacity with respect to the ability of the planet's water resources to accommodate increasing populations. Carrying capacity is the maximum number of inhabitants (humans included) that an area can support. Accordingly, the planet's carrying capacity is ultimately a scientific construct. Heretofore, and for the foreseeable future, carrying capacity is consistently expanded by human invention and technology. All of this may seem rather nebulous to investors looking at water as a thematic investment strategy. But it is critical for two very important reasons. First, in absolute terms, the water resources on the planet are a mission-critical constraint on the scientific determination as to just how many inhabitants can survive on Earth. Second, and more to the point, the notion of survival explicit in the concept of carrying capacity can be a relative term, especially with respect to the human population. In other words, should the carrying capacity seek to maximize the number of people "surviving" on the planet, albeit at the lowest possible denominator, or optimize some measure of the quality of life for a smaller, more sustainable human population?

The carrying capacity theory of relativity is known as "cultural" carrying capacity. Cultural carrying capacity is by definition less than simple carrying capacity because it encompasses a conscious decision to attain a higher standard of living in lieu of existential survival, that is, to make greater individual demands on the environment as a trade-off to supporting greater numbers. As such, the concept interjects choice into the equation. Choice is a matter of values that are dependent on culture, and cultural values are exactly the impetus behind the formation, structure, and development of our societal institutions. The cultural carrying value is likely to be drastically altered by the economic crisis. The economic and political winds favor a change in the institutional economics of water. But perhaps a larger question is just how will the world respond to the economic crisis relative to changing values associated with cultural carrying value and the way that core values affect the institutions of all types of governance.

Institutional Dimensions of Water

The institutional dimensions of water governance have been advanced as one of the drivers of the developing water industry and the concomitant attraction of investing in water.

Economic prosperity has a propensity to create a divergence between private and social returns, with private returns on top. The advent of a severe financial readjustment such as that experienced by the credit and liquidity crisis unfolding since 2008, and the commensurate political fallout, reverses the priorities and causes a convergence, with private returns falling and social return rising.

Could the rebalancing of social versus private returns swing the pendulum toward water as a public good? Yes, it could, but I do not believe that it will. Instead, I am hopeful that a reevaluation of global governing institutions for the financial system will be extended to other institutional dimensions. For example, the move from an era of water surplus to one of scarcity has not even begun to be institutionally recognized with respect to water. And, hopefully, legitimate institutions will replace the mosaic of nongovernmental organizations that currently seek to set water policy.

The legislative framework associated with the new administration's infrastructure initiatives is a specific example of new institutional dimensions impacting water. All of this portends some interesting possible changes to the "water industry in transition," as we have so often described it. This truly historic global economic situation elicits some concluding points of thought for water investors:

1. Since both the public and private sectors face a severe credit crisis, look for a renewed interest in the economics of public-private partnerships.

2. As a means of financing, municipalities may rediscover the attraction of special-purpose water and sewer bonds to investors based on stable, and likely increasing, water rates.

3. Regulators may "accommodate" the markets by responding with an upward bias in allowed returns in water rate cases.

4. Increased financing costs may provide an impetus for water and wastewater utilities to set rates closer to the market value of water.

5. The attractiveness of tax-free municipal bonds will likely be enhanced under a Democratic administration.

6. Water and sewer municipal bonds provide an attractive way to invest in water utilities without subjecting the investor to equity risk, where increased capital spending could have a negative impact on earnings.

7. Rationalizing the financial structure of water utilities may lead to a rapid acceleration of consolidation in the water provision business.

Water Infrastructure Financing

The global water infrastructure needs and requirements have been presented in detail as a major investment driver for a broad range of water companies. In the United States, much of the water infrastructure is approaching the end of its asset life cycle. Accordingly, capital renewal is the subject of a great deal of consternation among water professionals. Both as a tool to boost the U.S. economy and the follow-through on political platforms, infrastructure projects are likely to get a financial boost in the next (at least) four years. Whether the programs will favor water or other infrastructure projects remains to be seen.

The "New" New Deal

A major component of the economic recovery plan going forward is public spending and job creation through infrastructure spending. In an initiative similar to the Work Projects Administration of the New Deal, legislation is being considered to establish a new system through which the federal government can finance infrastructure projects. As a major component of this plan, public-private partnerships are being strongly considered by policy makers. While it is far from putting the stamp of approval on privatization, this should go a long way in advancing a funding mechanism that fell from favor when credit was free flowing.

For the water and wastewater industry, the areas of spending focus are likely to be in transmission and distribution, inflow and infiltration correction, structural correction of combined and sanitary sewer overflows, sewer replacement and rehabilitation, and collection and stormwater infrastructure.

Municipal Bonds

The focus on investing in water has centered on equities. This is because equities provide the most straightforward vehicle to realizing the gains associated with water market fundamentals. Obviously there are a number of other investment approaches such as convertible preferreds and bonds. Tax-exempt municipal bonds could be of interest to investors only if they become a viable method of raising capital for otherwise unfunded regulatory mandates and infrastructure needs. The attraction of these investments is largely a function of the outcome of the economic crisis that has created a number of dislocations in the market for financial instruments and the possible changes to the tax rates.

While the municipal bond market is one of the largest securities markets in the world, it remains an asset class that is often overlooked by many investors. This is most likely the result of both a lack of exposure to new bond issues and familiarity with the process. Municipal bonds are generally bought and sold not on an organized exchange but in the over-the-counter market. They are priced based on maturity, liquidity, yield, and, currently perhaps most important in the wake of the financial crisis, credit quality. Yield, traditionally the primary factor in analyzing the merits of a municipal bond, may in some cases be out of balance with creditworthiness. In other locations, concern of fiscal credibility is a harsh reality.

Municipals can be broadly classified into general obligation and revenue bonds. Water, wastewater, and/or stormwater systems or projects can be financed with either. General obligation bonds are issued by a governmental authority that has the power to levy taxes for repayment of the bonds. Revenue bonds are issued to finance a specific project or purpose, such as a water or sewer plant expansion or new construction that will generate income (through rates) that are dedicated to the repayment of the bonds.

Currently, though the fluctuations can be wild, municipal bonds in general are yielding a historically high premium to treasuries. That is substantially above the historical relationship and cannot last. The logic is that reversion to the mean relationship between municipal and treasury yields will occur through some combination of U.S. treasuries falling (raising their yields) or municipal bonds rallying (lowering their yields). Treasuries have rallied dramatically as a flight to safety in the wake of the global financial crisis. But with the monumental "rescue" package, numerous bailout deals (Bear Stearns, AIG, Citicorp, and likely more), and a seemingly never-ending extension of cash and guarantees to one after another collapsing credit market, the U.S. treasury doesn't quite look like the same safe haven that it is purported to be. It is not logical to assume that investors would elevate the safety of a municipality over that of the U.S. government, nor is it rational to ignore a tax-free yield. Again, it is the relational disconnect that creates the investment opportunity, not a win-or-lose asset class allocation strategy.

The other side of the argument is that the financial crisis (which impacts income, property, and sales taxes) is only going to exacerbate long-strained municipal budgets by making it even harder and more expensive to raise critical capital through the municipal bond market. This could raise the historically low default rate relative to alternative corporate bonds. Also, bond insurance is a huge issue, that is, the guarantee that the interest payments and principal on the bonds will be paid in case of default. The municipal bond insurers, not to mention the credit rating agencies, were not immune to the subprime mortgage debacle and insured riskier security lines beyond municipal bonds. Investors in existing water bonds must be wary of the developing risks that, in a perverse way, create some of the opportunity. At least an essential-purpose water or sewer bond is less dependent on widely fluctuating local economic conditions and more on the efficacy of the rates charged (but watch out for a bond highly dependent on water or sewer connection fees in this dismal real estate development market).

The years of relatively cheap financing for governments not only ushered in an era of complicated structured products but also, in my opinion, diverted significant funds away from critical water and sewer projects into more politically transparent public projects. Having said that, I am not making the judgment that airport expansions and toll roads are not worthy projects. I am simply saying that lowered borrowing costs seem to have been disproportionately distributed by city and local governments. This is yet another area where institutional changes could be very positive for the water industry.

Globalized Water Policy

This also points to another interesting observation with respect to the management of global water resources. For a biocentric mentality toward intrinsic value to prevail, that value must be shared on a global level. Ideally, there would be a unitary standard of living embraced across differing sovereignties.

Carbon Footprints and Watermarks

The advent of a "Kyoto Protocol" for water is unlikely. But several of the key trends that have been discussed give a hint of a positive change in that direction. Watershed management, with its methodology that takes into account all threats to human health and ecological integrity within a watershed, is an example. While creating a "global watershed" for regulatory purposes is nonsensical, a standardized regulatory approach based on the watershed as the regulatory unit is feasible. If based on a biocentric methodology, standardized watershed institutions can: (1) lead to more environmentally effective results, (2) provide greater opportunities for trading and other market based approaches, (3) reduce the cost of improving water quality, and (4) foster more effective implementation of total maximum daily loads (TMDLs). Since TMDLs are directly tied to carrying capacity, would not the aggregate of all watershed-wide TMDLs represent the planet's water-carrying capacity?

Again, one problem is the notion of cultural carrying capacity. The unique environmental, cultural, economic, and political attributes of a watershed must be considered, and these values cannot be standardized. Nonetheless, this approach could serve to provide at least a partial market value for certain water management activities. Other market- or performance-based initiatives could serve as a proxy for globalized water policy as well.

Cap and Trade for Water?

President Obama raised some eyebrows, in his preelection comments, when he stated that his program of a 100 percent auction on a cap-and-trade system for the emission of greenhouse gases would necessarily cause electricity rates to "skyrocket." This has prompted a revisitation of the possibility of a cap-and-trade methodology applied to water quality regulation. My interest is always piqued whenever I hear about the inevitability of price increases in conjunction with the implementation of a market solution to an environmental problem. The notion of a cap-and-trade approach to water resources is not new, but it evokes several questions of immediate interest. First, can the momentum of cap-and-trade in the carbon market spill over to the water market? And second, might a cap-and-trade system applied to water have a desirable monetization effect that would assist in establishing an intrinsic value for water?

The first question is largely political. Given the increase in regulatory oversight and the commensurate focus on enforcement, the political landscape is fertile for institutional change. The second question is economic. It is likely that water rates will not increase appreciably until inflation creeps back into the picture. In the interim, one way to encourage infrastructure projects is to pursue funding mechanisms that hint at market solutions, yet are administered by the public sector. A cap-and-trade system is such a program. Economists believe that no intrinsic value exists for any good or service except its price, which is a reflection of its supply and demand and not of any inherent characteristics. Absent a functioning market for water, a cap-and-trade program is a move in this direction. Water dischargers have the option to reduce contaminants in their own operations or to purchase water pollution credits from another source at a potentially lower price. Such a program can be combined with the Total Maximum Daily Load (TMDL) program and/or integrated into the watershed methodology that the Environmental Protection Agency (EPA) is moving to.

As the cost of achieving water quality standards is quantified, this will serve to add another element for establishing an intrinsic value of water. Despite a push by various political factions, the trend is toward incentive-based or market-based water regulations. And those last words are key: *market-based regulations.* This translates into market efficiency **within** an institutional (likely governmental or quasi-public) framework. It is not an ideological preoccupation with the process orientation of free markets. And it is not a denial of water as a human right. A modification of the institutional approach to water regulation is a recognition that market forces (pricing), unfettered by politically imposed constraints, contain information that can be acted upon by stakeholders, which, in turn, leads to the desired performance.

A cap-and-trade system applied to water could, if properly structured institutionally, have a desirable monetization effect that would assist in establishing an intrinsic value for water. The intrinsic value contained in a price would serve to provide a more concrete basis for water activities and certainly would aid in the analysis and valuation of water stocks as an emerging asset class.

Picking Water Stocks

The normal focus with respect to investing in water is through traditional equity investments in publicly traded companies. But times are certainly not normal. The financial crisis has brought to light more investment disconnects and failed correlations than can be imagined. Where we often look to some regulatory, technological, or structural rationale imbedded in a particular water stock, the credit crisis has drawn attention to interest rate plays. One is in the area of municipal bonds, and in particular municipal water and sewer bonds.

While water index–based exchange-traded funds afford the investor an extremely attractive option that was not available just several years ago, a studious investor can augment such a benchmark with specific stock preferences. Given the enormous expanse of the water industry, however, it is a daunting challenge to fully embrace all of the intricacies associated with individual stock selection. It is important to consider your methodology and investment approach to water-related companies.

The observation—often rising to the level of defeatist criticism—that it is difficult, if not impossible, to find absolutely "pure" water investments among the hundreds of public companies across the globe is frustratingly accurate. This is acknowledged and accepted as a reality associated with the current state of the industry. But if the reader takes just one thing away, it is hoped that it is the recognition that the existing approach to water must change. And since our future depends on looking at the glass half full, that change necessarily equates to opportunity.

Despite the objective of highlighting specific companies through the categorical lists referenced to a particular discussion, the tables cannot be all-inclusive. While it is the intent to aid investors in targeting the companies that are of water-related investment interest, stocks are included that may trade in accordance with fundamentals that are unrelated to their water industry exposure. In addressing the need to cull the list of water stocks to the most water-representative companies possible, if a particular water segment is well covered, then the need to include companies with relatively less water-related revenue is diminished.

An example of a well-covered segment would be pumps. Since there are a number of direct water pump plays, there is little need to drop down on the list to include companies that are less exposed to water. At the other end of the spectrum, the paucity of pure desalination plays necessitates that the list of companies engaged in this important sector be given a certain amount of latitude in order to capture the potential. In other words, the greater the potential, the greater the latitude for inclusion if investment availability is a factor. Further, given the dynamics of the water industry, it is the intent to be very much forward looking in anticipation of discovering those companies that will likely transition toward a more significant correlation with the water theme. Investors are strongly encouraged to avail themselves of some workable volume of information, research, analysis, current events, and so on, and watch for water initial public offerings going forward.

The obligatory notice that any security mentioned does not constitute a recommendation to buy or sell is tempered with suitability requirements designed to narrow the universe under consideration and eliminate obvious outliers. The propriety of any specific investment is critically dependent on the investors' unique situation. In addition, there is no intentional speculative element to the tables. With respect to U.S. exchange-traded securities, this would necessarily exclude pink sheet and other over-the-counter stocks, including such listed securities of even the most credible foreign companies. It is always recommended that, aside from American Depositary Receipts (ADRs) and American Depository Shares (ADSs), investors should purchase foreign securities directly on the foreign exchange in which the companies are domiciled.

An appropriate methodology would be to search the dozens of water indexes for confirmation of the investment clarity associated with a given stock. And, by and large, a key component of substantiating the water exposure of a particular company is through repeated listings, thereby assessing the multiplicity of segments in which the company operates. Water stock picking does not exist in a vacuum.

When I first started investing in water, virtually the only option was through a water utility. There were few predominantly water treatment companies, there were no companies that advertised the virtues of desalination, there was no awareness of water infrastructure plays, and there certainly were not any diversified global companies that strategically and publicly targeted water as a separate growth segment of their business.

Intrinsic Value

There is no shortage of uncertainty in the stock market. The global financial markets have entered a phase of such utter turmoil and conflicting crosscurrents that it does little good to prognosticate as to what the macroeconomic future holds. In the broader context, the death of securitization, the freeze-up in the credit markets, the myriad of deflationary forces, and the specter of increased governmental involvement are long-term trends that are likely to impact stock valuations for a very extended period, likely years. The specifics are equally ominous: industries lining up for life-preserving bailouts, unemployment soaring upward to perhaps double-digit levels, declining interest rates that have little stimulative impact, a comatose consumer, and a spiraling global economic slowdown.

Rather than dwell on the steepness of the drop, the likely intermediate-term direction of the global economy, and the impact of an Obama administration, it seems more appropriate to examine what a bottom in water stocks might look like. Granted, as we have often discussed, many water stocks trade like industrials. So despite the fundamental fact that we need water to survive, both literally and figuratively, there has been no safe haven in water. We have never professed that water is recession-proof. And while logic dictates that an enormous amount of global water usage should be price inelastic, the problem is that there is no market price for water. It is because of these conflicting points that a rather curious notion came to mind with respect to the current financial situation and the price of water stocks. Namely, is there intrinsic value in the water business that can shed light on the current price level of water stocks?

In other words, is there a floor to water stocks that can be relied upon independent of the frantic attempt to rationalize a slowdown in forever free-falling earnings estimates? After all, the notion of value in a single-digit price-to-earnings ratio is only as meaningful as the earnings projections plugged into the formula—not much comfort in an environment where all the rules are out the window. Needless to say, not many black-box hedge fund models paid attention to the statistical relevance of so many standard deviations away from normal.

Having said all that, intrinsic value is only a theoretical floor, or at least a foundational value that can provide some comfort even in the descent down the bottomless pit of downward spiraling negative feedback loops. But intrinsic value has a variety of meanings. The definition of *intrinsic value* is conceptually clear but practically lacking. With respect to stocks, the intrinsic value is the actual value of a security, as opposed to its market price or even book value. One way to look at it is that the market value is the price that investors are willing to pay for the company, whereas the intrinsic value is what the company is actually worth. But, especially in today's market, "actual worth" is as meaningful as determining just when the recession started.

In ecology, intrinsic value is based on the notion that the environment and life forms have value entirely independent of any anthropogenic value in use. While closer to the intrinsic value of water, as the molecule whose anomalous properties sustain life on the planet, this definition does little for incorporating the economic value of water. In fundamental analysis, the intrinsic value of a firm (and therefore its stock) is its underlying value separate from its market value and based on both quantitative factors (such as projected earnings, revenue, and cash flow) and qualitative factors (such as management, intellectual property, and intangible assets like brands). Many of the qualitative factors are not accurately reflected in the market price. This is the methodology chosen for the current discussion.

The key premise is that the intrinsic value of a firm provides an indication of whether the stock is under or overvalued. Since there is no "market" price for water, it is even more difficult to "build" an intrinsic value for water stocks. The conclusion is that the intrinsic value of water is vastly different than the methodology for calculating the intrinsic value of water stocks. Accordingly, intrinsic value is admittedly a rather subjective calculation based on a variety of considerations, all of which impact the critical projection of future earnings. The qualitative factors include market leadership (brand), regulatory-driven technological emphasis, trends in water resource management, concentration in the water industry, investor demand for water stocks, institutional initiatives, and the correlation to water demand. But no matter how you look at it, many water stocks are trading at or below values that would be considered intrinsic levels. This is a watershed event for long-term investors.

The Age of Ecology—Again or Finally

Make no mistake—the blatant contradiction between the advancement of an age of ecology and investing in water has not gone unnoticed. In fact, it has been a source of angst for many of the 25 years that I have studied water. After all, what better indictment of perpetuating man's mastery over all that is nonhuman than a book on profiting from water? My cynical side points out that there has already been at least one age of ecology in the industrial era. Let's hope the next one is not just a sequel. A historical account of the ecology movement, while fascinating, is well beyond the scope of this book.[2] Nonetheless, it is my firm belief that whether we practice "shallow ecology" or "deep ecology," at least the narrative is about ecology.

A central tenet of the water investment theme is that a growing world population and global economy would drive the rapid expansion of virtually all aspects of the water business: infrastructure, treatment methods, new technologies, alternative supplies, privatization, and so on. Yet despite unprecedented economic progress on a global scale, environmental issues have been largely neglected as a critical component of continued growth. For such a basic proposition as clean water for the planet, why has the industry dedicated to addressing this need in the new millennium not received more attention? What has happened to the much-heralded Age of Ecology?

One of the most serious deficiencies of our market economy is the failure to incorporate the various environmental costs of increasing resource use, be they radiation hazards, the loss of genetic diversity or aesthetics, the modification of the climate, the pollution of the air we breathe, or the contamination of the water we drink. For instance, if one user pollutes a stream, the pollution moves downstream to affect other users, and if one user pumps water from a common groundwater source, other users' pumping costs are affected. Without including these costs, our economic indicators give falsely optimistic signals and the market makes choices that put society inefficiently at risk.

Market failure with respect to third-party effects, or externalities, is often cited as reason enough to throw out the application of economics to ecology and to support governmental intervention in environmental issues. When private and social rates of return diverge, private decision makers will not allocate optimally. Such concerns are warranted—the potential for externalities is one of the most powerful arguments economists use to justify nonmarket alternatives.

But if government intervention is required, the governance must be more stewardship than control. Unfortunately, water management and water-related institutions seldom achieve either a separation between fact and value or the assignment of responsibility for making these two different kinds of judgments to those best qualified to make them. The divergence of social and private costs and/or benefits result as much from the "rules" established by institutions as it does from the methodology used to measure such costs. The gist of the attack is that globalization, as the World Trade Organization "rules" are advancing it, is gaining ground at the expense of, among other things, the environment.

The problem is that as economic activity expands, there seems to be an almost cavalier denial of the impact that such economic globalization has on our natural resources. Much of this oversight stems from the historical prevalence of a mechanistic explanation of how nature works; that is, the lack of ecological considerations. Armed with such an explanation, economic progress has developed as the goal of modern societies to be achieved only through the management of nature. Simple observation tells us that something is not working and the stakes are monumental. It is not that energy, minerals, and water cease to exist when humans use them, but that they cease to exist in the previous concentrations. Societies based on the rapid exhaustion of storages face the possibility of lasting just as long as those storages. A global economy must necessarily take this into critical consideration.

Globalization is not per se the antithesis of ecology. A diminishing role for national borders and the gradual fusing of separate national markets into a single global marketplace is not the process-oriented enchantment with the free market that it appears to be. More accurately, globalization, accelerated by the Internet and the free flow of information, is exposing serious flaws in the world's environmental institutions. Since the beginning of the industrial revolution, the marketplace has been seen as the mechanism to raise the standard of living. Based on this, the fundamental assumption of public policy has been that continued economic growth was a sufficient means of ensuring that all members of the economy would participate in rising levels of living. While environmentalism is not commonly seen as an income distribution problem, it is closely linked with changes in the distribution of income; developing countries are not likely to be interested.

As a result, when the global marketplace begins to divide up the economic pie, many countries view ecological problems as something that the rich countries must absorb; enter the debate over globalization. But in the twenty-first century, this rhetoric must be quickly dismissed. Donald Worster's metaphor—the Age of Ecology—suggests that, while economics ruled the twentieth century, ecology will rule in the twenty-first century. We are not off to a good start. Regardless of the metaphor, reality suggests that economics must have a significant validating role. It is this fusion of ecology and economics that will reorder the cultural paradigm and facilitate an understanding of our interconnectedness with nature. The assumptions of economic society must be fused with its biological underpinnings; this is the essence of biocentrism. At no other time in history has this been so apparent. At no other time in history has it been so critical. Even if the most ardent skeptic views environmental concerns as an appeal to emotion, denial does not escape the reality that there is simply no substitute for water. Its value will ultimately far exceed that of oil; it *is* the world's most valuable resource. Our speck in the cosmos developed as Planet Earth, but it will be sustained as we know it only in the context of Planet Water.

Appendix A

Water Contaminants

Refer to Chapter 13 for more information on water contaminants.

Table A.1   Microbial Contaminant Candidates

Microbial Contaminant Name	Information
Calicivirus	Virus (includes norovirus) causing mild self-limiting gastrointestinal illness
Campylobacter jejuni	Bacterium causing mild self-limiting gastrointestinal illness
Entamoeba histolytica	Protozoan parasite that can cause short- as well as long-lasting gastrointestinal illness
Escherichia coli (0157)	Toxin-producing bacterium causing gastrointestinal illness and kidney failure
Helicobacter pylori	Bacterium sometimes found in the environment capable of colonizing human gut that can cause ulcers and cancer
Hepatitis A virus	Virus that causes a liver disease and jaundice

(*Continued*)

Table A.1 (*Continued*)

Microbial Contaminant Name	Information
Legionella pneumophila	Bacterium found in the environment, including hot water systems, causing lung diseases when inhaled
Naegleria fowleri	Protozoan parasite found in shallow, warm surface and groundwater causing primary amebic meningoencephalitis
Salmonella enterica	Bacterium causing mild self-limiting gastrointestinal illness
Shigella sonnei	Bacterium causing mild self-limiting gastrointestinal illness and bloody diarrhea
Vibrio cholerae	Bacterium found in the environment causing gastrointestinal illness

Table A.2 Chemical Contaminant Candidates or CCL3 Candidates

Contaminant Name		Information About the Contaminant
a-Hexachlorocyclohexane	319-84-6	Component of benzene hexachloride (BHC) and formerly used as an insecticide
1,1,1,2-Tetrachloroethane	630-20-6	Industrial chemical used in the production of other substances
1,1-Dichloroethane	75-34-3	Industrial chemical used as a solvent
1,2,3-Trichloropropane	96-18-4	Industrial chemical used in paint manufacture
1,3-Butadiene	106-99-0	Industrial chemical used in rubber production
1,3-Dinitrobenzene	99-65-0	Industrial chemical used in the production of other substances
1,4-Dioxane	123-91-1	Solvent or solvent stabilizer in the manufacture and processing of paper, cotton, textile products, automotive coolant, cosmetics, and shampoos
1-Butanol	71-36-3	Used in the production of other substances, and as a paint solvent and food additive
2-Methoxyethanol	109-86-4	Used in consumer products, such as synthetic cosmetics, perfumes, fragrances, hair preparations, and skin lotions

Table A.2 (*Continued*)

Contaminant Name		Information About the Contaminant
2-Propen-1-ol	107-18-6	Used in the production of other substances, and in the manufacture of flavorings and perfumes
3-Hydroxycarbofuran	16655-82-6	Carbamate and pesticide degradate; the parent, carbofuran, is used as an insecticide
4,4'-Methylenedianiline	101-77-9	Used in the production of other substances and as a corrosion inhibitor and curing agent for polyurethanes
Acephate	30560-19-1	Insecticide
Acetaldehyde	75-07-0	Used in the production of other substances, and as a pesticide and food additive
Acetamide	60-35-5	Used as a solvent, solubilizer, plasticizer, and stabilizer
Acetochlor	34256-82-1	Used as an herbicide for weed control on agricultural crops
Acetochlor ethanesulfonic acid (ESA)	187022-11-3	An acetanilide pesticide degradate; the parent, acetochlor, is used as an herbicide for weed control on agricultural crops
Acetochlor oxanilic acid (OA)	184992-44-4	An acetanilide pesticide degradate; the parent, acetochlor, is used as an herbicide for weed control on agricultural crops
Acrolein	107-02-8	Used as an aquatic herbicide, rodenticide, and industrial chemical
Alachlor ethanesulfonic acid (ESA)	142363-53-9	Alachlor ESA is an acetanilide pesticide degradate; the parent, alachlor, is used as an herbicide for weed control on agricultural crops
Alachlor oxanilic acid (OA)	171262-17-2	Alachlor OA is an acetanilide pesticide degradate; the parent, alachlor, is used as an herbicide for weed control on agricultural crops
Aniline	62-53-3	Used as an industrial chemical, as a solvent, in the synthesis of explosives, rubber products, and in isocyanates
Bensulide	741-58-2	Used as an herbicide
Benzyl chloride	100-44-7	Used in the production of other substances, such as plastics, dyes, lubricants, gasoline, and pharmaceuticals

(*Continued*)

Table A.2   (*Continued*)

Contaminant Name	Information About the Contaminant	
Butylated hydroxyanisole	25013-16-5	Food additive (antioxidant)
Captan	133-06-2	Fungicide
Chloromethane (Methyl chloride)	74-87-3	Used as a foaming agent and in the production of other substances
Clethodim	110429-62-4	Used as an herbicide
Cobalt	7440-48-4	Naturally occurring element formerly used as cobaltus chloride in medicines and as a germicide
Cumene hydroperoxide	80-15-9	Used as an industrial chemical and is used in the production of other substances
Cyanotoxins (3)		Toxins naturally produced and released by cyanobacteria ("blue-green algae"); various studies suggest three cyanotoxins for consideration: Anatoxin-a, Microcystin-LR, and Cylindrospermopsin
Dicrotophos	141-66-2	Used as an insecticide
Dimethipin	55290-64-7	Used as an herbicide and plant growth regulator
Dimethoate	60-51-5	Used as an insecticide on field crops (such as cotton), orchard crops, vegetable crops, in forestry, and for residential purposes
Disulfoton	298-04-4	Used as an insecticide
Diuron	330-54-1	Used as an herbicide
Ethion	563-12-2	Used as an insecticide
Ethoprop	13194-48-4	Used as an insecticide
Ethylene glycol	107-21-1	Used as an antifreeze, in textile manufacturing, and is a canceled pesticide
Ethylene oxide	75-21-8	Used as a fungicidal and insecticidal fumigant
Ethylene thiourea	96-45-7	Used in the production of other substances, such as for vulcanizing polychloroprene (neoprene) and polyacrylate rubbers, and as a pesticide

Table A.2   (*Continued*)

Contaminant Name		Information About the Contaminant
Fenamiphos	22224-92-6	Used as an insecticide
Formaldehyde	50-00-0	Used as a fungicide, may be a disinfection by-product, and can occur naturally
Germanium	7440-56-4	Naturally occurring element commonly used as germanium dioxide in phosphors, transistors, and diodes, and in electroplating
HCFC-22	75-45-6	Used as a refrigerant, as a low-temperature solvent, and in fluorocarbon resins, especially in tetrafluoroethylene polymers
Hexane	110-54-3	Used as a solvent and is a naturally occurring alkane
Hydrazine	302-01-2	Used in the production of other substances, such as rocket propellants, and as an oxygen and chlorine scavenging compound
Methamidophos	10265-92-6	Used as an insecticide
Methanol	67-56-1	Used as an industrial solvent, a gasoline additive, and as antifreeze
Methyl bromide (Bromomethane)	74-83-9	Used as a fumigant as a fungicide
Methyl tert-butyl ether	1634-04-4	Used as an octane booster in gasoline, in the manufacture of isobutene, and as an extraction solvent
Metolachlor	51218-45-2	Used as an herbicide for weed control on agricultural crops
Metolachlor ethanesulfonic acid (ESA)	171118-09-5	An acetanilide pesticide degradate; the parent, metolachlor, is used as an herbicide for weed control on agricultural crops
Metolachlor oxanilic acid (OA)	152019-73-3	An acetanilide pesticide degradate; the parent, metolachlor, is used as an herbicide for weed control on agricultural crops
Molinate	2212-67-1	Used as an herbicide
Molybdenum	7439-98-7	Naturally occurring element commonly used as molybdenum trioxide as a chemical reagent

(Continued)

Table A.2   (*Continued*)

Contaminant Name		Information About the Contaminant
Nitrobenzene	98-95-3	Used in the production of aniline and as a solvent in the manufacture of paints, shoe polishes, floor polishes, metal polishes, explosives, dyes, pesticides, and drugs (such as acetaminophen); in its redistilled form (oil of mirbane), used as an inexpensive perfume for soaps
Nitrofen	1836-75-5	Used as an herbicide
Nitroglycerin	55-63-0	Used in pharmaceuticals, in the production of explosives, and in rocket propellants
N-Methyl-2-pyrrolidone	872-50-4	Solvent in the chemical industry, and is used for pesticide application and in food-packaging materials
N-nitrosodiethylamine (NDEA)	55-18-5	A nitrosamine used as an additive in gasoline and in lubricants, as an antioxidant, as a stabilizer in plastics, and also may be a disinfection by-product
N-nitrosodimethylamine (NDMA)	62-75-9	A nitrosamine formerly used in the production of rocket fuels; is used as an industrial solvent and an antioxidant, and also may be a disinfection by-product
N-nitroso-di-n-propylamine (NDPA)	621-64-7	A nitrosamine and may be a disinfection by-product
N-Nitrosodiphenylamine	86-30-6	A nitrosamine chemical reagent that is used as a rubber and polymer additive and may be a disinfection by-product
N-nitrosopyrrolidine (NPYR)	930-55-2	A nitrosamine used as a research chemical and may be a disinfection byproduct
n-Propylbenzene	103-65-1	Used in the manufacture of methylstyrene, in textile dyeing, and as a printing solvent, and is a constituent of asphalt and naptha
o-Toluidine	95-53-4	Used in the production of other substances, such as dyes, rubber, pharmaceuticals, and pesticides
Oxirane, methyl-	75-56-9	An industrial chemical used in the production of other substances
Oxydemeton-methyl	301-12-2	Used as an insecticide

Table A.2 (*Continued*)

Contaminant Name		Information About the Contaminant
Oxyfluorfen	42874-03-3	Used as an herbicide
Perchlorate	14797-73-0	Both a naturally occurring and man–made chemical; most of the perchlorate manufactured in the United States is used as the primary ingredient of solid rocket propellant
Permethrin	52645-53-1	Used as an insecticide
PFOA (perfluorooctanoic acid)	335-67-1	Used for its emulsifier and surfactant properties in or as fluoropolymers (such as Teflon), fire-fighting foams, cleaners, cosmetics, greases and lubricants, paints, polishes and adhesives and photographic films (known as C8)
Profenofos	41198-08-7	Used as an insecticide and an acaricide
Quinoline	91-22-5	Used in the production of other substances, and as a pharmaceutical (antimalarial) and as a flavoring agent
RDX (Hexahydro-1,3,5-trinitro-1,3,5-triazine)	121-82-4	Used as an explosive
sec-Butylbenzene	135-98-8	Used as a solvent for coating compositions, in organic synthesis, as a plasticizer, and in surfactants
Strontium	7440-24-6	Naturally occurring element and is used as strontium carbonate in pyrotechnics, in steel production, as a catalyst, and as a lead scavenger
Tebuconazole	107534-96-3	Used as a fungicide
Tebufenozide	112410-23-8	Used as an insecticide
Tellurium	13494-80-9	Naturally occurring element and is commonly used as sodium tellurite in bacteriology and medicine
Terbufos	13071-79-9	Used as an insecticide
Terbufos sulfone	56070-16-7	A phosphorodithioate pesticide degradate. The parent, terbufos, is used as an insecticide

(*Continued*)

Table A.2   (*Continued*)

Contaminant Name		Information About the Contaminant
Thiodicarb	59669–26–0	Used as an insecticide
Thiophanate–methyl	23564–05–8	Used as a fungicide
Toluene diisocyanate	26471–62–5	Used in the manufacture of plastics
Tribufos	78–48–8	Used as an insecticide and as a cotton defoliant
Triethylamine	121–44–8	Used in the production of other substances and as a stabilizer in herbicides and pesticides, in consumer products, in food additives, in photographic chemicals, and in carpet cleaners
Triphenyltin hydroxide (TPTH)	76–87–9	Used as a pesticide
Urethane	51–79–6	Paint ingredient
Vanadium	7440–62–2	Naturally occurring element and is commonly used as vanadium pentoxide in the production of other substances and as a catalyst
Vinclozolin	50471–44–8	Fungicide
Ziram	137–30–4	Fungicide

SOURCE: EPA (2008)

Appendix B

Acronyms and Abbreviations

ADRs and ADSs	American Depositary Receipts and American Depository Shares
AMR	automatic meter reading
AWWA	American Water Works Association
BAC	biologically active carbon
BAT	best available technology
BMP	best management practice
BOD	biochemical oxygen demand
BOD_5	5-day biochemical oxygen demand
BRIC	Brazil, Russia, India, China (countries)
CAA	Clean Air Act
CAFO	concentrated animal feeding operation
CCL	Contaminant Candidate List
CSO	combined sewer overflow
CWA	Clean Water Act

(Continued)

CWNS	Clean Watersheds Needs Survey
CWSRF	Clean Water State Revolving Fund
D/DBP	disinfectant/disinfection by-product
DBP	disinfection by-product
DBPR	Disinfection By-Product Rule
DDD	disruptive decentralized development
DE	Diatomaceous Earth
DO	dissolved oxygen
DWS	Drinking Water Standard
EDR	electrodialysis reversal
EPA or U.S. EPA	Environmental Protection Agency
ESWTR	Enhanced Surface Water Treatment Rule
ETF	exchange-traded fund
GAC	granular activated carbon
GC	gas chromatography
GC/MS	gas chromatography/mass spectrometry
GIS	geographic information system
GWDR	Groundwater Disinfection Rule
GWR	Groundwater Rule
HAA	haloacetic acid
HDD	horizontal directional drilling
HF	hyperfiltration (reverse osmosis)
I/I	infiltration and inflow
ICR	Information Collection Rule
IPO	initial public offering
LAACE	Latin America, Africa, Central Europe (regions)
LEED	Leadership in Energy and Environmental Design (U.S. Green Building Council)
MCL	maximum contaminant level
MCLG	maximum contaminant level goal
MF	microfiltration
mg	milligram(s)
mg/L	milligram(s) per liter (equivalent to ppm)
mgd	million gallons per day
mL	milliliters
MTBE	methyl tertiary butyl ether
NF	nanofiltration
NGO	nongovernmental organization
NOAA	National Oceanic and Atmospheric Administration
NPDES	National Pollutant Discharge Elimination System
NPDWR	National Primary Drinking Water Regulations
NSDWR	National Secondary Drinking Water Regulations

O&M	operation and maintenance
PCE	tetrachloroethylene
POE	point of entry
PPCPs	pharmaceuticals and personal care products
POTW	publicly owned treatment works
POU	point of use
POUR	point of use–reuse
ppb	parts per billion; 10^9 (μg/L or micrograms per liter)
ppm	parts per million; 10^6 (mg/L or milligrams per liter)
ppt	parts per trillion; 10^{12} (ng/L or nanograms per liter)
PWS	Public Water System
RfD	reference dose
RO	reverse osmosis (hyperfiltration)
SDWA	Safe Drinking Water Act
SRF	State Revolving Fund
SSO	sanitary sewer overflow
SWRO	seawater reverse osmosis
SWTR	Surface Water Treatment Rule
TCE	trichloroethylene
TCR	Total Coliform Rule
TDS	total dissolved solids
THM	trihalomethane
TMDL	Total Maximum Daily Load
TOC	total organic carbon
TTHMs	total trihalomethanes
UF	ultrafiltration
U.S. EPA	United States Environmental Protection Agency
UV	ultraviolet
VOCs	volatile organic chemicals
WEF	Water Environment Federation
WHO	World Health Organization
WMA	Watershed Management Area
WTO	World Trade Organization
WWTP	wastewater treatment plant
μg/L	microgram(s) per liter (equivalent to ppb)

Appendix C

Metric Conversions and Flow Equivalents

1 acre-foot = 325,851 gallons
1 acre-foot = 43,560 cubic feet
1 million gallons = 3.0691 acre-feet
1 cubic meter = 35.31 cubic feet
1 cubic foot = 0.02832 cubic meters
1 gallon = 0.1337 cubic feet
1 cubic foot = 7.48052 gallons
1 gallon = 3.785 liters
1 cubic foot = 28.32 liters

1 cubic meter = 1,000 liters
1 cubic meter = 264.2 gallons
1 liter of water = 1 kilogram
1 liter = 0.03531 cubic feet
1 liter = 0.2642 gallons
1 liter = 1.057 quarts
1 liter = 33.8140 ounces
1 cubic foot of water = 62.4 pounds
1 gallon of water = 8.34 pounds

1 gallon = 3.785×10^{-3} cubic meters
1 million gallons per day (mgd) = 3,785 m^3/day
1 million gallons per day (mgd) = 133,681 ft^3/day

1 million gallons per day (mgd) = 3.0689 acre-feet per day
1 cubic foot per second (cfs) = 7.48052 gallons per second
1 cubic foot per second (cfs) = 448.83 gallons per minute (gpm)
9/5 °C +32 = °F
5/9 °F −32 = °C

Glossary

Activated carbon A highly porous form of charcoal that, after being subjected to intense heat, can be used to adsorb large quantities of specific contaminants in water. The granules (granular activated carbon [GAC]) have a high capacity, given the enormous surface area, to selectively remove trace and soluble contaminants from water.

Absorption The uptake of water or dissolved chemicals by a cell or an organism; the process by which one substance is trapped throughout the volume of another, usually a liquid, by solution or chemical reaction.

Acre-foot A unit for expressing large quantities of water and defined as equivalent to the volume of water to cover one acre of land to a depth of one foot.

Activated sludge Refers to a biological process; a wastewater treatment method in which carbonaceous organic matter of wastewater provides an energy source for the production of new cells for a mixture of microorganisms. Bacteria make up about 95 percent of the activated sludge biomass. In addition, certain microorganisms obtain energy by oxidizing ammonia nitrogen to nitrate nitrogen in the process known as nitrification.

Adsorption A physical process by which contaminants are held on the surface of a solid substance for example, activated carbon.

Advanced treatment Purification processes used after or during secondary wastewater treatment to remove nutrients or additional solids and dissolved organics; also called tertiary treatment.

Aeration A physical treatment process in which air is thoroughly mixed with water or wastewater for purification.

Aerobic In the presence of air or available molecular oxygen.

Algae Microscopic single-celled plants that contain chlorophyll and live floating or suspended in water; phytoplankton. The biological activities of algae significantly affect the pH and dissolved oxygen of water.

Algal bloom Visible overgrowth of algae in lakes or reservoirs, due to eutrophication.

Alum Aluminum sulfate, one of the most commonly used chemical coagulants used for water treatment.

Anaerobic In the absence of air or available molecular oxygen.

Anion A negatively charged ion in an electrolyte solution, for example, chloride (Cl^-).

Aquifer A geologic formation that exhibits the permeability (porosity and fractures) to transmit and yield groundwater in amounts sufficient to be used as a usable water supply (*see also* Groundwater).

Bacteria Microscopic single-celled plants that do not contain chlorophyll and do not nourish themselves by photosynthesis.

Best available technology (BAT) The best technology treatment techniques or other means that the EPA administrator finds, after examination for efficacy under field conditions and not solely under laboratory conditions, are available (taking cost into consideration). For the purpose of setting maximum contaminant levels for synthetic organic chemicals, any BAT must be at least as effective as granular activated carbon (GAC).

Best available technology economically achievable Technology-based standard established by the Clean Water Act (CWA) as the most appropriate means available on a national basis for controlling the direct discharge of toxic and nonconventional pollutants to navigable waters. In general, BAT effluent limitations guidelines represent the best existing performance of treatment technologies that are economically achievable within an industrial point source category or subcategory.

Best management practices (BMPs) Structural, nonstructural, and managerial techniques that are recognized to be the most effective and practical means to control non–point source pollutants, yet are compatible with the productive use of the resource to which they are applied. BMPs are used in both urban and agricultural areas.

Biochemical oxygen demand (BOD) The amount of oxygen required by microorganisms (mainly bacteria) to decompose (biodegrade) organic matter in water. BOD is a measure of the amount of organic pollution.

Biosolids The solid materials resulting from wastewater treatment that meets government criteria for beneficial use, such as for fertilizer and soil amendments. Biosolids consist mostly of living organisms but can contain other contaminants as well. Accordingly, treatment and processing are required under stringent EPA (see Part 503 Rule) and state regulations. Biosolids are one of the most studied materials that have ever been regulated by the EPA. The term *biosolids* is distinct from sewage sludge in that biosolids are a by-product of sludge that can be beneficially and safely recycled.

Black water Liquid and solid human body waste and the carriage water generated through toilet usage.

Cation A positively charged ion in an electrolyte solution; for example, sodium ion (Na^+).

Centrifugal pump A mechanical device that adds energy to a liquid using a rapidly rotating impeller in a specially shaped casing. As the rotating impeller spins the water, centrifugal force builds up enough pressure to force the water through the discharge outlet. Centrifugal pumps are a common type of pump used for water treatment and distribution.

Chloramines Compounds formed by the reaction of hypochlorous acid (or aqueous chlorine) with ammonia.

Chlorine residual The amount of chlorine compounds that remain in water or wastewater after disinfection, providing continued sanitary protection in the distribution system.

Clarifier A large circular or rectangular sedimentation basin or settling tank in which heavier suspended solids settle to the bottom and the clarified water or wastewater is drawn off the top; also called settling basins or sedimentation basins.

Coagulants Treatment chemicals that cause very fine particles to clump together into larger particles, thereby facilitating the separation of solids from the water by settling, skimming, draining, or filtering. The chemicals neutralize the electrical charges of the suspended particles, causing destabilization (collision) and clumping (flocculation).

Coagulation The process of adding coagulant chemicals in the formation of settleable flocs.

Combined sewer A pipeline infrastructure that transports a mixture of surface runoff, human domestic wastes (sewage), and sometimes industrial wastes. Wastewater and runoff in a combined sewer may occur in excess of the sewer capacity and cannot be immediately treated. The excess is frequently discharged directly to a receiving water body without treatment, or to a holding basin for subsequent treatment and discharge.

Consumptive use That part of water withdrawn from available supplies that is evaporated, transpired by plants, incorporated into products, used on crops, consumed by humans or livestock, or otherwise removed without direct return to an immediate water resource system or environment; also referred to as water consumed.

Contaminant Any physical, chemical, biological, or radiological substance or matter in water (definition in CFR Section 141.2 146.3).

Conventional filtration The mainstay of traditional water treatment for substantial particle removal (filtration). The process is generally as follows: coagulant chemicals, flash mixing, coagulation, flocculation, sedimentation, and filtration.

Corrosion inhibitor A substance that slows the rate of corrosion of metal plumbing materials by water, especially lead and copper materials.

Desalination The removal of salts from saline water to provide freshwater.

Disinfection The process designed to kill or inactivate most microorganisms in water, including essentially all pathogenic bacteria. Chlorine is, by far, the most prevalent oxidant used in disinfection in the United States. However, the concern over carcinogenic by-products of the chlorine disinfection method has created strong interest in disinfection alternatives, such as chlorine dioxide, chloramines, ozone, mixed oxidants, and ultraviolet radiation. It should be noted that most disinfectants have the potential for harmful by-products under the right conditions.

Disinfection by-product A compound formed by the reaction of a water treatment disinfectant with natural organic matter (a "precursor" found in all surface and groundwaters) in a water supply.

Effluent Water or some other liquid (raw, partially or completely treated) flowing from a reservoir, basin, treatment process, or treatment plant.

Electrodialysis The process where the salts are extracted from the feedwater by using a membrane with an electrical current to separate the ions. The positive ions go through one membrane, while the negative ions flow through a different membrane, leaving the end freshwater product.

Eutrophication The degradation of water quality due to an increase in the nutrient (primarily nitrogen and phosphorus) levels of a lake or other body of water that results in excessive plant (principally algae) growth and decay. Low dissolved oxygen in the water is a consequence of eutrophication. Cultural eutrophication is the subset caused by human activities.

Filtration A process for removing particulate matter from water by passage through porous media; technically distinct from separation.

Flocculation The gathering together of fine particles in water by gentle mixing after the addition of coagulant chemical to form clusters or flocs.

Geographic information system (GIS) A computerized database system containing information on natural resources and other factors that can be analyzed and displayed in spatial or map format. GIS technology is increasingly used in watershed management.

Greywater Wastewater, other than sewage, from water usage in activities such as clothes and dish washing, bathing, and sinks.

Groundwater Subsurface water that is present below the water table in soils and geologic formations that are fully saturated (*see also* Aquifer).

Hard water Specifically refers to the total concentration of calcium and magnesium (salts) in water (measured in terms of grains per gallon [gpg]). Water hardness is a relative scale ranging from soft water (under 1 gpg or 17.1 mg/L) to very hard water (over 10.5 gpg or 180 mg/L).

Heavy metals Metallic elements with high atomic weights, for example, mercury, zinc, copper, silver, chromium, cadmium, arsenic, and lead. They are of particular concern because they can damage living things at low concentrations and tend to bioaccumulate in the food chain.

Industrial sources Nonmunicipal sources generating wastewater that is discharged to surface waters. The types of wastewaters generated at a facility depend on the specific activities undertaken at a particular site, and may include manufacturing or process wastewaters, cooling waters, sanitary wastewater, and stormwater runoff.

In-situ infrastructure rehabilitation The replacement and repair of water, wastewater, and/or stormwater pipeline systems through in-place rehabilitation techniques as opposed to more costly and disruptive traditional approaches. So-called trenchless rehabilitation and replacement technologies include cured-in-place pipe (CIPP), fold-and-form pipe, slip lining, pipe bursting, microtunneling, and horizontal directional drilling (HDD).

Ion exchange A water treatment process in which ions are preferentially adsorbed from a solution for equivalently charged ions attached to resin (small solid structures).

Irrigation The controlled application of water for agricultural or vegetative purposes through constructed systems to supply water requirements not satisfied by precipitation.

Large water system A water system that serves more than 50,000 persons.

Maximum contaminant level (MCL) The maximum permissible level of a contaminant in water that is delivered to the free-flowing outlet of the ultimate user of a public water system, except in the case of turbidity, where the maximum permissible level is measured at the point of entry to the distribution system.

Maximum contaminant level goal (MCLG) The maximum level of a contaminant in drinking water at which no known or anticipated adverse effect on the health of persons would occur, and which allows an adequate margin of safety. MCLGs are nonenforceable health goals.

Membrane bioreactor (MBR) A membrane bioreactor is a combination of suspended-growth activated sludge biological treatment and membrane separation treatment. The use of MBR in wastewater applications has grown rapidly as a cost-effective alternative to secondary clarifiers (conventional activated sludge) and tertiary filters.

Micron A unit of length equal to one millionth of a meter or one thousandth of a millimeter. One micron equals 0.00004 of an inch.

National Pollutant Discharge Elimination System (NPDES) A national program in the United States under Section 402 of the Clean Water Act for regulation of discharges of contaminants from point sources to receiving water bodies; discharges are authorized by an NPDES permit, which is the regulatory agency document issued by either a federal or state agency.

Non–point source pollution Pollutants or contaminants discharged over a wide land area such as a watershed as opposed to a specific, identifiable point source. These are forms of diffuse pollution caused by sediment, nutrients, and organic and toxic substances (such as pesticides) originating from land-use activities, which are carried to lakes and streams by surface runoff. Non–point sources include agricultural stormwater runoff, return flows from irrigated agriculture, city streets, residential property, construction, land disposal, and saltwater intrusion.

Organic matter Carbon compound–based substances made by living organisms (plant and animal residue). A precursor in the formation of trihalomethanes when combined with chlorine in the water disinfection process.

Osmosis The passage of a liquid from a weak solution to a more concentrated solution across a semipermeable membrane. The membrane allows the passage of the solvent (water) but not the dissolved solids (solutes).

Ozone disinfection The disinfection of water or wastewater, utilizing ozone (O_3) as an alternative to other disinfection methods. The oxidation potential of ozone is second only to fluorine. Accordingly, it is an effective disinfectant for a wide range of pathogens and achieves the primary disinfection goal for the categories regulated under the Surface Water Treatment Rule (SWTR). Ozone is highly unstable and therefore must be generated on-site.

Pathogen A disease-producing agent in a living organism; viruses, bacteria, parasites, or fungi that cause disease.

Part 503 rule The federal biosolids rule contained in 40 CFR Part 503; biosolids that are to be land applied must meet these strict regulations and quality standards governing their use and disposal. The Part 503 rule has different provisions for each class of biosolids (Class A and Class B) but generally contains numerical limits for metals in biosolids, pathogen and vector attraction reduction standards, management practices and frequency of monitoring, and record keeping and reporting requirements for land-applied biosolids.

pH A measure of the relative acidity or alkalinity of water (or liquid). Mathematically, pH is the logarithm (base 10) of the reciprocal of the hydrogen ion concentration, $[H^+]$; that is, $pH = Log (1/[H^+])$. Pure water is neutral, with a pH of 7. Natural waters usually have a pH between 6.5 and 8.5.

Point-of-entry (POE) Refers to a water treatment device applied to potable water entering a house or building for the purpose of reducing contaminants in the drinking water distributed throughout the house or building.

Point-of-use (POU) Refers to a water treatment device applied to a single tap used for the purpose of reducing contaminants in drinking water at that one point of use.

Point-of-use-reuse (POUR) Refers to the emergence of sustainable techniques, particularly with respect to decentralized wastewater treatment systems. The premise of POUR technology is the on-site separation and biological treatment of household wastewater and reuse/recycling; a decentralized analogy to a membrane bioreactor at a centralized wastewater treatment plant.

Point source pollution Pollutants or contaminants that are discharged from a single stationary source, location, or fixed facility such as an industrial effluent discharge or sewage outflow pipe. *NPDES:* Any discernible, confined, and discrete conveyance, including but not limited to, any pipe, ditch, channel, tunnel, conduit, well, discrete fissure, container, rolling stock concentrated animal feeding operation (CAFO), landfill leachate collection system, vessel or other floating craft from which pollutants are or may be discharged.

Potable water Water of a quality that is safe and satisfactory for drinking and cooking.

Primary wastewater treatment The first stage of the wastewater treatment process, where mechanical methods are used to remove pollutants. Solid material in wastewater settles out during this process.

Prior appropriations doctrine A property rights system for allocating water to private interests utilized by the early settlers and miners and prevalent in the relatively arid western states. John Locke is attributed with laying the foundation for the American doctrine of prior appropriation. The prior appropriations doctrine is based on the concept of "first in time, first in rights." The first person to take a quantity of water had a senior priority right to the water. The embedded principle of "beneficial use," however, required that a person's right is limited to the amount of water actually put to beneficial use; appropriative rights can be lost through nonuse. In addition, the rights can be separated from the land and sold or transferred. The prior appropriations doctrine is contrasted with the riparian rights doctrine.

Publicly owned treatment works (POTW) A treatment works, as defined by Section 212 of the CWA, that is owned by the state or municipality. This definition includes any devices and systems used in the storage, treatment, recycling, and reclamation of municipal sewage or industrial waste liquids. It also includes sewers, pipes, and other conveyances only if they convey wastewater to a POTW treatment plant. Privately owned treatment works, federally owned treatment works, and other treatment plants not owned by municipalities are not considered POTWs.

Public water system A system for the provision to the public of piped water for human consumption, if such system has at least 15 service connections or regularly serves an average of at least 25 individuals at least 60 days out of the year. The term includes: (1) any collection, treatment, storage, and distribution facilities under control of the operator of such system and used primarily in connection with such system; and (2) any collection or pretreatment storage facilities not under such control that are used primarily in connection with such system. A public water system is either a "community water system" or a "noncommunity water system."

Reclaimed wastewater Municipal wastewater effluent that is treated to for a specific, beneficial use; also called recycled or reused water.

Recycled water Water that is used more than once before it is discharged into the hydrologic cycle.

Reverse osmosis (RO) An advanced method of water or wastewater treatment that relies on a semipermeable membrane to separate water from constituent contaminants. Pressure is used to reverse the normal osmotic process, resulting in the solvent's moving from a solution of higher concentration to one of lower concentration. The membrane allows the passage of the solvent (water) but not the dissolved solids (solutes).

In desalination, the process of removing salts from water using a membrane. With RO, the product water passes through a membrane with a pore size that salts are unable to pass through. The rejected salt waste brine is removed and must be disposed of.

Riparian rights doctrine A system for allocating water to private interests based on rights of the owner whose land abuts water. The doctrine has its origins in English common law and is prevalent in the eastern United States, where surface water is relatively more abundant. Riparian water rights differ from state to state and often depend on whether the water is a river, lake, or ocean. Specifically, persons who own land adjacent to a stream (riparian) have the right to make reasonable use of the stream; riparian users of a stream share the flow among themselves with no application of priority of use (compare to the Prior appropriations doctrine). Riparian water rights cannot be sold or transferred for use on nonriparian land.

Secondary wastewater treatment Treatment following primary wastewater treatment involving the biological process of reducing suspended, colloidal, and dissolved organic matter in effluent from primary treatment systems. Secondary wastewater treatment generally removes 80 to 95 percent of the biochemical oxygen demand and suspended matter and may be accomplished with biological or chemical-physical methods. Activated sludge and trickling filters are common in secondary treatment and remove about 90 percent of the oxygen-demanding substances and suspended solids. Disinfection is the final stage of secondary treatment.

Salinity The total amount of minerals (salts) dissolved in water and measured by TDS (*see* definitions of freshwater, brackish water, and seawater under Total dissolved solids).

Sanitary sewer A sewer that transports only wastewaters (from domestic residences and/or industries) to a wastewater treatment plant.

Septic system An on-site system designed to treat and dispose of domestic sewage; a typical septic system consists of a tank that receives wastes from a residence or business and a system of tile lines or a pit for disposal of the liquid effluent that remains after decomposition of the solids by bacteria in the tank.

Sewer system An infrastructure network of underground systems of conduits (pipes and/or tunnels) that collect and transport wastewaters and/or runoff; gravity sewers carry free-flowing water and wastes; pressurized sewers carry pumped wastewaters under pressure.

Softener A point-of-entry device that reduces water hardness by replacing calcium and magnesium ions with sodium ions.

Surface water All water naturally open to the atmosphere (rivers, lakes, reservoirs, streams, impoundments, seas, estuaries, etc.) and all springs, wells, or other collectors that are directly influenced by surface water.

Tertiary wastewater treatment The additional treatment of effluent beyond that of primary and secondary treatment. It involves specific biological, physical, and chemical separation processes to remove organic and inorganic substances that resist conventional treatment and may involve alternative disinfection methods such as ozone or ultraviolet radiation.

Total dissolved solids (TDS) All of the solid material dissolved in water. TDS is measured on a sample of water that has passed through a very fine mesh filter to remove suspended solids. The water passing through the filter is evaporated, and the residue represents the dissolved solids.
> Freshwater: Water with <1,000 mg/L of TDS; generally, however, more than 500 mg/L of TDS is undesirable for drinking and many industrial uses.
> Brackish water: Water with >1,000 to 25,000 mg/L of TDS
> Seawater: Water with >25,000 mg/L of TDS

Total Maximum Daily Load (TMDL) The total pollutant loading from point and non–point sources that a water body can assimilate. Assimilative capacity is the amount of pollutants that a water body may absorb while maintaining corresponding water quality classification and standards, including protection of aquatic life and human health.

Transmission lines The pipeline infrastructure that transports raw water from its source to a water treatment plant. After treatment, water is pumped into transmission pipelines that are connected to the distribution infrastructure grid system.

Turbidity The cloudy appearance of water caused by the presence of suspended and colloidal matter. Technically, turbidity is an optical property of the water based on the amount of light reflected by suspended solid particles. Turbidity can significantly impact the efficacy of treatment methods and water quality.

Ultraviolet (UV) disinfection The disinfection of water or wastewater by using UV light as an alternative to other disinfection methods. A UV disinfection system transfers electromagnetic energy from a mercury arc lamp to an organism's genetic material, thereby destroying the cell's ability to reduce.

Volatile organic compounds (VOCs) Volatile organic compounds are compounds that have a high vapor pressure and low solubility. The most frequently occurring VOCs in groundwater are perchloroethylene (industrial solvent), methyl tertiary butyl ether (fuel oxygenate), and chloroform (by-product of chlorination). Maximum contaminant levels for many VOCs have been established by the EPA and the states because of adverse human health effects.

Wastewater The used water and solids from a community (including used water from industrial processes) that is not suitable for use unless it is treated and flows to a treatment plant. Stormwater, surface water, and groundwater infiltration also may be included in the wastewater that enters a wastewater treatment plant. The term *sewage* usually refers to household wastes but is being replaced by the term *wastewater*.

Water rights A highly specialized type of real property that legally varies widely from the local to federal level and by type, such as natural rights, appropriative rights, or sovereign control. In the context of the institutional structure governing a market-driven, efficient allocation of water, water rights must be well defined, enforceable, and transferable.

Watershed The land area that drains water (contributes runoff) to a particular stream, river, or lake. There are an infinite number of watersheds on Earth.

Watershed management The optimization, through integrated planning, of the water resource goals of an area defined by a natural drainage basin (watershed). Central to the term is a holistic approach to a broad array of goals, including sustainability, water quality, cost effectiveness, and human health, as well as innovation in implementation tools and protocols such as geographic information systems, land use, Total Maximum Daily Load studies, and watershed-based National Pollutant Discharge Elimination System permits.

Notes

Chapter 1: Water: Prerequisite for Life, and Living

1. C. A. Sullivan, J. R. Meigh, and T. S. Fediw, "Derivation and Testing of the Water Poverty Index Phase 1." Final Report (May 2002), Volume 1, Centre for Ecology and Hydrology (CEH); Natural Environment Research Council for the Department for International Development.

Chapter 2: The Global Water Condition

1. The pioneering work on estimating the human appropriation of NNP is attributed to P. M. Vitousek, P. R. Ehrlich, A. H. Ehrlich, and P. A. Matson, "Human Appropriation of the Products of Photosynthesis." *Bioscience* 36 (1986): 368–373.

2. A subsequent study by H. Haberl, K. H. Erb, F. Krausmann, et al., "Quantifying and Mapping the Human Appropriation of Net Primary Production in Earth's Terrestrial Ecosystems." *Proc Natl Acad Sci USA* 104 (2007): 12942–12947, extended the global-aggregate approach to a more detailed analysis based on terrestrial grid cells.

3. Ibid.

Chapter 3: Public Good, Commodity or Resource?

1. Tom Tietenberg, *Environmental and Natural Resource Economics,* Second Edition (Scott Foresman and Company, 1988.)
2. Terry Anderson, *Water Crisis: Ending the Policy Drought* (Cato Institute, 1983.)

Chapter 4: The Cost of Clean Water

1. *Infrastructure to 2030: Telecom, Land Transport, Water and Electricity* (Organization for Economic Co-operation and Development, July 2006; ISBN 9789264023987).
2. *Regional and Global Costs of Attaining the Water Supply and Sanitation Target (Target 10) of the Millennium Development Goals* (World Health Organization, 2008).
3. Guy Hutton and Laurence Haller, *Evaluation of the Costs and Benefits of Water and Sanitation Improvements at the Global Level* (World Health Organization, 2004).
4. *Clean Watersheds Needs Survey 2004; Report to Congress* (U.S. EPA, January 2008).
5. This convention is used to avoid any confusion with a privatized public utility. For example, take a state-owned Malaysian water utility. If the government is "privatizing" the public utility, it is offering ownership to the public, that is, investors, through a listing on a stock exchange.

Chapter 5: The Business of Water

1. In addition to the diversified companies engaged in the beverage category such as Nestlé, Coca-Cola, Group Danone, and Pepsi, there are a multitude of smaller bottled-water companies that possess widely differing prospects. A recent addition that is focused on the Chinese bottled-water market is Heckmann Corporation (HEK), which purchased China Water and Drink Inc. to gain access to the large and growing middle class in China.
2. R. Saleth and A. Dinar, *The Institutional Economics of Water: A Cross-Country Analysis of Institutions and Performance* (Washington, D.C.: World Bank Publications, 2004), 23–46. This exhaustive literature review evaluates the performance of water institutions and water policy reform through the empirical application of an "institutional ecology" framework.

Chapter 8: Decentralized Water and Wastewater Treatment

1. U.S. EPA, "Decentralized Wastewater Treatment Systems: A Program Strategy" (EPA 832-R-05-002, January 2005).
2. Ibid.

3. WaterTech Capital, LLC, "Home Water Treatment Markets" (March 2007).

4. Central Arizona–Phoenix Long-Term Ecological Research; Fourth Annual Symposium, "Land-Use Change and Ecological Processes in an Urban Ecosystem of the Sonoran Desert," Arizona State University, January 17, 2002.

5. L. Canter, R. Know, and D. Fairchild, *Ground Water Quality Protection* (Chelsea, MI: Lewis Publishers, Inc., 1988), 5–13.

Chapter 9: Water Infrastructure

1. U.S. EPA, "Clean Watersheds Need Survey (CWNS): 2008 Guide for Entering Stormwater Management Program (Category VI) Needs" (2008).

2. Ibid.

3. P. Gordon, J. Kuprenas, J. Lee, J. Moore, H. Richardson, and C. Williamson, "An Economic Impact Evaluation of Proposed Stormwater Treatment for Los Angeles County" (University of Southern California, November 2002).

4. Congressional Research Service, "Energy Independence and Security Act of 2007: A Summary of Major Provisions" (December 21, 2007).

5. Eleventh Annual Municipal Sewer & Water Survey, *Underground Construction* (February 2008), www.oildompublishing.com/uceditorialarchive/feb08/survey.pdf.

Chapter 10: Water Analytics

1. WaterTech Capital, LLC, "Water Instrumentation and Monitoring Markets." White Paper, May 2005.

2. "Information Collection Rule (ICR)," 61 *Federal Register* 24354 (May 14, 1996). The ICR study was the largest, longest and most carefully formulated water quality study undertaken by U.S. water utilities in support of future regulation of microbial contaminants, disinfection alternatives and disinfection byproducts.

3. See note 1.

4. Ibid.

5. "Water Infracture: Information in financing, Capital Planning, and Privatization, "GAO-02-764, Washington, D.C.: August 16, 2002.

6. C. Copeland and B. Cody, "Terrorism and Security Issues Facing the Water Infrastructure Sector." Congressional Research Service Report for Congress (May 21, 2003).

Chapter 11: Water Resource Management

1. Aldo Leopold, *A Sand County Almanac* (New York: Oxford University Press, 1949), 201–226.

2. The Report of the World Commission on Dams, "Dams and Development: A New Framework for Decision-Making" (November 16, 2000).

3. Gifford Pinchot, *The Fight for Conservation* (New York: Doubleday, Page & Company, 1910).

4. U.S. Department of the Interior, U.S. Geological Survey, "Irrigation Water Withdrawals for the Nation" (2000), www.ga.water.usgs.gov/edu/wuir.html.

5. M. El-Fadel, Y. El Sayegh, K. El-Fadl, and D. Khorbotly, "The Nile River Basin: A Case Study in Surface Water Conflict Resolution." *Journal of Natural Resources and Life Sciences Education* 32 (2003): 107–117.

6. S. Postel and A. Vickers, "Boosting Water Productivity," *State of the World: 2004* (Washington, D.C.: Worldwatch Institute, 2004), chap. 3.

Chapter 12: Desalination

1. *International Desalination & Water Reuse Quarterly* (February/March 2008).

Chapter 13: Emerging Issues

1. World Health Organization, "Arsenic in Drinking Water." Fact Sheet Number 210, Revised May 2001.

2. U.S. EPA, "Clean Water and Drinking Water Gap Analysis Report," (EPA 816-R-02-020, 2002); "Closing the Gap: Innovative Responses for Sustainable Water Infrastructure," (2003 EPA Water Infrastructure Forum).

Chapter 14: Water as an Asset Class

1. Roger G. Ibbotson and Paul D. Kaplan, "Does Asset Allocation Policy Explain 40 Percent, 90 Percent, or 100 Percent of Performance?" *Financial Analysts Journal* (January/February 2000).

2. Robert D. Arnott, Chairman, Research Affiliates, LLC. Quote appears in an interview on the Pimco website: www.pimco.com/LeftNav/Product+Focus/2005/Arnott+Fundamental+Indexing+Interview.htm.

Chapter 15: Climate Change and the Hydrologic (Re)Cycle

1. R. Spahni, J. Chappellaz, T. Stocker, et al., "Atmospheric Methane and Nitrous Oxide of the Late Pleistocene from Antarctic Ice Cores." *Science* 310(5752) (November 25, 2005): 1317–1321.

2. 2006 Annual Climate Review: U.S. Summary, June 21, 2007, National Climatic Data Center, NOAA.

3. T. Karl, N. Nicholls, and J. Gregory, "The Coming Climate." *Scientific American* (May 1997): 133–149.

4. J. Rose, S. Daeschner, D. Easterling, F. Curriero, S. Lele, J. and Patz, "Climate and Waterborne Disease Outbtreaks." *Journal AWWA* 92(9) (September 2000): 79–86.

Chapter 16: Forward–Looking Thoughts for Water Investors

1. S. Hoffmann, "Estimating Residential Demand for Water in the City of Denton." Unpublished Master's Thesis, University of North Texas, December, 1986.

2. For a detailed account of the history of ecology see Donald Worster's *Nature's Economy* and *The Background of Ecology* by Robert McIntosh.

About the Author

Stephen Hoffmann, a resource economist, is recognized for his expertise in the water industry in which he has been active for over 25 years. He is the founder of WaterTech Capital, an investment and consulting company that specializes exclusively in the water industry. Hoffmann was one of the earliest investors to recognize the investment potential of the global water business. In 1987 he published, "Water: The Untapped Market," which became the foundation for his premise that the economic value of water would become an area of growing investment interest as quantity and quality issues emerged worldwide.

Hoffmann, a long-time member of the American Water Works Association and the Water Environment Federation, has substantial consulting, operational, and financial experience with applications in water rate design, technology commercialization, strategic analysis, and water policy. He has served in numerous entrepreneurial and executive management positions within the water industry and has applied that knowledge as a broker, a registered investment advisor, and an investment banker.

Hoffmann writes and speaks extensively on water industry topics and has been a contributing editor to *U.S. Water News' Water Investment*

Newsletter for more than 14 years. Hoffmann is a cofounder and the principal architect of the pioneering industry benchmark, the Palisades Water Index, that serves as the tracking index for the first water exchange traded fund launched in 2005 by Invesco PowerShares.

Index